# Backroad Mapbook

## Welcome

Welcome to the Premier Edition of the Backroad Mapbook for Ontario's Algonquin Region! Inside this guidebook, you will find the most comprehensive outdoor recreation resource available for the Algonquin Region. Located in central Ontario, this region is comprised of Algonquin Provincial Park and its surrounding area. The most renowned geographic characteristic is the rolling highlands that are so often seen in professional photography of the area. The Ottawa Valley, with its large stands of pine trees, lies to the east of Algonquin Park. Also found in the east are the cottage destination towns of Trout Creek and South River. To the north of the park, the Mattawa River and its surrounding lowlands can be found.

The reference section found in this book includes information on several different activities such as lake and stream fishing, wilderness camping, provincial parks and conservation areas, paddling routes as well as multi-use trails (hiking/biking, horseback riding, cross-country skiing, snowmobiling/ATV, etc.). Countless hours have been spent in researching this book, making it the most complete compilation of outdoor recreation information you will find anywhere. This information can be enjoyed by anyone who spends time in the great outdoors.

The maps in this book highlight the logging/bush road networks, trails systems and recreation opportunities for the Algonquin Region. A unique feature of the maps is that all recreation activities are labelled, allowing for quick and easy referencing when researching a specific area. Further, no other source provides as much detail and accuracy on the road and trail networks of the Algonquin Region.

The opportunities are endless! Whether you like to fish, hike, paddle, ski, mountain bike or just explore the backroads, we are sure you will have as much fun using the Backroad Mapbook as we did in developing it!

## Forward

The Backroad Mapbook is truly a unique product. No other source covers the Algonquin Region with as much detail or information on outdoor recreation activities as this book.

The Backroad Mapbook is simple to use. There are two sections in the book, a reference section and the maps. If you know the activity you are planning, you simply turn to that reference section and find the activity you are interested in. If you are planning a trip to a specific area, you should consult the index or the map key to find the appropriate map(s) and look for the various recreation opportunities highlighted.

The maps have been developed and updated using a wide variety of sources including actual field research. Therefore, our maps are very detailed and show up to date information on the backroads and trail systems of the Algonquin Region. Continuous referral to our maps and the reference sections, will help you become acquainted with the area you are interested in.

By popular demand from GIS users, we have included UTM Grids for reference points. We must emphasis that these are for reference only. This generality is because we have to consult several different sources to create the maps.

Generally, outside of Algonquin Provincial Park there is a well established secondary road system that provides easy access to the backcountry. With numerous bush roads and trails, much of this part of the region is accessible. Although logging practices continue in Algonquin Provincial Park, printing of detailed road information would create significant management problems for the park. Travel on any non-designated public usage areas is prohibited within Algonquin Park.

We emphasis that our mapbook should only be used as an access and planning guide. We have gone to great lengths to ensure the accuracy of this book. However, over time, the road and trail conditions change. Always be prepared!

Please respect all private property and close any gates behind you.

## Acknowledgement

This book could not have been created without the hard work and dedication of the Mussio Ventures Ltd. staff, Kelly Briggs, Shawn Caswell, Trevor Daxon, Brett Firth and Brandon Tam. Without their hard work and support, this comprehensive mapbook would never have been completed as accurately as it was. We would also like to thank the following individuals for helping with the project: Heather K. Smith, Carmine Minutillo and Jeremy Pooler for their first hand research.

In addition, we would like to thank all those individuals, retailers, natural resources staff and tourism personnel for their knowledge and assistance in the production of this mapbook. We would also like to thank the Friends of Algonquin Park.

Most of all, we would like to thank Heather K. Smith, Nancy Jackson and Penny Mussio. Their patience and support helped us during the many hours spent researching and writing the Backroad Mapbook Series.

ISBN 0-9697877-9-0

**Cover and layout designs by Brandon Tam**

Published by:
Mussio Ventures Ltd
232 Anthony Court
New Westminster, B.C. V3L 5T5
P. (604) 520-5670 F. (604) 520-5630
E-mail: info@backroadmapbooks.com
or visit our web site:
(http://www.backroadmapbooks.com)

*Canadian Cataloguing in Publication Data*

Marleau, Jason, 1972-
Mussio Ventures presents Backroad mapbook:
Algonquin region

Includes index.
Written by Jason Marleau, Russell Mussio and Wesley Mussio.
ISBN 0-9697877-9-0

1. Outdoor recreation – Ontario – Algonquin Provincial Park Region – Guidebooks. 2. Recreation areas – Ontario – Algonquin Provincial Park Region – Maps. 3. Algonquin Provincial Park Region (Ont.) – Guidebooks. 4. Algonquin Provincial Park Region (Ont.) – Maps. I. Mussio, Russell, 1969- II. Mussio, Wesley, 1964- III. Mussio Ventures Ltd. IV. Title. V. Title: Backroad mapbook: Algonquin region. VI. Title: Algonquin region.

G1146.E63M87 1999     796.5'09713'147     C99-900813-7

## The Authors

Russell and Wesley Mussio welcome Jason Marleau to the Backroad Mapbook Series. Jason has joined us to spearhead the writing and research of the Ontario Backroad Mapbooks.

Jason (right) was born in Sudbury, Ontario and spent his childhood summers in Killarney Provincial Park at the family owned and operated marina. While growing up in Central Ontario, he had the opportunity to experience and enjoy Ontario's great outdoors. After graduating from the University of Ottawa, Jason spent a few years exploring British Columbia, where he met the Mussio brothers.

Russell (left) graduated from U.B.C. with a degree in Leisure and Sports Administration. He formed Mussio Ventures Ltd. in 1993 with his brother, Wesley, in order to publish, distribute and market the Backroad Mapbook Series.

Wesley (middle) is a Registered Professional Forester and a lawyer practising as a trial lawyer with the law firm Lindsay Kenney, in Vancouver, B.C.

Russell, Wesley and Jason are all avid outdoorsmen. Whenever they are not working on the Backroad Mapbook project, they are enjoying the great outdoors.

## Disclaimer

# Table of Contents

## Outdoor Recreation Reference Section

## Map Section

**Map Key & Legend**

# Freshwater Fishing

## (Lake and Stream Fishing)

## Lake Fishing

The Algonquin Region is famous for its quality fishing and attracts visitors from around the world. An endless array of canoe routes and trail systems dot the region and provide access to some of the most remote water bodies in central Ontario. In our guide, we provide information on over 900 freshwater fishing lakes. The higher elevation lakes support a colder environment making the lakes more suitable for trout, which are the predominant species of the region. From small cool brook trout ponds to large lake trout lakes, the Algonquin Region offers unlimited angling opportunities.

To access the interior lakes of Algonquin Provincial Park you must travel from one of the many interior access points that lie along the park's border. Parking is provided at all access points. Permits are required for both day and overnight use . Canoe routes are the main method of travel within the interior, although there are a few backpacking and cart trails that also travel to interior Algonquin lakes. Along the Hwy 60 corridor, a number of lakes can be accessed. Fishing is slower on these lakes due to the easy accessibility of the area.

Stocking has a long history in the Algonquin Region. In the past, many exotic species, such as grayling and smallmouth bass, have been attempted to be introduced into Algonquin Provincial Park. Grayling could not survive in the park environment, however, a number of natural trout lakes are now inhabited by smallmouth bass. Smallmouth usually place competitive pressure on brook trout forcing them to extinction in their natural environment. Brook trout and lake trout were also widely stocked throughout the park in an effort to increase angling opportunities. Stocking had little success and today park management focuses on restricting the expansion of non-native species and maintaining natural reproduction. Outside of Algonquin Park, brook trout and lake trout continue to be widely stocked in a number of areas. Most stocked lakes once supported natural trout species but were 'fished out'. Stocking is usually done on a two to three year cycle depending on the fishing pressure on the lake. Splake, the brook trout/lake trout hybrid, is also stocked in and outside of Algonquin Park. Splake provide decent angling opportunities in lakes that are suitable for trout species. Splake help reduce pressure on fragile natural lake trout lakes in the area and grow very quickly to good sizes. This makes them an attractive angling option.

A few of the more popular restrictions on some Algonquin Region lakes are slot size limits and seasonal fishing sanctuaries. A slot size limit is the restriction of what size of fish must be released and what size you can keep from a lake. For example, on Canoe Lake, in order to keep lake trout they must be less than 40cm (15.7 in) or greater than 55cm (21.7 in) in length. The idea is to release fish that are at a healthy maturity and the prime breeding stock of the lake, to give them the opportunity to reproduce. Seasonal fishing sanctuaries is one of the newer restrictions that have been brought into effect on various water bodies in the province. The idea of this regulation is to curb incidental and out of season catches of fragile species, such as lake trout, when fishing for other fish, like perch, which are available to anglers year round. In Algonquin Park, a few lakes have been designated voluntary catch and release lakes. A minimum of two fish can be kept in these lakes, although catch and release is highly recommended. The idea of the restriction is to preserve a quality fishery and promote more responsible angling practices. These regulations are having positive effects on fishing quality in the region and are in place for the benefit of future angling.

Expanded awareness of anglers has increased the practice of voluntary catch and release, which is vital for a healthy fishery in the popular Algonquin Region. Each species of sport fish has a regulated open and closed season. The closed period usually coincides with the spawning period of the fish to allow for regeneration of stocks without angling pressure. There are over 25 fish species that are angled for sport in the Province of Ontario and most species are regulated to some degree. The most popular species in the Algonquin Region are listed below:

1. **Atlantic Salmon** were native to Lake Ontario and became extinct by 1900 mainly due to over fishing by European settlers. There have been many attempts to introduce Atlantics into the Great Lakes and a few North Bay area lakes, although success has been limited. North Bay area Atlantics are locally known as Ouininache. Although the species is rare, the salmon are caught periodically in Trout Lake and Nosbonsing Lake, while trolling for other fish. The Ontario record is 11kg (24 lbs).

2. **Brook Trout** are native to the Algonquin Region and inhabit cool streams and smaller lakes throughout the region. Algonquin Park is renowned for its brook trout and has been the focus of numerous research projects. Anglers flood to the park annually in search of the beautiful trout. Brook trout are also known as speckled trout due to the red spots with blue halos on their sides. Brookies are often a fickle and difficult fish to catch and some of the most ardent anglers can be skunked during a day's outing for brook trout. Stream brook trout are generally small and rarely reach sizes in excess of 30cm (12 in), while lake brook trout can be found to 1kg (2.2 lbs) and sometimes larger. The most effective method of angling for brookies is fly fishing in spring and late September, before the seasonal closure. Insects make up a large portion of a brook trout's diet. It makes sense that fishing success would be greater if you imitate what the trout eats. Small spoons and spinners tipped with worms can also be productive and is the recommended set up when fishing for brook trout through the ice. The Ontario record brook trout was caught on a fly in the Nipigon River and weighed a whopping 6.58kg (14.5 lbs).

3. **Lake Trout** is one of the most sought after fish species in the province and is a prized fish in the Algonquin Region. In many parts of southern Ontario, lake trout populations have been in steady decline and have become extinct from numerous lakes that once thrived with lakers. The dramatic decline in Southern Ontario is due mainly to over harvesting by anglers. Pollution from the numerous cottages and motor boats on Ontario lakes has also affected lake trout. These detrimental effects are even evident on busy Algonquin Park lakes. Lake trout grow very slowly and mature at an older age (6-8 years of age) than most other species. The use of catch and release fishing can go a long way in helping maintain populations. Lakers can grow to sizes exceeding 6 kg (13 lbs) and can be found near the surface in spring when the temperature level throughout the lake is generally constant. As summer approaches, the trout retreat to colder water and to depths that require down rigging equipment to find them. Spoons, spinners, or anything that imitates the lake trout's main food source, the minnow, are good choices when angling for lakers. The Ontario record lake trout is 28.6kg (63.12 lbs).

4. **Largemouth Bass** are found in the Algonquin Region mainly in the warmer waters of the Ottawa Valley. The cooler lakes of most other parts of the region make unsuitable habitat for the warm water species. In lakes with largemouth bass, top water lures and flies can create a frenzy of action. Plastic jigs or any minnow imitation lure or fly can also be productive. Largemouth bass generally grow larger than its cousin, the smallmouth bass. The Ontario record largemouth is 4.7kg (10.43 lbs).

5. **Muskellunge** is the largest freshwater sport fish species in Ontario and can reach over 16kg (35 lbs) in size. Often referred to as "muskie," this warm water predator feeds mainly on other fish and frogs, mice, muskrat and the occasional waterfowl. The best method for finding these large fish is by trolling long plugs and lures in calm bays where they often cruise for food. Fall is the more productive time of year. The Ontario record muskellunge was caught in 1989 in Blackstone Harbour of The Massasauga Provincial Park and weighed 29.5kg (65 lbs). This great fish would not have made it to a record size if not for catch and release angling.

| Abbreviations Used Throughout the Book | |
|---|---|
| $ | Canadian Dollar |
| + | plus |
| 2wd | 2 wheel drive |
| 4wd | 4 wheel drive |
| cm | centimetres |
| ft | feet |
| ha | hectares |
| hr | hours |
| Hwy | Highway |
| kg | kilograms |
| km | kilometres |
| m | metres |
| min | minutes |
| Mnt | Mountain |
| Mt | Mount |
| Prov | Provincial |
| Rec | Recreation |
| RV | Recreational Vehicle |
| X-C | Cross-country |

6. *Northern Pike* is the cousin of the muskellunge and inhabits weedy, murky waters throughout Ontario. Northern pike often compete with the muskellunge, which is why most lakes do not have both species. In larger lakes, the two predators can co-exist. The main food source for pike is other fish, although they often take frogs, ducklings and small muskrat. Pike are very aggressive and readily strike fast moving spoons and spinners or anything imitating a good meal. Colourful spoons or flies can also be very productive baits. Northern pike can be found over 8kg (17.6 lbs) in size. Smaller piker are often referred to as 'Hammerheads'. The Ontario record northern pike is 19.11kg (42.13 lb).

7. *Rainbow Trout* are native to the Pacific Northwest and have been introduced into a few inland lakes and streams of the Algonquin Region. Rainbow trout usually average 35-45cm (14-18 in) in lakes and are generally smaller in streams. Fly fishing is the preferred method for small lake fishing, although small spinners and spoons can be productive. The Ontario record rainbow trout is 13.2kg (29.12 lbs).

8. *Smallmouth Bass* are the close cousin of the largemouth bass and were introduced to many of the lakes in the Algonquin Region. The smallmouth has a reputation of putting up a great fight when hooked. The smallmouth can be a very aggressive feeder at times and readily strike jigs, spinners, spoons and other fast moving lures that look like a good meal. The smallmouth can be found around structure such as shoals, islands and under water drop-offs at dusk or during overcast periods. The Ontario record smallmouth bass is 4.5kg (9.84 lbs).

9. *Splake* is a sterile cross between lake trout and brook trout. The hybrid was developed specifically to stock lakes uninhabited by other trout species or lakes where trout were extinct or near extinction. Splake are readily stocked in the Algonquin Region to reduce pressure on native trout lakes and to enhance angling opportunities. Like brook trout, splake grow very rapidly but they reach sizes similar to lake trout. Often, anglers don't know that they have caught a splake and mistake the hatchery fish for natural lake trout. Splake are most active in winter and in spring, just after ice off. Similar to lake trout, splake will strike shiny spoons and spinners and retreat to deeper water as summer approaches.

10. *Walleye or Pickerel* is perhaps the most prized sport fish in Ontario due in part to its acclaim as a great tasting fish. The walleye's diet is made up of mainly bait fish, although they do take leeches and other grub like creatures. Jigs are the lure of choice for walleye either through the ice or during open water season. Jigging in set locations is a productive method or trolling slowly along weed beds can also entice strikes. Walleye travel in loose schools and once you find them you should be able to catch more than one. They are most active during the darker times of day; therefore, early morning and evening are the most productive periods. The Ontario record walleye is 10.1kgs (22.25 lbs).

11. *Whitefish* are found in many lakes from the Great Lakes to the Hudson Bay in Ontario. The species is not known as a sport fish, although is increasingly becoming more popular. Similar to trout, whitefish feed mainly on insects, although they are much more aggressive and less spooky. Whitefish average 2-3kg (4.5-6.5 lbs) in size but the Ontario record is a stunning 6.53kg (14.38 lbs). Whitefish will readily strike spinners, spoons or other shinny lures. They can also be taken on the fly.

12. *Yellow Perch* are aggressive feeders and are best caught by still fishing worms with a float. Perch don't grow very big and only average 20-30cm (8-12 in) in size. They are fished more for their great eating quality than their size. Perch are found in many warm water lakes throughout the province and are active throughout the year, especially during ice fishing season. The Ontario record yellow perch is 1kg (2.25 lbs).

*Before heading out, be sure to check the Ontario Recreational Fishing Regulations Summary to ensure you are not breaking any laws. Penalties for offences can be severe including large fines, confiscation of vehicles and equipment, or even jail time.*

## Lake Vernon Area Lakes (Map 1)

There are numerous lakes in the Lake Vernon area that offer fishing for a wide variety of species, including trout, bass and pike. There are a number of larger lakes, such as Mary Lake, that provide the ideal setting for that great cottage weekend. If you prefer, hike-in or canoe access lakes are also available. Overall, the area is a great recreation playground for all ages to enjoy.

**Arrowhead and Little Arrowhead Lakes (G2)** are two distinctly different lakes, although they are located close to one another. Arrowhead Lake lies within Arrowhead Provincial Park and is a heavily used lake that offers fair fishing for smallmouth bass to 2kg (4.5 lbs) and slow fishing for small brook trout. Little Arrowhead Lake provides fair fishing for smaller sized lake trout and brook trout and is best fished through the ice.

**Buck Lake and Fox Lake (B2)** are busy cottage destination lakes in the summer and have been created by the damming of the Buck River. There is good fishing for smallmouth and largemouth bass to 3kg (6.5 lbs) and fair to good fishing for northern pike in the 3.5+ kg (8 lb) range. Spinner baits or any minnow imitation lure or fly can be productive. Both lakes can be accessed via Ravenscliffe Road.

**Clark and Palette Lakes (E2)** are two smaller lakes found to the west and east of Waseosa Lake and are easily accessed by roads. There is fair to good fishing at times for smallmouth bass that average 0.5-1kg (1-2 lbs) in both lakes.

**Clearwater Lake (F7)** can be found via Beaver Meadows or Clearwater Lake Roads and provides fair fishing for smallmouth bass in the 0.5-1kg (1-2 lb) range. There are a number of cottages along the lake.

**Devine and Fleming Lakes (G7)** are two of the smaller lakes in the area and both offer fair to good fishing at times for smallmouth bass in the 0.5-1kg (1-2 lb) range. Devine Lake also has a population of largemouth bass that can be aggressive for top water lures and flies.

**Fairy Lake's (G4)** shoreline makes up a beautiful part of the town of Huntsville and is a busy lake year round. There is a boat launch at the north end of the lake, which offers fair to good fishing for smallmouth bass to 2.5kg (5.5 lbs) and lake tout to 70+ cm (28 lb). The lake is stocked periodically with rainbow trout and has been stocked in the past with lake trout to supplement natural populations. Fishing for rainbows is generally slow. Ice fishing and trolling are the preferred methods of angling for lake trout. Try off Antler or One Tree Islands for smallmouth action.

**Fish and Oudaze Lakes (F1)** can be found off of Fish Lake Road and both lakes offer slow to fair fishing for brook trout to 35 cm (14 in). Oudaze Lake also provides good fishing at times for smallmouth bass to 1.5kg (3.5 lbs). Try a crayfish imitation fly or lure dragged slowly near the bottom for better results.

**Foote Lake (G1)** is found off Foote Lake Road and has cottages along its shoreline. The lake offers fair fishing for smallmouth bass in the 0.5-1kg (1-2 lb) range and slow fishing for brook trout. The lake has also been stocked with rainbow trout, although fishing for rainbow is generally slow.

**Lake Vernon (E4)** is one of the larger lakes in the area and is a busy cottage destination in summer. The lake receives heavy fishing pressure throughout the year and continues to offer good fishing for smallmouth and largemouth bass to 1.5kg (3.5 lbs). The lake also provides fair fishing for northern pike in the 3.5+ kg (8 lb) range and lake trout to 75+ cm (30 in) and average sized rainbow trout. The lake has been stocked with lake trout to supplement natural populations.

**Langford Lake (E1)** is found just outside the village of Novar off Long Lake Road. The lake offers fair fishing for average sized brook trout, which are best fished through the ice or in spring with flies or worms and a small shiny lure.

**Longs and Mainhood Lakes (C7)** are two smaller cottage country lakes found off of Hwy 141, which provide fair to good fishing for average sized smallmouth bass. Longs Lake also has a small population of brook trout available, although fishing is generally slow.

**Mary Lake (E7)** is a busy cottage destination lake year round. There is good fishing at times for smallmouth bass to 1.5kg (3.5 lbs) and fair fishing for lake trout to 75+ cm (30 in). The lake is stocked almost annually with lake trout and periodically with rainbow trout. There is also a small population of brook trout and fishing for brook tout and rainbow trout is generally slow. Ice fishing for trout can be one of the more productive methods. In summer, trout are difficult to find and must be trolled for.

**Mayflower Lake (F2)** is a small lake found within Arrowhead Provincial Park and offers slow fishing for small brook trout. The lake is best fished in the spring, just after ice off.

**Nutt Lake (A7)** is a small cottage destination lake found off of Hwy 141. The lake offers slow fishing for marginal sized smallmouth bass.

**Round Lake (B1)** can be accessed off Fern Glen Road and can be busy in the summer. The lake provides good fishing at times for smallmouth and largemouth bass to 1.5kg (3.5 lbs) and fair to good fishing for smaller northern pike. Spinner baits or minnow imitation lures or flies are productive. There is also a small population of brook trout as well as whitefish and perch in the lake.

**Rose Lake (C7)** can be found via a road off of Old Muskoka Road and offers good fishing at times for smallmouth bass that average 0.5-1kg (1-2 lbs). Any minnow imitation lure or fly can be productive.

**Skeleton Lake (A6)** is one of the larger and more popular lakes in the area and is found off County Road 3 or Hwy 141. There are a few boat launch sites onto the lake and a number of cottages along its shoreline. The lake offers good fishing at times for average sized smallmouth bass and fair fishing for walleye and lake trout. Lakers can be found to 75 cm (30 in) and walleye to 3.5kg (8 lbs). The lake has been stocked with rainbow trout in the past and there remains a small brook trout population. Watch for lake trout slot size restrictions.

**Solitaire Lake (D2)** forms the southern border of J. Albert Bauer Provincial Park and can be accessed via a road off County Road 8. There is fair to good fishing at times for natural lake trout to 65 cm (26 in). Trolling in spring can produce decent results. The lake is part of a fall to spring fishing sanctuary in order to preservation the fragile lake trout stocks.

**Waseosa Lake (E2)** has a number of cottages along its shoreline and can be accessed by a number of different roads just off Hwy 11. The lake offers fair to good fishing for smallmouth bass to 1.5kg (3.5 lbs) and fair fishing for brook trout to 45 cm (18 in). The lake is stocked every few years with rainbow trout and fishing for rainbows can be good in the spring, after ice off. There remains a small population of natural lake trout, which can be found in the 75 cm (30 in) range.

## Lake of Bays Area (Map 2)

The Lake of Bays area lies just west of Algonquin Park and is renowned for its many lakes and endless outdoor recreation opportunities. Many of the lakes in the area are deep, cold, water bodies, which make ideal habitat for lake and brook trout. Like many of the lake trout stocks in the southern part of the province, the lake trout in the Lake of Bays area are under constant pressure. The increased practice of catch and release fishing will help in preserving lake trout fishing for the future.

**Ashball Lake (G5)** is a small lake found off County Road 12 not far from Hwy 35 and offers fair fishing for small northern pike. Spinner baits, top water lures/flies or a minnow imitation can be productive.

**Beetle and Martencamp Lakes (F2)** can be accessed via a road off Hwy 60 just before Algonquin Park. Martencamp Lake is stocked every few years with brook trout and offers fair to good fishing for average sized brookies in the spring. Beetle Lake also holds a population of brook trout and fishing is fair in the spring.

**Bella and Rebecca Lakes (C1)** are two cottage destination lakes that both offer good fishing at times for smallmouth bass to 2+ kg (4.5 lbs) and fair fishing for lake trout to 70+ cm (28 in). Bella Lake contains a naturally reproducing strain of lake trout and has slot size restrictions on lakers to help maintain stocks. Rebecca Lake is stocked periodically with lake trout to reinforce existing stocks and also contains a fair population of walleye.

**Big Hoover Lake (F1)** can be located by an old logging road/trail near the south end of Oxbow Lake and offers good to very good fishing for nice sized smallmouth bass. There is not much fishing pressure on the lake during the year and the bass are usually quite active.

**Blue Chalk and Red Chalk Lakes (F7)** can be accessed via a road off Paint Lake Road and offer slow to fair fishing for small brook trout. Blue Chalk Lake has been stocked with lake trout in the past to supplement natural stocks and fishing for lakers to 70 cm (28 in) is fair in the spring, just after ice off. Red Chalk Lake has a good population of largemouth bass in the 0.5-1kg (1-2 lbs) range that are regularly found much bigger. Blue Chalk Lake is part of the winter/spring fishing sanctuary to help preserve natural lake trout stocks.

**Buchanan Lake (A4)** is found just off East Browns Road and is surrounded by private property. Permission must be obtained to enter the area. There is fair fishing for brook trout to 30 cm (12 in) at the lake.

**Burns and Docker Lakes (E3)** are two small hidden lakes that are difficult to access and offer fishing for average sized brook trout. Docker Lake can be accessed via a rough 4wd road, while Burns Lake can only be walked to. Both lakes provide good brook trout fishing in winter and spring.

**Camp and Flossie Lakes (G2)** are two connected lakes that make great camp and cottage lakes. The lakes provide fair fishing for lake trout to 70 cm (28 in) and for brook trout to 35 cm (14 in). Trolling in spring with small spoons can be productive. Watch for slot size restrictions on lake trout.

**Charcoal Lake (G6)** is a hidden lake located near Hwy 35, just after Dorset and is stocked every few years with brook trout. Fishing for brookies in the 20-30 cm (8-12 in) range is fair through the ice or in spring, just after ice off.

**Chub and Paint (Deer) Lakes (E7)** are easily accessed off Paint Lake Road and provide fair fishing for smallmouth bass in the 0.5-1kg (1-2 lb) range and slow fishing for brook trout. Paint Lake has been stocked with splake, which provide fair fishing through the ice and in the spring.

**Cod and Wilbur Lakes (G4)** can be accessed via a rough road from either Hwy 35 or Hwy 60 and are stocked every few years with brook trout. Fishing for brookies to 30 cm (12 in) is good through the ice or in spring, just after ice off.

**Cooper Lake (D3)** is located just to the north of the village of Dwight and offers fair fishing for smallmouth bass in the 0.5-1kg (1-2 lb) range. A good road off Hwy 60 leads to the lake.

**Dotty and Oxbow Lakes (D1)** can be accessed from County Road 8 and have a number of camps and cottages along their shorelines. The lakes offer good fishing for smallmouth bass that average 0.5-1kg (1-2 lbs) and fair fishing for lake and brook trout. Lake trout are stocked periodically in both lakes and can be found to 65 cm (26 in) in size. Brookies are much smaller than their lake trout counterpart, although can be found in the 30 cm (12 in) range. Try trolling or near creek mouths.

**Doughnut Lake (G1)** can be found via a rough road that travels south to Camp Lake and provides fair fishing in the spring for stocked brook trout. There is an island on the lake that makes a great picnic spot.

**Dunn Lake (A7)** can be found via a few different roads off South Portage Road. There are cottages along the lake's shoreline and the lake offers fair fishing for average sized smallmouth bass.

**Eastell Lake (D2)** is part of the J. Albert Bauer Provincial Park and can only be accessed on foot through sometimes, heavy bush. The lake contains brook trout and fishing is good in the spring, just after ice off or through the ice in winter.

**Eighteen, Seventeen, Sixteen and Fifteen Mile Lakes (E3)** can each be accessed via rough roads off of Hwy 60 and each offer good fishing for smallmouth bass to 1.5+ kg (3.5 lbs). Fifteen, Sixteen and Seventeen Mile Lakes offer fair fishing for natural lake trout to 70 cm (28 in) and Eighteen Mile Lake provides good fishing for lakers in winter and spring. Fifteen Mile Lake is part of a winter fish sanctuary to protect natural lake trout stocks.

**Ermine Lake (G1)** is found in Algonquin Park and has been stocked with splake in 1997 due to low brook trout populations. Reports on fishing success for splake are sketchy, although should improve in the 2nd and 3rd year after stocking.

**Gostling Lake (F5)** is a small lake found near Hwy 35 and offers slow fishing for small brook trout.

**Grandview Lake (C7)** is a smaller lake found near the south end of Lake Of Bays and provides fair fishing for marginal sized smallmouth bass. Try a spinner bait or minnow imitation for better results.

**Grindstone and Wren Lakes (G7)** are two Frost Centre Lakes that can be found just off Hwy 35. Both lakes are stocked every two years with splake and provide good fishing for average sized splake through the ice and in the spring, just after ice off. Wren Lake also has a fair population of smallmouth bass that average 0.5-1kg (1-2 lbs).

**Hardwood (Clinto) Lake (G4)** are both found off of County Road 12 and are popular cottage destination lakes that offer fair fishing for natural lake trout to 65+ cm (26 in) in size. Rainbow trout have been stocked in both lakes, although fishing is generally slow and there is a small population of brook trout available in Crozier Lake. There is slot size restrictions for lake trout on Clinto Lake, while Crozier Lake is part of the winter/spring fishing sanctuary to preserve lake trout stocks.

**Harp and Walker Lakes (A3)** can be found via roads just off Hwy 60, east of Huntsville. Both lakes provide fair fishing for smallmouth bass to 1.5kg (3.5 lbs). Harp Lake is stocked every few years with lake trout and fishing for lakers can be good through the ice or in spring, just after ice off. The lake also has a small population of brook trout available, although fishing is slow. Walker Lake has a small population of lake trout and was stocked with rainbow trout in 1996. Fishing for both species is relatively slow.

**Insula and Martin Lakes (E7)** are two semi-wilderness lakes that are surrounded mainly by crown land. Martin Lake can be accessed via a rough 4wd road and a short portage found at the south side of the lake can take you to Insula Lake. Both lakes offer fair to good fishing at times for small brook trout, while Martin Lake also provides good fishing for largemouth bass that average 0.5-1kg (1-2 lbs). Insula Lake is usually better for brookies since it takes a little more work to get to.

**Lake of Bays (C7)** is synonymous with cottage country and is a busy water body during summer months. Hwys 117 and 35 both travel along the lake's shoreline, where a number of access points to the lake can be found. The lake receives a lot of angling pressure year round, and continues to maintain an exciting sport fishery. Smallmouth bass fishing is good for bass to 2.5kg (5.5 lbs). Try off points and near islands. The lake has been stocked in the past with lake trout, although currently relies solely on natural reproduction. Fishing for lakers to 75 cm (30 in) is fair in winter and in the spring. Rainbow have been introduced in the past and brook trout were once found in the lake.

**Lasseter and Lee Lakes (C3)** are two small hidden lakes that contain the elusive brook trout. Lasseter Lake can be easily accessed via a road off Hwy 60 and offers fair fishing for small brookies. Lee Lake is much more difficult to get to, as it is accessed by a rough 4wd road. The lake provides good fishing at times for brook trout to 35 cm (14 in) in size. Ice fishing or fly fishing in spring is best for brookies.

**Little Shoe and Lost Lakes (G7)** are two small, secluded lakes that offer good fishing for small brook trout. Little Shoe Lake can be accessed by about a 200m portage from the marsh area west of Wheeler Lake. Lost Lake must be bushwhacked to from the end of an old logging road. Small nymph patterns in spring work well.

**Limburner Lake (G4)** is a small lake that is stocked every two years with brook trout. It is found just off County Road 12 between Clinto and Crozier Lakes and. Brookies average 20-30 cm (8-12 in) and fishing can be good through the ice or in spring, just after ice off. Try small spoons jigged through the ice or nymph pattern flies in spring.

**Longline Lake (E6)** can be easily accessed off Hwy 117 and is stocked with splake every few years. Fishing for splake is fair through the ice and in spring. There is also a small population of brook trout in the lake, although fishing is generally slow.

**Lumber and Thumb Lakes (G2)** are two secluded lakes that are mostly fished in the winter. Thumb Lake has been stocked with brook trout, while both lakes offer fair to good fishing for average sized brookies. Spring fishing with nymph fly patterns or worms can be productive.

**Mink Lake (E7)** is a secluded lake that is most often visited by snowmobile. The lake offers fair fishing for small brook trout through the ice or in spring, just after ice off.

**Otter Lake (G5)** is a popular lake that offers fair fishing for smallmouth bass and small northern pike. There is also a small population of brook trout in the lake, although fishing is quite slow.

**Oxtongue Lake (F3)** passes under Hwy 60 and is a busy lake in summer. Fishing for smallmouth bass to 2+ kg (4.5 lbs) is good and fair for lake trout to 70+ cm (28 in). The lake has been stocked with rainbow trout and fishing for average sized rainbows is fair in spring. There is also a small population of brook trout available in the lake. A small pond at the southernmost tip of Oxtongue Lake offers fair to good fishing for small brook trout.

**Peninsula Lake (B3)** is found off Hwy 60, just outside of Huntsville. The lake provides good fishing at times for smallmouth bass to 2kg (4.5 lbs) and was once stocked with rainbow trout. Cottage docks provide excellent cover for nice sized smallmouth bass. Also try around Hills Island near any major drop-offs.

**Tasso and Toad Lakes (F1)** are found at the end of County Road 8 and are popular cottage/camp lakes. Despite the rough access, both lakes offer fair fishing for smallmouth bass to 1.5kg (3.5 lbs) which Tasso Lake also offers fishing for brook trout and lake trout. Fishing for lakers to 80 cm (30 in) and average sized brookies is fair in the spring but can be quite slow in the summer months.

**Upper Raft Lake (A1)** is a hidden, difficult to access lake that supposedly has been stocked with rainbow trout. Fishing reports vary and the fishing quality is currently unknown.

**Upper Oxbow Lake (E2)** is another hidden lake that offers good fishing for brook trout that average 20 cm (8 in). The lake is stocked every few years and is best fished with small flies or worms.

**Verner Lake (A1)** can be accessed via a rough 4wd road and/or on foot. The lake has been stocked with brook trout at one time and offers good fishing as times for average sized brookies. The lake is best fished through the ice or in spring with artificial flies.

## Kawagama Lake Area (Map 3)

The Kawagama Lake area lies west of Algonquin Park's southern panhandle and is home to the Leslie M. Frost Centre and the Haliburton Forest Reserve. The area is characterized by the rolling hills of the Haliburton Highlands and offers numerous outdoor recreation possibilities. The lakes of the area are mostly cool lakes similar to that of Algonquin Park. Brook trout, lake trout and smallmouth bass are the predominant species of the region.

**Arbuckle and Fisher Lakes (A3)** are two secluded lakes that can be accessed via rough 4wd roads/trails and provide good fishing at times in winter and spring for average sized brook trout. The easiest access is in winter by snowmobile.

**Avery, Bruin and Orley Lakes (A7)** are three small Frost Centre lakes that are stocked with splake every two years. Fishing for average sized splake can be good through the ice or in spring, just after ice off. Try small spoons through the ice and streamer patterns in the spring. There are rustic campsites available at each lake.

**Ban (Band) Lake (G4)** is a small, secluded lake found in the Haliburton Forest and offers good fishing for small brook trout. The lake is stocked every two years and is mainly fished in the winter through the ice.

**Bear and Livingstone Lakes (D3)** can be accessed via roads and can be busy during summer months. There are a number of cottages on both lakes and fishing for smallmouth bass to 2+ kg (4.5 lbs) is good especially during overcast periods. Both lakes have been stocked with lake trout, with Bear Lake being stocked almost every two years. Fishing for lakers is fair through the ice or by trolling in spring. There is also a small population of brook trout in each of the lakes, although fishing is slow. Livingstone is an alternate access point to the Rockaway Canoe Route. Watch for slot size restrictions on lake trout.

**Big Porcupine and Bonnechere Lakes (F1)** can be busy by Algonquin Park standards from the spring through fall due to the minimal distance portages that are required to access the lakes. There are a number of rustic campsites found on both lakes and fishing is fair for brook trout and lake trout in the spring and slows considerably as summer progresses. Brookies average 25-30 cm (10-12 in) and lake trout can be found to 55 cm (22 in).

**Birchy Lake (G7)** is a small secluded lake found just south of Kennisis Lake and offers slow fishing for small brook trout.

**Black Cat and Cat Lakes (D7)** are accessible by portage only and are stocked every few years with brook trout. Fishing for brookies is fair and can be good at times through the ice or in spring. There are a number of rustic campsites available for use on both lakes.

**Bluebell and Hilly Lakes (C1)** are located in Algonquin Park and offer good fishing in the spring for small brook trout. The lakes can only be accessed by canoe and low maintenance portages. There is a rustic campsite available on Bluebell Lake.

**Bone Lake (F6)** can be accessed via the Kendra Lake Trail and offers fair fishing for smallmouth bass in the 0.5-1kg range. Try a spinner bait or minnow imitation for better results.

**Bright and Niger Lakes (A2)** are located near the western Hwy 60 entrance to Algonquin Park and are stocked periodically with brook trout. Niger Lake is easily accessed via a rough road and Bright Lake can be accessed via rustic portage from Niger Lake. Fishing for brook trout to 30 cm (12 in) is fair and can be good through the ice or in spring, just after ice off.

**Clear Lake (D7)** is found in the Leslie M. Frost Centre and can only be accessed via portage. The lake offers fair fishing for natural lake trout to 70 cm (28 in) and has a number of rustic campsites available for overnight use. The lake is part of the winter/spring fishing sanctuary in order to protect deplete lake trout stocks.

**Crown Lake (E1)** can be accessed via a 4wd road and is located only a few kilometres from Algonquin Park. The lake offers fair fishing for brook trout that average 25-35 cm (10-14 in) and is best fished through the ice or in spring, just after ice off.

**Crozier (McFadden) Lake (A4)** lies off of County Road 12 and offers fair fishing for natural lake trout to 65+ cm (26 in) in size. Rainbow trout have been stocked in both lakes, although fishing is generally slow. There is a small population of brook trout available in the lake. Crozier Lake is part of the winter/spring fishing sanctuary.

**Crystalline, Roger and Sunrise Lakes (C1)** are three small fishing lakes that can be accessed by 4wd roads. Crystalline Lake is the only lake that can not be accessed by road and must be portaged to from one of the other lakes. Roger and Sunrise Lakes are stocked periodically with brook trout, while all three lakes offer fair to good fishing in the spring for brook trout to 30 cm (12 in).

**Dividing Lake (G2)** takes quite a bit of work to get to, although in the spring you could be well rewarded. Fishing for average sized brook trout is good in the spring and can be good in the fall. There are two rustic campsites at the lake and the lake's western shore is part of the Dividing Lake Provincial Nature Park that preserves a stand of beautiful old growth white pine trees.

**East Jeannie Lakes (C4)** are two small lakes located off a road from County Road 12 and are stocked every few years with brook trout. Fishing for brookies in the 20-30 cm (8-12 in) range is fair.

**East Paint Lake (C7)** is one of the lesser visited lakes in the Frost Centre due to the 1300m (4,265 ft) portage from Red Pine Lake. East Point Lake is stocked every few years with splake and offers good fishing through the ice and in spring for fish that average 30 cm and can be found much bigger. There is a beautiful island campsite at this lake.

**Ernest, Herb and Gunn Lakes (A7)** are all connected by short portages in the northern portion of the Leslie M. Frost Centre. All three lakes provide good fishing for smallmouth bass and the odd largemouth bass to 1.5kg (3.5 lbs). Spinner baits and most minnow imitations can work well. There are rustic campsites available on each lake.

**Fletcher Lakes (B3)** can both be accessed off County Road 12 and are popular lakes that are stocked every few years with lake trout. Fishing for lakers to 75 cm (30 in) is fair through the ice or by trolling in spring

**Glennies Pond, Shoelace Lake and Wallace Pond (C7)** are three secluded, portage access lakes that are stocked every few years with brook trout. They offer good fishing through the ice and in the spring, just after ice off for brookies to 35 cm (14 in). There are rustic campsites available at Shoelace Lake and Glennies Pond, which is the slowest lake to fish.

**Goodwin (Loon), Johnson and Kelly Lakes (F5)** lie with the Haliburton Forest Reserve and are accessible by roads. Each of the lakes are inhabited by lake trout and bass. Lake trout stocking still occurs Goodwin Lake. The lakes offer fair fishing for average sized lake trout and bass. All three lakes have smallmouth bass, while Johnson Lake also hosts a small population of largemouth bass. Kelly Lake is part of the winter/spring fishing sanctuary and there are slot size restrictions for lake trout on Johnson Lake.

**Harvey Lake (A5)** can be accessed via a road and has a few cottages along its shoreline, although the majority of the shore is crown land. The lake has been stocked in the past with splake and there is a natural population of brook trout. Fishing is fair for splake and slow for brook trout.

**Havelock Lake (F5)** can be accessed by trail within the Haliburton Forest Reserve and is one of the better lake trout lakes within the area. The lake reaches depths of 30m (100 ft) and has been stocked in the past with lake trout. Fishing is good through the ice or by trolling in spring. There is a picnic area at the lake.

**Heron Lake (A1)** is located within Algonquin Park near the Hwy 60 corridor and is stocked every few years with splake. Fishing for splake is fair, while fishing for smallmouth bass that average 0.5-1kg (1-2 lbs) can be good.

**Hinterland Lake (D3)** is a remote lake that can only be accessed on foot through dense forest. A rustic trail did exist at one time, although over the years it has overgrown and may be difficult to locate. The lake is rarely visited and provides very good fishing for smallmouth bass in the 1+ kg (2 lb) range.

**Kawagama Lake (C5)** is one of the largest lakes in the region and provides the starting point to the Rockaway Lake and Hollow River Canoe Routes. There are many access points to the lake including a public boat launch. The lake offers good fishing for smallmouth bass to 2+ kg (4.5 lbs) and fair fishing for natural lake trout. Rainbow trout have been stocked in the past and brook trout were once native to the lake. These trout are rarely caught. For active smallmouth bass, try off one of the many islands with a jig or crayfish imitation. There are slot size restrictions on the lake.

**Kennisis Lakes (F7)** are easily accessed via roads, although Little Kennisis Lake lies within the Haliburton Forest boundary. Both lakes offer slow fishing for lake trout to 75 cm (30 in) and fair fishing for smallmouth bass. The lakes have many cottages along their shorelines and can be quite busy during the summer months.

**Kimball Lake (D3)** has a few camps along its shoreline but is mostly surrounded by crown land. The lake can only be accessed via portage from neighbouring Bear Lake along the Rockaway Lake Canoe Route. The lake offers good fishing for smallmouth bass to 2.5kg (5.5 lbs) and fair fishing for lake trout that average 40-45 cm (16-18 in) in size. There is also a fair population of brook trout in the lake that can reach up to 40 cm (16 in) in size.

**L'Azure Lake (E6)** can be accessed via road within the Haliburton Forest Reserve. It has a number of campsites available for use. Smallmouth and largemouth bass were introduced many years ago and fishing is fair for bass to 2+ kg (4.5 lbs).

**Little Coon Lake (G1)** is a small, beautiful Algonquin lake that has a great camping spot on its southern shore. The site is often occupied on weekends, although if you're lucky you can have this lake all to yourself. Fishing at the lake is fair for lake trout and small brook trout.

**Louie Lakes (D2)** are two small lakes that can be accessed via a rough road and offer slow to fair fishing for brook trout. Louie Lake is also stocked every few years with splake.

**Lost, Nugget and Sprucehen Lakes (B4)** can be easily accessed by a road or short trail within the Haliburton Forest. Fishing is fair and can be good in winter or spring. Lost and Nugget Lakes have been stocked with splake and still have small brook trout available. Sprucehen Lake is stocked with brook trout. Smallmouth bass can also be found in Lost Lake.

**Luck and Wolf Lakes (D1)** can be accessed by rough roads and offer fair fishing for brook trout to 40 cm (16 in). Luck Lake has been stocked in the past with brook trout. Wolf Lake has a few cottages/camps along its shoreline, while Luck Lake is surrounded by crown land.

**MacDonald Lake (G6)** lies within the Haliburton Forest and can be accessed by a road. These lakes are unique due to the fact that the lake trout that inhabit the lakes are a unique strain that is not found anywhere else. These Haliburton Forest lake trout are generally smaller and more plentiful than other lake trout. MacDonald Lake is the most productive lake with good fishing for lakers to 40 cm (16 in). Smallmouth and largemouth bass have invaded all the lakes and fishing can be good at times. Please practice catch and release whenever possible to help preserve the Haliburton Forest lake trout. There are size restrictions for lake trout.

**Maple Leaf Lake (A1)** is found in Algonquin Park and is stocked every few years with splake. The lake, which offers camping, can only be accessed via the Western Uplands Backpacking Trail. Fishing for average sized splake is fair during spring, just after ice off.

**Merdie Lake (F3)** is a small, remote lake that can only be reached by canoe and rustic portage. The lake is rarely visited other than the odd ice fisherman and provides good fishing for average sized brook trout.

**Mouse Lake (A7)** can be accessed via a rough, gated road off the Sherborne Access Road. The lake has been stocked with rainbow trout.

**Nehemiah and Ronald Lakes (B7)** are two small secluded lakes found in the Leslie M. Frost Centre and are stocked ever few years with brook trout. Fishing for brookies that average 20-25 cm (8-10 in) is good through the ice and in spring, just after ice off. Nehemiah Lake can be accessed via the Sherborne Access Road and a 455m (1,493 ft) portage can take you to Ronald Lake. There are rustic campsites available on both lakes.

**Nunikani and Red Pine Lakes (C7)** are two of the larger lakes in the Frost Centre and can only be accessed by portage from one of the neighbouring main lakes. Red Pine Lake has a number of cottages and camps along its shoreline, although there are still rustic campsites available on many of the lake's islands. Nunikani Lake is undeveloped and also has a number of rustic campsites available. Both lakes provide good fishing at times for smallmouth bass that average 0.5kg (1 lb) and fair fishing for natural lake trout to 65 cm (26 in).

**Park Lake (A1)** is located near the western entrance to Algonquin Park and can be accessed by canoe and a low maintenance portage. The lake offers fair fishing for smallmouth bass in the 1kg (2 lb) range.

**Poorhouse Lake (C3)** can be found via a road off County Road 12 and offers fair fishing for stocked brook trout. Brookies average 25-30 cm (10-12 in) in size. The lake is stocked every two years.

**Powderhorn and Island Lakes (D6)** are within the Haliburton Forest and are only accessible by trail. Powderhorn Lake is a shallow lake that offers fair fishing for smallmouth bass in the 0.5-1kg (1-2 lb) range and Island Lake provides fair fishing for stocked brook trout.

**Rabbit Lake (C7)** is a small hidden lake that can only be found by a 170m portage from the southern shore of Nunikani Lake. There is a rustic campsite available and the lake is stocked every two years with brook trout. Fishing for average sized brookies is good through the ice and in spring, just after ice off.

**Ragged Lake and Parkside Bay (E1)** can be easily accessed via a 240m (787 ft) portage from Smoke Lake, a main access point to the southern interior of Algonquin Park. There are numerous campsites located on both water bodies, which can be quite busy all season long. Fishing is slow for brook trout and fair in the spring for average sized lake trout. Smallmouth bass can be found in the 0.5-1+ kg (1-2 lb) range and fishing is generally fair throughout the warmer months.

**Raven Lake (A7)** is one of the larger lakes in the area and can be easily accessed off Hwy 35. There are many cottages along the lake's shoreline, although there remains a few rustic campsites available for overnight use. Fishing for lake trout to 75 cm (30 in) is slow and good at times for smallmouth bass to 2.5kg (5.5 lbs).

**Rockaway Lake (F2)** can be accessed by a grueling 2,745m (9,005 ft) portage from Kimball Lake and is bordered by the Dividing Lake Provincial Nature Park to the north. The park preserves old growth white pine trees that are best viewed along the portage to Minkey Lake. The lake offers fair fishing for brook trout to 45 cm (18 in) and is part of the Rockaway Lake Canoe Route. An Algonquin Park permit is required for the rustic campsite available at the north end of the lake.

**Sampson Pond (C7)** is hidden at the end of a 340m (1,116 ft) portage found at the south end of Red Pine Lake. The lake offers good fishing for smallmouth bass that can be found in the 0.5+ kg (1 lb) range.

**Shawandasee Lake (B1)** is within Algonquin Park's management area and can only be accessed by canoe and a low maintenance portage. The lake offers good fishing in spring for brook trout to 30 cm (12 in).

**Slipper and Stocking Lakes (D5)** are two similar lakes but only Stocking Lake can be accessed by road within the Haliburton Forest Reserve. Slipper Lake can be found by portage from Stocking Lake or from Kawagama Lake. Both lakes are inhabited by lake trout and brook trout and offer fair fishing for lakers and good fishing at times for brook trout. Lakers are generally small and brook trout can be found to 45 cm (18 in). Both lakes are part of the winter/spring fishing sanctuary and there are minimum size restrictions on brook trout.

**Snap Lake (G5)** is a small, secluded lake that was stocked with rainbow trout at one time and still holds a fair population of trout. The lake can be accessed via the Snap Lake Trail from Stocking Lake Road.

**Sunken Lake (A6)** can be found off County Road 8 and has a number of cottages along its shoreline. The lake has been stocked with rainbow trout. The fishing for rainbows is good in the spring but slows considerably as summer progresses. Brook trout also inhabit the lake and fishing is fair for brookies through the ice or in spring.

**Surprise and Verner Lakes** can be accessed via rough 4wd roads and or on foot. Both lakes have been stocked with brook trout at one time and offer good fishing at times for average sized brookies.

**Sward Lake (E2)** is a small remote lake that can be accessed by a 4wd road. The lake offers fair fishing for small brook trout, which are best fished through the ice or in spring. Try small silver spoons through the ice and worms or nymph fly patterns in spring.

**Troutspawn Lakes (C2)** can be found via a rough road to Troutspawn Lake, while Little Troutspawn Lake requires some bushwhacking to reach it. Little Troutspawn Lake is stocked every few years with brook trout. Fishing for brookies to 35+ cm (14 in) is fair. Try a small silver spoon through the ice or nymph pattern flies in spring.

**Wolf Lake (G6)** in the Haliburton Forest offers a wide variety of sport fish species to entice the angler. There is a fair population of smallmouth bass and lake trout in the lake as well as a small population of brook trout. The lake has also been stocked quite regularly with splake and fishing can be good through the ice or in spring for small splake. There are a few campsites available at the lake.

## Haliburton Area Lakes (Map 4)

Haliburton Lake lies to the western side of Algonquin Park's southern panhandle admid the rolling hills common to the area. There are numerous secluded and picturesque lakes inside and outside Algonquin Park that can be the perfect setting for a wilderness getaway. The predominant sport fish species is the lake trout and brook trout. Please practice catch and release whenever possible to help preserve the quality of the fishery for these fragile species.

**Beanpole and Coburn Lakes (D5)** can be found via a rough 4wd road and have both been stocked with rainbow trout. Coburn Lake has also been stocked periodically with splake and fishing for splake and or rainbow trout is fair in spring and winter, while Beanpole Lake offers slow fishing for rainbow trout.

**Beaver and Dog Lakes (A6)** are found in the Haliburton Forest. These two small lakes offer fair fishing for smallmouth bass in the 0.5kg (1 lb) range. Try spinners or minnow imitation flies or lures.

**Bivouac and Noname Lakes (A4)** can be accessed from North Road in the Haliburton Forest. Bivouac Lake is stocked every few years with splake and fishing is fair for splake and slow for native brook trout. Noname Lake offers slow fishing for native brook trout and has been stocked in the past with rainbow trout. There are a few rustic campsites available on Bivouac Lake.

**Black (Eyre) Lakes and Clear Lake (A6)** lie within the Haliburton Forest and can be easily accessed by a 2wd road. These lakes are unique due to the fact that the lake trout are a unique strain that is not found anywhere else. These Haliburton Forest lake trout are generally smaller and more plentiful than other lake trout. The fishing on Clear Lake can be a little slow. Little Black and Black Lake offer fair fishing for these small lake trout. Smallmouth and largemouth bass have invaded all the lakes and fishing can be good at times. There are size restrictions on the lake trout.

**Blue Lake (A7)** is one of the more developed lakes within the Haliburton Forest and has a number of campsites available for use. The lake is stocked with rainbow trout and fishing for rainbows to 1kg (2 lbs) is good, especially in spring.

**Boundary (Martin) and East Lakes (E5)** can be accessed via a 4wd road and offer fair to good fishing through the ice or in spring for brook trout that average 25-35 cm (10-14 in) in size. Boundary Lake is stocked every two years while East Lake contains a natural population of brook trout.

**Camp Lake (E2)** is a small interior Algonquin lake that offers good fishing for lake trout. The lakers in this lake are generally smaller than what you find in larger lakes due mainly to the size of the lake.

**Cauliflower Lake (G2)** can be a popular Algonquin Park interior lake in spring when trout season opens. Fishing for both lake trout and brook trout is fair and can be good at times, just after ice off. The main access point to the lake is from Hay Lake via a 995m (3,265 ft) portage. There are four backcountry campsites available at the lake.

**Clydegale Lake (E1)** is a large lake by Algonquin standards and is a popular destination lake for southern interior canoe trippers. There are six rustic campsites available on the lake and fishing is fair in the spring for brook trout to 40+ cm (16 lb). The bugs are intense throughout the park in late May to early July but they seem even worse on Clydegale Lake. If you are on the lake during bug season, camp on one of the two island sites if possible to take advantage of winds.

**Depot and Raden (Raddan) Lakes (A5)** are both stocked every few years to enhance sport fishing in the lakes. Depot Lake has a number of campsites along its shoreline and is stocked with splake. Fishing is good for splake in winter or spring. There also remains a small population of brook trout within the lake. Raden Lake is stocked with brook trout and is a little more difficult to access. Fishing is usually slower than in Depot Lake.

**Dog, Duck and Little Birchy Lakes (A7)** can be accessed via rough roads and then by short trails. Fishing for brookies that average 25-35 cm (10-14 in) is good through the ice or in spring. While ice fishing try small spoons and in the spring nymph fly patterns or worms can be productive. The lakes are stocked every few years with brook trout.

**Dutton Lake (A5)** is stocked every two years with splake and can be found via a road in the Haliburton Forest Reserve. Fishing for splake is fair through the ice or in spring, just after ice off. There are a number of campsites located at the lake.

**Florence and Frank Lakes (B1)** are small Algonquin Park southern interior lakes that are probably more often passed through by canoeists en route to other destinations. There are no campsites on the Florence Lake, although there is a nice site on Frank Lake Both lakes provide fair to good fishing at times for small brook trout.

**Freezee Lake (B5)** is a secluded and rarely visited lake that can be accessed by trail only, as only a portion lies within the Haliburton Forest Reserve. There is brook trout in the lake.

**Green Canoe Lake and Ike's Pond (B7)** can be found via a 4wd road and are stocked every few years with brook trout. Fishing for brookies to 35 cm (14 in) can be good at times.

**Gregory's Pond (F6)** is stocked every two years with splake and provides good fishing. The pond is not as small as you would think and can be accessed via a 4wd road.

**Guilford Lake (B7)** is found via road just to the east of Redstone lake and is stocked every few years with splake. Fishing for nice sized splake is fair throughout the winter and in spring. Try jigging a small silver spoon while ice fishing or by trolling in spring.

**Haliburton and Oblong Lakes (D7)** are two lakes that still contain natural lake trout strains. Fishing for lakers is fair, although can be slow at times. Fishing for smallmouth bass in the 0.5-1kg (1-2 lb) range is fair. There is slot size restrictions for lake trout from Haliburton Lake and Oblong Lake is part of the winter/spring fishing sanctuary.

**Harburn Lakes (C7)** can be accessed via a rough road and are stocked every few years with brook trout. Brookies in the 25-30 cm (10-12 in) range are found in the lake and fishing can be good at times. Winter and spring are the most productive periods.

**Harry, Rence and Welcome Lakes** all lie within Algonquin Park and can attract a number of fishermen in the spring when trout season opens. The main access route is from Rock Lake and there is one difficult portage of 1,870m (6,135 ft) along the Galipo River to Welcome Lake. Brook trout can be found in all three lakes and fishing is generally good for brook trout to 40 cm (16 in) in the spring and at times in the fall. All three lakes are designated catch and release lakes and only artificial lures can be used as bait. Welcome and Rence Lakes also have size restrictions on brook trout. There are a number of rustic campsites on each lake.

**Lake Louisa (A1)** is one of the larger lakes in Algonquin Park's southern interior and has a number of regularly used campsites. The lake is quite scenic and fishing is generally fair in spring for lake trout to 55 cm (22 in). Trolling a spoon or streamer fly are productive methods for fishing. During summer months, the lake sees few visitors.

**Little Cauliflower Lake (G2)** is a small, secluded interior Algonquin Park lake that has a great rustic island campsite. Access is by portage only from the east or the west of the lake and both portages are fairly lengthy. Fishing for brook trout to 35 cm (14 in) is good, especially in the spring.

**Little Hay Lake (G3)** is located within Algonquin Park and can be accessed via Hay Creek and a 995m (3,265 ft) portage from Hay Lake. There is a rustic campsite at the lake and fishing for average sized smallmouth bass is good and can be very good at times.

**McGarvey Lake (G1)** offers fair fishing for lake trout to 75 cm (30 in) and is found in the southern Algonquin interior. There are three beautiful campsites at the lake with one being a nice island site. The lake can be busy in spring when trout season opens.

**Madawaska Lake (D3)** lies within the southern Algonquin Park interior and is a good base for exploration of the South Madawaska River. There are three rustic campsites available and fishing for lake trout to 65+ cm (26 lb) and average sized brook trout is good in the spring. Fishing can also be fair in the fall before the trout season closure. The lake's northern bog section is a common area to spot moose.

**Marsh (Marsden) and Upper Pelaw Lakes (A7)** are partially within the Haliburton Forest Reserve and are close in proximity but offer different experiences. Upper Pelaw Lake has a number of cottages along its shoreline and offers fair fishing for smallmouth bass and the odd lake and brook trout. Marsh Lake can only be accessed via portage from Upper Pelaw Lake and provides fair fishing for natural lake trout and slow fishing for smallmouth bass and brook trout. There are slot size restriction for lake trout on Marsh Lake.

**Morrow and Ross Lake (C7)** are both stocked every two years with splake and provide fair to good fishing at times for average sized splake. Ross Lake also has a fair population of smallmouth bass in the 0.5kg (1 lb) range. Ice fishing for splake is popular on both lakes and Spring can also be a productive period.

**North Grace Lake (A1)** is found in the southern Algonquin interior and offers fair to good fishing at times in the spring for average sized brook trout and lake trout to 65+ cm (26 in). There are three campsites on the lake.

**North Lake (D6)** has been stocked with lake trout at one time but is now part of the winter/spring fishing sanctuary to help preserve natural lake trout strains. Fishing for lakers is generally slow and fair for smallmouth bass in the 0.5-1kg (1-2 lb) range.

**Pen Lake (D1)** is easily accessed via a 375m (1,230 ft) portage from Rock Lake, one of the busier access points to Algonquin Park. There are a number of campsites available at the lake and fishing is fair in the spring, just after ice off for lake trout to 70+ cm (28 lb) and brook trout that average 25-35 cm (10-14 in).

**Percy Lake (E7)** has cottages along its shoreline and can be found via a road. The lake is stocked every two years with lake trout and fishing for lakers to 75 cm (30 in) is fair and can be good at times. Try trolling in spring or ice fishing in winter. Smallmouth bass to 2+ kg (4.5 lbs) are also found in the lake in good numbers. Action usually increases at dusk and during overcast periods.

**Prottler Lake (F1)** in a small interior Algonquin lake that is not as busy as most of the neighbouring lakes due to the 1,630m (5,348 ft) portage to access the lake from Galeairy Lake to the north. There are two rustic campsites available at Prottler Lake and fishing is fair for lake trout, brook trout and good at times for smallmouth bass. The decline of the trout fishery is due in part to the introduction of smallmouth bass into the lake.

**Rainbow Lake (C4)** lies partially within Algonquin Park and partially within the Haliburton Forest Reserve. The lake can only be accessed through the Forest Reserve via trail and is stocked periodically with splake. Fishing for nice sized splake can be good in winter and spring and there is also a fair population of smallmouth bass in the lake.

**Redstone Lakes (A7)** are popular cottage destination lakes that offer fair fishing for natural lake trout to 75 cm (30 in) and good fishing at times for smallmouth bass in the 0.5-1kg (1-2 lb) range. Both lakes are easily accessed via roads and there is slot size restrictions.

**Stringer Lake (A1)** can be accessed via a 290m (951 ft) portage from North Grace Lake in the southern Algonquin Park interior. There are a few rustic campsites available on the lake and due to past over harvesting of the brook trout population, the lake is currently closed to fishing.

**Wildcat Lakes (A3)** are two remote lakes that can be accessed by vehicle. Wildcat Lake lies within the Haliburton Forest and there is a rough road leading to the lake, while South Wildcat Lake can be accessed via a 4wd road. Wildcat Lake is stocked every two years with splake and fishing can be good in the winter and spring. There are a few rustic campsites on the lake. South Wildcat Lake offers fair fishing for natural lake trout and is part of the winter/spring fishing sanctuary. Both lakes still have small populations of native brook trout available.

## Lake St. Peter Area Lakes (Map 5)

This area lies east of Algonquin Provincial Park's southern panhandle and is a great area for both provincial park and crown land camping. Along with Algonquin Park, Lake St. Peter Provincial Park is easily accessible and both offer plenty of recreation opportunities including good fishing. There are numerous lakes in the area that are surrounded by crown land that provide fishing and wilderness camping opportunities.

**Amable Lakes (C2)** can be found via a 4wd road and provide good fishing at times for largemouth bass in the 0.5-1kg (1-2 lb) range. The lakes are surrounded by crown land.

**Back and Indian Lake (G4)** are two small brook trout lakes that can be accessed by 4wd roads. Ice fishing and spring fishing is productive. In summer, trout become more subdued but can be coaxed into hitting flies and smaller spoons. Sizes are relatively small with the odd 30+ cm (12in) trout caught.

**Benair Lake (C7)** is located just outside the southern tip of Algonquin Park and has a number of camps and cottages along its shoreline. It can be accessed via Elephant Lake Road and provides fair fishing for walleye and muskellunge, as well as good fishing at times for smallmouth and largemouth bass in the 1kg (2 lb) range.

**Big McGarry, Big Lighthouse, Chainey Lakes and Leather Root Lake (E7)** are all small brook trout lakes that can be accessed by good forest roads. All five of the lakes have been stocked with brook trout. Fishing success can vary between the lakes but in general you will experience fair results in winter and spring. Sizes also vary but an average trout is usually in the 20-25 cm (8-10 in) range. In spring, try fly fishing for better results.

**Big Mink Lake (D6)** is a long, thin lake that is stocked regularly with lake trout and can be accessed via a road from Hwy 127. Fishing for lake trout is fair in winter and spring and good for smallmouth bass to 2kg (2.5 lbs). The lake is entirely surrounded by crown land, which makes for a rustic and wilderness setting.

**Big Rock Lake (A7)** is an interior Algonquin Park lake that is found in the southern panhandle of the park. The lake can be accessed via portage from Kingscote Lake to the west or from Byers Lake to the east. Fishing at the lake can be quite good in the spring for average sized lake trout.

**Billings Lakes (A5)** are two Algonquin Park lakes that do not see many visitors throughout the year. Due to the number and distance of the portages along both the southern and northern routes to the lakes, they provide good fishing for brook trout to 35+ cm (14 in). There is a rustic campsite available at Billings Lake.

**Branch and Byers Lakes (A6)** are two lakes found in the southern interior of Algonquin Park. The lakes are somewhat connected and provide good fishing for average sized lake trout and brook trout in the 25-35 cm (10-14 cm) range. Larger brookies can be found in these lakes and there are a few rustic camping sites available on Byers Lake.

**Cannon Lake (G7)** can be accessed off a dirt road west of Maynooth. The lake is surrounded by private land and permission must be obtained to access the lake. There are northern pike and smallmouth bass in the lake in fair numbers. Fishing is generally fair for smaller fish.

**Coughlan Lake (G1)** can be found north from Cross Lake via a 2km trail. A logging road travels near the lake but not right to it. Coughlan Lake is stocked every few years with splake and fishing is often good through the ice and in spring for nice sized splake.

**Cross Lake (G2)** offers a car top boat launch on the lake's southern shore. The access road is found off the west side of Hwy 523. There are a number of camps on the lake's shore but fishing is still good for nice sized smallmouth bass. Bass are caught up to 2.5kg annually, although average 0.5-1kg (1-2 lbs). Lake trout also inhabit this lake. Fishing can be fair in winter or in spring, just after ice off. Little Cleo's and other minnow imitation lures are the most productive. Some decent sized lakers are caught annually.

**Drizzle and Hay Lakes (B3)** are the largest lakes in the area and make up one complete water body. The access point can be found via a gravel (2wd) road at Hay Lake, which doubles as an access point to Algonquin Park. Fishing for smallmouth and largemouth bass to 2.5kg (5.5 lbs) is good and can be very good at times. There are many bays and inlets along with log and rock structure that attracts lunker bass. Fishing for lake trout to 75+ cm (30 lb) is fair with the best success coming by trolling spoons in spring. All three lakes are part of the winter/spring fishing sanctuary to protect fragile lake trout stocks.

**Hawk Lake (G3)** is a secluded brook trout lake that can be accessed by walking through dense bush from Cross Lake Road (Hwy 523). Fishing for average sized brookies is fair throughout the year with ice fishing in winter or fishing just after ice off being the most productive periods.

**Kingscote Lake (A7)** is the access point for the southern interior of Algonquin Park and is found by following the Kingscote Lake Road from Elephant Lake Road. There are seven different campsite locations on the lake and fishing for lake trout and brook trout is fair in the spring and slows significantly as summer progresses. The portage at the north end of the lake opens a variety of interior tripping options.

**Lake St. Peter (E4)** can be found off Hwy 127, north of the village of Maynooth. The northern portion of the lake is a part of Lake St. Peter Provincial Park, however, a number of cottages can also be found on the lake's southern shore. The park offers full amenities and is a beautiful place to camp or picnic. Fishing on the lake is fair throughout the year for average sized smallmouth bass. The lake also supports a natural strain of lake trout. The lake used to be stocked with lake trout in the past. Today, Lake St. Peter relies on natural reproduction; therefore, it is imperative to practice catch and release whenever possible. Fishing for lakers is fair during winter and in spring. In summer, fishing success decreases dramatically. Lakers are found up to 80 cm (31 in) in size. Watch for slot size restrictions and special winter regulations.

**McCoy Lake (A1)** is a small lake found off Hwy 127 and is stocked periodically with splake. Fishing for splake is fair in the spring or through the ice for splake that average 30-40 cm (12-16 in) in size.

**McKenzie Lake (E3)** has a number of cottages along its northern shoreline, although is still a productive fishing lake. A good gravel road leads to the public access point on the lake's northern point. The lake's southern point lies within Lake St. Peter Provincial Park's northern boundary. Fishing for smallmouth bass can be quite good for bass averaging 0.5-1kg (1-2lbs). Many larger bass in the 2.0+ kg (4.5 lb) range are caught yearly. Lake trout are caught up to 60 cm (24 in) in length. Ice fishing is the most productive method for lakers, although spring trolling can also provide decent results. Watch for special regulations on the lake.

**Meach Lakes (D5)** are two average sized brook trout lakes that can be accessed via a 4wd road. Fishing can be good through the ice or in spring for brook trout to 40+ cm (16 lb) in size. Trolling a small silver spoon or fly fishing with nymph and streamer patterns can increase your chances significantly.

**Minnow Lakes (A7)** are two small lakes that can only be accessed by portage from Kingscote Lake in Algonquin Park. 300m (984 ft) down the portage from Kingscote Lake there is a 400m (1,312 ft) portage north to Lower Minnow Lake and from there it's another 300m to Upper Minnow Lake. There are no campsites on the lakes but fishing for brook trout in the 20-30 cm (8-12 in) range can be good in the spring.

**Mitchell Lake (F6)** lies mainly on private property, although the lake's northern shore is crown land. The lake is stocked every few years with brook trout. Fishing success is fair through the ice and in spring for average sized brookies. You must cross across private land to find the lake, be sure to obtain permission before entering.

**Moore Lake (F1)** is a large remote smallmouth bass lake. The only access to the lake is a rough 4wd road found off Hwy 60. The road doesn't give you direct access to the lake, however, it will get you to the small creek that flows out of the lake. From the road it is about 300m (984 ft) to the lake. Due to its remoteness and the rough road travel, the lake receives little pressure. Fishing is very good for nice sized smallmouth bass in the 1-2.5kg range. Some bigger fish have been caught in this lake.

**North Cahiny Lake (F3)** can be found by following the small creek that flows into McKenzie Lake's eastern shore. It is a rough 400m (1,310 ft) bushwhack but it is worth the effort. The lake offers good fishing and sometimes great fishing for smallmouth bass. Bass average 1.5kg (3 lbs) but can be found bigger. The quality of this fishery is due solely to the lack of pressure it receives since there are no roads to the lake.

**Oxbend and Sandox Lake (E6)** are two secluded lakes that can only be accessed by snowmobile or on foot through heavy bush. Both lakes are stocked periodically with splake, which can grow to good sizes in these lakes. Fish in the 60+ cm (24 lb) range have been caught here. Fishing is fair through the ice and in spring, just after ice off. Silver spoons are the most productive lure in winter.

**Pat and Silversheen Lake (D4)** are two small brook trout lakes found west of Lake St. Peter. A dirt road travels right by Silversheen Lake, whereas Pat Lake must be walked to from the road. Both Lakes are stocked every few years with brook trout, which average 20-25 cm (8-10 in) and are periodically found bigger. Fishing is good through the ice and in spring, after ice off. In spring, try a nymph pattern or a small silver spinner.

**Pell Lake (G1)** is a small brook trout lake that is stocked every few years with brook trout. The only access to the lake is by snowmobile in winter or by a trail from Coghlan Lake. The trail actually leads to Lyell Long Lake, however, you can cut north about 250m to Pell Lake. Brookies can be found to 40+ cm (15.5 lb), although are generally much smaller. Ice fishing can be good at times.

**Scorch Lake (A6)** is a remote interior Algonquin Park lake that can be found up a small creek from Branch Lake. There are no campsites at the lake, although if you do make the journey you will be rewarded with good fishing for lake trout, especially in spring.

**Soaking Lake (D3)** is a small, secluded lake that can be found via a 4wd road and offers fair fishing for small brook trout. Ice fishing is popular and if you can get down the soggy roads in the spring, you should have fair to good success. The road to the lake may be difficult to find due to the maze of logging offshoot roads in the area.

**South Little Mink Lake (C7)** is found within the southern boundary of Algonquin Park and can be accessed on foot down an old road into the park. The lake offers slow fishing for small lake trout and fair fishing for brook trout in the 25-35 cm (10-14 in) range.

**Watt Lake (D7)** can be accessed via a 4wd road. Watt Lake is one of the few lakes in the area that offers fishing for largemouth bass. Fishing is generally good for Largemouth that are found in the 1-2kg (2-4.5 lb) range. These bass hit top water flies hard. They also take minnow imitation lures quite aggressively.

**Wicklow Lake (G3)** does not have direct road access, although a logging road does come close to the lake. It is about a 300m (984 ft) walk to the lake through thick bush. Wicklow is stocked every few years with brook trout and fishing is good through the ice and in spring, after ice off. Try nymph patterns or mayfly dry's in spring. A little cleo jig through the ice provides good results in winter.

## Papineau Lake Area (Map 6)

The Bark Lake area lies within the Madawaska Highlands and provides great scenery. There area a number of bigger lakes in the area, including Bark Lake, that provide good fishing opportunities. There are also a few hike-in or paddle access lakes that can provide great outdoor recreation experiences.

**Baldcoot and Littlecoot Lake (G4)** are two secluded lakes that can be accessed via snowmobile or by foot through dense bush. A 4wd road approaches the lakes, although ends about 1.5km from the lakes. Baldcoot Lake has a naturally reproducing strain of brook trout available, while Littlecoot is stocked every few years with splake. Fishing in Baldcoot is fair for generally small brookies. Success in Littlecoot is good through the ice or in spring, just after ice off. Splake can be found in the 35+ cm (14 in) range in Littlecoot Lake.

**Bennet Lake (G3)** used to be stocked with brook trout every few years, although the stocking program was never a big success. Today, you'll find smallmouth bass in fair numbers. Bass average 0.5-1kg (1-2 lbs) and are best caught by a minnow or crayfish imitation lure or fly. Evening and overcast periods increase success.

**Buck Lake (E5)** is a secluded lake that can be accessed via snowmobile or on foot. Northern pike reside in the lake in good numbers and are regularly found roaming the shoreline as evening approaches. Most pike are small but they can reach up to 3kg (6.5 lbs) in size. Lake trout have recently been stocked, although reports on angling success vary. The lake is part of the winter/spring fishing sanctuary.

**Cardwell Lake (A5)** can be accessed by a dirt road and has a few camps along its shoreline. Both smallmouth and largemouth bass are found in the lake in fair numbers. The lake is also stocked semi-annually with rainbow trout, although fishing is fair. For best results, try near the mouth of feeder streams with a fly. Small spinners are also productive.

**Davis Pond (C4)** is a small pond that is stocked every few years with brook trout. Fishing for small brookies is fair throughout the year. For best results try a nymph pattern or mayfly pattern in spring. A 4wd road leads to the pond but most of the fishing occurs during winter.

**Echo Lake (F4)** can be accessed via a 4wd road that travels through private land. The north shore of the lake is private property, although the majority of the shoreline is crown land. The lake was stocked at one time with brook trout. Currently the lake is a part of an annual fishing sanctuary to aid ailing brook trout populations.

**Fraser Lake (G7)** offers fair fishing for smallmouth bass in the 0.5-1kg (1-2 lb) range and for northern pike to 60 cm (24 in). Walleye can also be found up to 70 cm (28 in), although fishing is generally slow. Walleye success picks up during winter months. Try jigging with white or yellow colours. The narrows, around Welsh Island can be a productive spot. A public access point is located on the lakes eastern shore.

**Graphite Lake (A7)** is a popular summer lake that offers fair fishing for small northern pike. These hammer handle pike can be aggressive at times. Spinners, spoons or jigs can all produce results. A road off Hwy 62 leads to the lake, where a public boat launch is available on the lake's northern shore. The lake is surrounded by private land.

**Hicks and Potash Lake (C2)** are two brook trout fishing lakes that can be accessed by snowmobile or on foot through dense bush. Both lakes are stocked every few years with brook trout and fishing can be good through the ice in winter or in spring, just after ice off. Small jigs or silver spoons can be productive through the ice.

**Inright, Johnson and Yuill Lakes (B2)** are three small, secluded brook trout lakes that can only be accessed by snowmobile or on foot through heavy bush. A small stream flows out of Inright Lake into Harris bay, which you can follow to the lake. A 4wd logging road ends about 200m from Yuill Lake. A stream from Johnson Lake can be followed from the access road. All three lakes are stocked regularly with brook trout and provide fair to good fishing in winter and in spring. Sizes reach up to 30 cm (12 in).

**Kamaniskeg Lake (F2)** can be found off Hwy 60, west of the village of Combermere. The lake is very scenic and has several cottages along the lake's shoreline. There is a public boat launch available at the northwest end of the lake. Fishing is good for smallmouth bass in the 1-2kg (2-4.5 lb) range with larger bass to 3kg (6.5 lbs) caught annually. Lake trout are a much sought after species on Kamaniskeg Lake. Fishing for lakers is generally slow, although picks up during ice fishing season. Lakers can be found to 80 cm (30 in) in the lake. Watch for slot size restrictions for lake trout as well as special winter regulations. Northern pike and walleye are also found in the lake in fair numbers.

**Little Papineau Lake (B3)** can be accessed via a dirt road from Cross Lake Road (Hwy 523). The lake offers fair fishing for small northern pike with some fish caught in the 2-3kg (4.5-6.5 lb) range. Smallmouth bass can be aggressive feeders during overcast periods and are found to 2kg (4.5 lbs). Most of the lake is surrounded by crown land.

**McCormick Lake (D3)** can be accessed by snowmobile or on foot from the Papineau-Kamaniskeg Lake Road. The lake was once stocked with brook trout, although it hasn't been stocked in several years. The lake produced average sized brookies at one time, although current information on the fishing quality of the lake is sketchy.

**Poplar Pond (C3)** is a small pond that is found east of Papineau Lake. Access to the pond is limited to snowmobile or on foot. It is about a 300m (984 ft) walk from the road to the pond. Fishing is fair throughout the year and best in spring, after ice off. The pond is stocked every few years with brook trout and as recently as 1998. The average size of trout caught is generally small, at 20-25 cm (8-10 in) in size.

**Purdy Lake and James Lake (E3)** are two lakes that can be accessed via road not far off Hwy 62. Purdy Lake is a popular cottage destination lake that is stocked with lake trout. Lakers can be found up to 65 cm (26 in) and are best caught through the ice. Fishing is fair during winter, but slow during the rest of the year. Purdy Lake also has a fair population of smallmouth bass, which can be found up to 2kg (4.5 lb) in size. Fishing is best in the evening or during overcast periods. Be sure to check special lake trout regulations for Purdy Lake. James Lake is a small lake that is located just north of Purdy Lake. The lake is stocked every few years with brook trout. Fishing can be good in winter and spring for brookies up to 30+ cm (12 lb) range.

**Papineau Lake (C3)** is a popular summer destination lake. The scenery and fishing is quite good, despite the several cottages that line the lake's shoreline. Largemouth bass to 2kg (4.5 lbs) are found in good numbers throughout the lake, while fishing for average sized northern pike is fair. Best results occur during overcast periods and in the evening. Lake trout are found to 70 cm (28 in) in the lake and fishing is fair through the ice or in spring, after ice off. There are two public boat launches onto the lake. One on the north side and one on the south side of the lake. Check regulations for slot size and winter restrictions.

**Salmon Trout Lake (C7)** offers fair fishing for smallmouth bass in the 0.5-1kg (1-2 lb) range. Walleye are also found in the lake but in low numbers. Fishing for walleye is usually slow. Much of the lake is surrounded by private land, although there is a public boat access on the lake's eastern shore.

**Stringer Lake (G6)** can be found off Fort Stewart Road, southeast of Hwy 62. Much of the lake is surrounded by private land but there is a public access area on the lake's north shore. Fishing is fair for small walleye and northern pike. Still jigging is a productive method for finding the roaming walleye in this lake.

**Whiteduck Lake (F3)** is stocked almost annually with rainbow trout. Fishing for rainbow in the 25-30 cm (10-12 in) range can be good at times, especially in spring. To increase your success try fly fishing with the current hatch as rainbow are selective feeders. The lake can be accessed via a dirt road off Hwy 62.

## Latchford Bridge Area (Map 7)
The Latchford Bridge area offers plenty of different angling opportunities from trout to bass and northern pike. The higher elevation characteristic of the area is prime habitat for trout. Brook trout are predominantly found in the smaller lakes in the area, while lake trout can be found in the larger, cooler lakes. Warm water fish species share a few lakes with lake trout and are also found in murky lower level lakes. Similar to many southern Ontario trout lakes, over fishing in some lakes has reduced some natural lake trout populations to extinction. Be sure to practice catch and release whenever possible.

**Beaches, Beaudrie and Dodds Lake (C7)** are three small trout lakes that are stocked every few years with brook trout. All three lakes are best accessed by snowmobile of on foot. Be sure not to trespass, as some areas near these lakes are private lands. Some big brookies have been pulled out of all three lakes but especially Beaudrie Lake. Ice fishing close to shore or other shallow structure can be very effective.

**Buck and Deep Lake (G2, G1)** are two small, secluded lakes. The lakes are stocked regularly and provide good angling opportunities. Fly fishing can be very productive. Try a small nymph pattern or mayfly. Small spoons are the preferred method through the ice.

**Cameron (Eneas) Lake (F4)** can be found off Hwy 515, west of the village of Quadeville. The lake offers slow fishing for small walleye. Several cottages are found along the lake's shoreline and there is no designated public access point to the lake.

**Charlotte Lake (E2)** is a cottage destination lake that offers fair fishing for small northern pike. Smallmouth bass are also found in fair numbers and average 0.5-1kg (1-2 lbs) in size. Charlotte Lake was also one of the few natural lake trout lakes in the area. Unfortunately, over harvest of lakers brought the natural stock to extinction. Today the lake is stocked with lake trout and fishing for lakers can be good at times for nice sized trout. Winter and early spring are the most productive periods.

**Diamond Lake (B3)** is stocked every few years with lake trout, which can grow to good sizes. Diamond Lake was a natural lake trout lake, however, over fishing depleted natural stocks to unsustainable levels. Today, the lake has become a stocked lake trout fishery. Ice fishing is still the most productive method on this lake.

**Dropledge and Marquardt Lake (C6)** are two small lakes set amid the picturesque Madawaska Highlands. These remote lakes can only be accessed on foot or on snowmobile in winter. Brook trout are stocked in both lakes every few years, which provides for good angling opportunities. Fly fishing can be very productive at times.

**Graham and Serpent Lake (G5)** are two brook trout lakes with different characteristics. Graham Lake is accessible mainly by snowmobile in winter or on foot and offers a natural brook trout fishery. The walk from the nearest road is about 1km. Serpent Lake is stocked almost annually with brook trout, which provides a better fishery. The trout don't grow very big but they can be aggressive, especially in winter or spring. Fly fishers will definitely find this lake a pleasure to fish if they can match the hatch. For spincasters, try small spoons or spinners for good action.

**Gun and Halfway Lake (A2)** are found north of the village of Combermere. Both lakes are stocked every few years with splake and provide fair fishing for the hybrid species. Splake can reach sizes in the 45+ cm (18 in) range. Halfway Lake has a number of cottages along its shoreline, while Gun Lake is more secluded. Gun is surrounded by crown land and is much smaller than Halfway Lake. Ice fishing is popular on both lakes.

**Hardwood Lake (D7)** is found not far from Hwy 28. The lake is stocked every few years with splake that can grow to some decent sizes. The fast growing hybrid is very aggressive in winter and in spring, after ice off. Try jigging a small spoon or even a light coloured jig through the ice.

**Lorwall Lake (G1)** has a number of cottages along its shoreline and is a popular summer destination lake. Walleye are found in this lake in fair numbers, although fishing can be slow. Still jigging near shoals or drop-offs can increase production.

**McKeek Lake (A3)** is part of the York River and the Madawaska River system. The lake has a number of cottages along its shoreline but a public access point can be found on McPhees Bay on the east side of the lake. Fishing is fair for average sized smallmouth and largemouth bass. Northern Pike also inhabit the lake in fair numbers and range in size from small hammer handles to about the 70+ cm (28 in) range. The weedy bays of the lake are ideal for both pike and bass species. Minnow imitation lures or jigs can increase success.

**Raglan (White) Lake (C5)** is a lake trout lake that has become solely dependant on stocking for its angling opportunities. The lake is stocked every few years with lake trout and provides fair fishing during ice fishing season and in spring. Lakers can grow to sizes exceeding 70+ cm (28 lb). There is a public boat launch at the north end of the lake that can be accessed via a 4wd dirt road. Much of the lake's shoreline is crown land and rustic camping opportunities are available.

**Salt Lake (A1)** is a small brook trout lake that is wedged in the York River Highlands. It can be accessed via a 4wd road then on foot. The lake is stocked every few years with brook trout. Success is generally good in winter and in spring.

**Turtle Lake (G7)** can be accessed via trail from a dirt road or from the bank of the Madawaska River. Turtle Lake is a beautiful, small lake that is stocked almost annually with brook trout. Ice fishing is often good as well as fishing in the spring. Wilderness camping opportunities are available at the lake.

**Wadsworth Lake (A1)** is a popular summer cottage lake that can be busy at times. There is a public boat launch at the lake's north shore. Lake trout were stocked in the lake in 1997 and fishing quality has picked up from the days when over fishing decimated the population. The current fishery is a stocked fishery and should provide decent angling opportunities in the years to come.

## Lake Clear Area (Map 8)
The Lake Clear area is a scenic outdoor playground. Lake Clear itself is a popular cottage destination lake that can provide plenty of summer fun. The Lower Madawaska River, which is the sight of countless whitewater adventures, flows through the southern portion of the area. Brook trout are the predominant sport fish species in the area and there are some good opportunities for decent sized trout. Ice fishing is popular and one of the more successful angling methods for brookies.

**Addington and Dugan Lake (E4, D4)** are two brook trout lakes that can only be accessed by foot or snowmobile. Addington offers fair fishing for natural brook trout that average 20-25 cm (8-10 in) in size. Dugan Lake is stocked almost annually and provides good fishing through most of the winter and spring months. Fishing slows during the summer period but picks up again for the last few weeks of September. Both lakes are surrounded by crown land and rustic camping opportunities are available.

**Archies Lake (F3)** is located just north of Garvin Lake and is a small secluded brook trout lake. The lake is stocked almost annually and fishing can be good at times. Winter and spring as well as the last few weeks of the season (in September) are productive periods. Fly fishing can increase your success on this lake dramatically.

**Big Limestone Lake (G7)** lies partially within the Centennial Lake Provincial Nature Reserve. The lake is stocked annually with lake trout, which can be found in the 45+ cm (18 lb) range. Fishing is good throughout winter and early spring, although late fall can be the most productive time of year. Access to the lake is limited by snowmobile or in spring and summer via rough trail.

**Buckskin Lake (A2)** is a fairly large lake for brook trout and is stocked every few years. Brookies can grow to good sizes reaching 35+ cm (14 in). Ice fishing is always productive, while fishing in the spring, just after ice off can also be fair.

**Burns Lake (F4)** is one of the few remaining natural lake trout fisheries in the area but fishing success is slow. The lake can be accessed via a dirt road from Hwy 41. There is a public access on the lake's south shore. Ice fishing is closed and the lake is part of the winter/spring sanctuary.

**Canoe Lake (B4)** is stocked almost annually with brook trout. Brookies can be found in the 25 cm (10 in) range and can grow bigger. The lake can be accessed by trail from a 4wd road. Canoe Lake sits amid the picturesque lower Madawaska Highlands and is surrounded by crown land. Wilderness camping opportunities are available at the lake.

**Donahue and Garvin Lake (F3)** are two brook trout lakes that can be accessed by 4wd road. Both lakes offer fair fishing for average sized brook trout with the odd good sized brookie caught annually. Much of the shorelines of both lakes is private land and permission must be obtained to cross private property.

**Elanor and Tooeys Lake (G4)** are two lakes that are stocked almost annually with brook trout. Tooeys Lake lies off Hwy 42, while Elanor Lake can be accessed via road and a short walk. Fishing in Elanor Lake is usually better than in Tooeys Lake due to the fact that it is a little more off the beaten path. There is also a nice picnic area on Tooeys Lake. Fishing is fair in these lakes for generally small brook trout.

**Godin Lake (E5)** can be accessed on foot through dense bush or by snowmobile in winter. The lake is stocked every year with brook trout, which results in a good fishery. Brookies are most aggressive in winter and spring, although the last few weeks of September can be the best time of year. Try a small spoon in the shallows when ice fishing or flies and small spinners throughout the year. The lake's southern stream mouth is often a good holding area for nice sized brookies.

**Highland Lake (C3)** is one of the few lakes in this area that is inhabited by a warmwater sportfish species. The majority of the lake is surrounded by crown land and the only access is by snowmobile or on foot. The lake offers good fishing for small northern pike. The odd big fish can be found. Top water minnow lures or flies can be a lot of fun on this lake.

**Lake Clear (C1)** is a popular summer destination and is one of the larger lakes in the area. Fishing is a big attraction of the lake, which offers three public access points for small trailers. The lake offers a little bit of everything for fishermen. Panfish are an easy catch making the lake enjoyable for kids. Smallmouth bass up to 3kg (6.5 lbs) can be found in good numbers. Fishing for northern pike also offers good for pike up to 5kg (11 lbs) in size. Walleye and lake trout also inhabit the lake, although in smaller numbers. Fishing for walleye is fair for fish in the 1-2kg range and slow for lake trout to 80+ cm (30 in) in size. In the spring of 1998, lake trout were also stocked to help supplement current populations. There are special restrictions on Lake Clear to help preserve the lake's fishery. Watch for the winter/spring sanctuary period and slot size restrictions.

**McHale Lake (A6)** can be found just off a dirt road, west of the village of Griffith. The lake is stocked almost annually with brook trout. Fishing success is usually quite good for trout in the 20-30 cm (8-12 in) range. Try small spoons or white jigs through the ice.

**Morrow Lake (G7)** is stocked annually with lake trout. Fishing is usually good through the ice and in spring for lakers that average 35-40 cm (14-16 in) in size. The access to the lake is by a rough road. Try fishing off the lake's northern point for cruising lakers.

**Schavens and Little Trout Lake (D3)** are two trout lakes that are found south of Hwy 512. Schavens Lake is located at the end of a dirt road and is stocked every few years with splake. Fishing is usually good in the winter and spring for nice sized splake. Little Trout Lake is found east of Schavens Lake. Access to the lake is limited to snowmobile in winter or on foot during spring and summer months. The lake is stocked every few years with brook trout and fishing is generally good in the winter and spring. Trout in the 25 cm (10 in) range are not uncommon.

**Twin Lakes (G4)** are two small lakes that are found off Hwy 41. Lower Twin Lake is stocked annually with rainbow trout and Upper Twin Lake with brook trout. Although the lakes are close to the highway, they can be productive, especially in spring. In late fall, rainbow fishing in Lower Twin Lake can also be good. Trout are generally small in both lakes, however, the odd 35+ cm (14 in) trout can be taken. Fly fishing can increase your chances of success.

## Calabogie Area Lakes (Map 9)

Forested rolling hills surround the many cool, small lakes that dot the landscape. In these lakes, brook trout are the main sport fish species. Whether you enjoy vehicle access or hike-in fishing, the Calabogie area has it all. Brookies do not grow to great sizes but anglers enjoy good success on many lakes .

**Bailey Lake (G7)** is stocked annually with brook trout and provides a good fishery especially in winter and spring. The lake can only be accessed by snowmobile or on foot, which helps reduce angling pressure. The lake is set between scenic highlands and is surrounded by crown land. Wilderness camping is possible.

**Barry, Battery and Belanger Lake (G7)** are three small trout lakes that are located south of Calabogie Lake. Belanger Lake can be accessed by rough road and is stocked almost annually with brook trout. Fishing is often good for brookies in the 25-30 cm (10-12 in) range. Battery Lake can be found via a 4wd road not far from the other two trout lakes. Battery offers fair fishing for sized splake, which are aggressive in early spring.

**Black Donald Lake (B7)** is one of the larger lakes in the area and offers a few public access points. There are several cottages on Black Donald Lake, however, a significant portion of the shoreline is crown land. A few of the islands on the lake are part of Centennial Lake Provincial Nature Reserve Park. Fishing is good for smallmouth bass in the 0.5-1.5kg (1-3.5 lb) range. Try off islands or points along the lake for added success. Walleye average 40 cm (16 in) and can be aggressive during overcast periods. Hammer handle northern pike can be found roaming the numerous bays on this lake. Larger pike are often caught by lucky anglers.

**Calabogie Lake (G6)** lies off Hwy 508. The lake is a popular cottage destination that offers decent fishing opportunities. Northern pike are found to 6kg (13 lbs) with fair fishing throughout the year. Try along the shallows as evening approaches for better success. Smallmouth bass can reach sizes of 2.5kg (5.5 lbs) but there have been rumors of many bigger bass. Crayfish imitations and jigs are good for smallmouth. Walleye are the most sought after species in the lake. Fishing for walleye is generally fair but success can increase during overcast periods. Walleye are found to 3kg (6.5 lbs). Be sure to check the regulations for restrictions.

**Centre and Holmes Lake (D6)** sit side by side and can be accessed via dirt road. It is a short walk to each lake, however, the fishing is worth it. In spring, brook trout are quite aggressive and will chase small spinners or streamers. The lakes are stocked every few years.

**Constant Lake (A1)** offers fair fishing for walleye and northern pike. Walleye can be found up to 4kg (9 lbs) and northern pike to 5+ kg (11 lbs). Many cottages line the shore of this rural lake and most of the surrounding shoreline is private land. Smallmouth bass in the 0.5-1kg (1-2 lb) range can also be found in fair numbers. For perch ethusiasts, fishing is usually good throughout the year.

**Elbow Lake (F7)** is located south of the Madawaska River and can be found by following the small feeder creek from the lake that flows into the Madawaska. Snowmobiles are the best way to find the lake. The lake is stocked every few years with brook trout and provides fair fishing most of the year. In spring, try small spinners or flies.

**Green Lake (B6)** used to be a natural lake trout lake but over fishing brought the natural stocks to extinction. Currently the lake is being stocked but fishing is usually slow for small lakers. There is a public access point at the lake's southern end.

**Heifer and Steer Lake (A7)** are two small lakes that are stocked with brook trout every few years. Fishing for brookies is often good for trout in the 25+ cm range. The popular lakes can be accessed via snowmobile or on foot and are surrounded by crown land.

**Long and Minnow Lake (G7, F7)** are stocked annually with rainbow trout. Long Lake can be accessed via a road, while Minnow Lake can be found by a 4wd road that follows a power line. Fishing can be good in both lakes in spring and late fall. Angling success usually increases when using flies. Small nymph patterns work well in spring.

**Long and Murphy Lake (A5, B4)** are stocked every few years with brook trout. Fishing through the ice can be good at times for average sized brookies, which vary in size from very small to the 30 cm (12 in) range. Spring fishing can also be productive.

**Marble, Scully and Shiner Lake (D6)** are three gems set to the east of Black Donald Lake. The three lakes are often overlooked for fishing opportunities and provide fair to good fishing for small brook trout. A few brookies are found in the 30+ cm (12 in) range and are real scrapers. Ice fishing is quite productive or try in the spring.

**Norway Lake (G4)** has a few cottages along its shoreline. Fishing can be good for smallmouth bass in the 0.5-1kg (1-2 lb) range. Walleye can be found in the lake to 2kg, although fishing is generally slow. Northern pike also inhabit the lake and are found in fair numbers. Most of the pike are small but the odd lunker is produced.

**Oriole Lake (E6)** is a secluded lake found west of Calabogie Lake. The lake is set amid crown land and is stocked annually with rainbow trout. Fishing is generally fair for rainbows in the 25+ cm (10 in) range. Try fly fishing or small spinner/spoons.

**St. Pierre Lake (E6)** can be found off Hwy 508 and is stocked every few years with brook trout. Fishing is fair for average sized brook trout. Winter and spring are the most productive periods.

**Stubinski Lake (C7)** is a small little lake found not far off Hwy 508. The lake is stocked almost every year with brook trout and is really only fished by locals. The lake lies on crown land is a pleasure to fish as fishing is often good. Try a small spinner or a fly for better results.

**Wabun Lake (E7)** offers fair fishing for stocked lake trout on the lake's southern shore. There is a public access point that is found off Hwy 508. Wabun Lake is just north of the Madawaska River and is surrounded by crown land. Success usually increases in winter or spring.

## Burk's Falls Area (Map 10)
The Magnetawan River and many of its headwater tributaries area found in the Burk's Falls area. The logging industry helped establish the small community and today, the steady flow of summer tourism aids Burk's Falls economy. The community is on the doorstep to Algonquin Park's western side and sees its fair share of Algonquinites annually. The area is an outdoor recreation paradise offering everything from fishing to snowmobiling for year round fun.

**Bay (Bucktooth) and Clear Lake (G7, E7)** have cottages along their shorelines and offer fair fishing for smallmouth bass in the 0.5kg (1 lb) range. Clear Lake has recently been stocked with rainbow trout (in 1998), which should result in decent angling opportunities in the years ahead. Bay Lake has been stocked with lake trout and offers fair fishing for small lakers as well as walleye, which can reach 4kg (9 lbs). Ice fishing is the most productive method for lake trout.

**Bernard and Pool Lake (B1)** are two popular summer destination lakes found north of the town of Burk's Falls. Bernard Lake is one of the larger lakes in the area and there are many cottages along its shoreline. The lake is stocked with lake trout, which provides for fair fishing at certain times of year. Smallmouth bass are also found in fair numbers. Smallmouth can often be found holding under docks and other manmade structure. Lake trout can be found to 70+ cm (28 in), while smallmouth can often be caught in the 1.5kg (3.5 lb) range. Pool Lake is a much smaller lake that is found to the southeast of Bernard Lake. Smallmouth bass fishing is fair for bass in the 0.5-1kg (1-2 lb) range. A number of cottages are also found along the lake.

**Bluesky Lake (G1)** is found off a dirt road east of the village of Sundridge. Fishing is fair for small brook trout and can be quite slow. Fishing in spring or the last few weeks of September can increase success.

**Buck and Raven Lakes (G2)** are somewhat secluded, however, they can be reached by 4wd roads. Lower and Upper Raven Lakes are stocked almost annually with splake, which reach 75+ cm (30 in) in size. Fishing can be good through the ice and in spring. The neighbouring Buck Lake continues to host a natural lake trout population. Lake trout average 45 cm (18 in), although can be found to 60 cm (24 in). Fishing in Buck Lake is generally slower than in the Raven Lakes. Be sure to practice catch and release for lake trout when possible.

**Calm and Groom Lake (G6)** have several cottages along their shorelines. The lakes are still quite scenic and offer fair fishing for smallmouth bass. Bass can be found to 2kg (4.5 lbs). These lakes see quite a bit of angling pressure but overcast periods can still be quite productive.

**Compass Lake (B7)** lies off the Seguin Trail and offers fair fishing for smallmouth bass n the 0.5-1kg (1-2 lb) range. Try topwater flies and lures during overcast periods for exciting action.

**Crooked and Tea Lake (F2, E2)** are two small trout lakes that are inhabited by lake trout. It is unknown whether natural lake trout still exist in Tea Lake, however, brook trout can still be found in the lake. Crooked Lake has been stocked with brook trout and fishing is fair for brookies to 25+ cm (10 in). Lake trout angling is currently closed to help re-establish the low population. Incidental catches must be released without harm.

**Deer and Three Mile Lake (E5, D5)** are popular cottage country lakes that offer fair fishing for walleye. Walleye can be found to 3kg (6.5 lbs), although average 0.5-1kg (1-2 lbs). Jigging is the most effective method for finding cruising walleye. On Three Mile Lake, Garden Island can be a good walleye holding area. Lake trout exist, although are difficult to catch on Three Mile Lake. Smallmouth bass also inhabit the lakes and average 1kg.

**Doe Lakes (A6)** are two popular cottage destination lakes that can be accessed off paved roads. Fishing is fair for walleye that can be found up to 3kg (6.5 lbs) in size. Smallmouth bass can be quite aggressive during overcast periods and fishing can be good at times. Bass average 0.5-1kg (1-2 lbs) but can be caught up to 1.5kg. Northern pike also inhabit the lakes and average 2-3kg. Try along the shallows in evening for bigger northerns.

**Emsdale Lake (G7)** can be accessed by dirt road. The lake offers good fishing at times for average sized smallmouth bass. The lake has been stocked with lake trout and fishing is usually fair for nice sized lakers. Spring trolling is a productive time of year for cruising lakers.

**Fifteen and Fourteen Lake (G5)** are two small lakes that can be accessed by dirt road. Both lakes have been stocked in the past with rainbow trout. Fishing is generally slow but can pick up in spring.

**Frank Lake (F3)** was once a natural brook trout lake. A few reports still claim brookies inhabit the lake, however, they are scarce. Rainbow trout were also stocked in the lake at one time.

**Grass, Island and Loon Lake (G2, F2)** are three lakes that have a few cottages along their shoreline and can be accessed by dirt roads. Fishing for trout can be good. Grass Lake continues to sustain a natural lake trout and brook trout population. The lake trout wer edangerously close to collapse, however, the introduction of a winter sanctuary has helped save the species. Island and Loon Lake are now both stocked with lake trout. Lake trout on Loon Lake are generally smaller than Island Lake's. Natural brook trout are found to 40 cm and lake trout to 80 cm (30 in) in Island Lake.

**Hassard Lake (G5)** lies off Hwy 518, north of the village of Kearney. The lake is inhabited by smallmouth bass and provides fair fishing at times for smallmouth to 1.5kg (2.5 lbs). Try crankbaits along shoreline structure for aggressive smallmouth.

**Jack's Lake (C3)** offers fair fishing for nice sized walleye that can be found up to 2kg (4.5 lbs). Fishing for smallmouth bass is also fair for bass in the 0.5kg (1 lb) range. Access to the lake is by road and there are numerous cottages on the small lake.

**Kemick Lake (C4)** is a small lake found near of Burk's Falls. The lake provides fair fishing for smallmouth bass in the 0.5kg (1 lb) range. Try poppers or top water lures for added excitement. Access is by paved road.

**Larson Lake (D4)** is surrounded by private land and permission must be obtained before accessing the lake. The lake provides slow fishing for brook trout.

Mason and Himbury Lake (F3, G6) can be accessed by roads and offer fair fishing for smallmouth bass that average 1kg. Mason Lake is surrounded by private land, while the north shore of Himbury Lake is crown land.

Mayer and Spry Lake (G7) can be good fishing lakes for smallmouth bass in the 0.5-1kg (1-2 lb) range. Many bigger bass are also found in these lakes. Most of Mayer Lake's shoreline and all of Spry Lake is crown land. These two bass lakes are often overlooked by anglers looking for trout or walleye.

North Lake (G1) can be accessed by a 4wd road. The western half of the lake is private land, while the eastern half is crown land. Fishing is fair for average sized brook trout and lake trout. Both species are natural to the lake and it is imperative to follow regulations to maintain this fishery. The lake is part of a winter/spring fishing sanctuary.

Pickerel Lake (D2) offers fair fishing for walleye and northern pike. Walleye can be found exceeding 2.5kg (5.5 lbs), while northern pike can top 3.5kg (7.5 lbs). Smallmouth bass are also found in the lake in fair numbers and fishing can be good at times. Smallmouth average 0.5-1kg, although can be found to 3kg (6.5 lbs) in size. Try crayfish lures or flies worked on the bottom near drop-offs for big bass action. Pickerel Lake has numerous cottages along its shoreline but is still a relaxing and pleasing lake to fish.

Sand Lake (G4) is one of the larger lakes in the Kearney area and is a popular summer destination lake. Many cottages line the shoreline, however, the scenery is still quite enjoyable. Fishing is fair for lake trout to 70 cm (28 in) and for smallmouth bass to 2.5kg (5.5 lbs). The lake is stocked every few years with lake trout. Ice fishing for lakers is the most productive method to catch the elusive fish.

Widgeon Lakes (F1) are two secluded trout lakes. Widgeon Lake can be accessed by a dirt road, while Little Widgeon can be found via canoe and short portage. Widgeon Lake offers good fishing for stocked splake. Little Widgeon provides fair fishing for natural brook trout. Brookies average 25-30 cm (10-12 in) in size.

## Rain Lake Area (Map 11)

Rain Lake lies in Algonquin Provincial Park amid the deciduous highlands of the park's west side. There are plenty of opportunities for both provincial park and crown land camping. Brook trout and lake trout inhabit the small cool lakes of this area. There is canoe access to the lakes within the park boundary and numerous hike-in lakes outside of the park.

Bee Lake (C1) is fairly inaccessible and it is unknown whether trout inhabit the lake. However, the larger unnamed lake directly south of Bee Lake holds brook trout. A rough 4wd road/trail leads to the unnamed lake where brook trout fishing can be good.

Burnt Island Lake (E3) is part of 'Yonge Street' as the canoe route is called from Canoe Lake to Big Trout Lake. Burnt Island is one of the bigger lakes in the park and has several superb campsites to choose from. There are some big lake trout in the lake but they are hard to find. Fishing is fair for smaller lakers early in the year and can be good some days. Wind plays a factor in your angling success on this lake. Smallmouth bass are also found in the lake and in pretty good numbers. When lake trout retreat to the depths of the lake in summer, try the rock drop-offs and bays for 0.5-1.5kg (1-3.5 lb) smallmouth bass.

Butt and Little Trout Lake (E2, F1) are two lakes that lie in a popular western Algonquin interior access area. Butt Lake is the larger of the two lakes and offers fair fishing for lake trout and brook trout. Lake trout can be found larger than 60 cm (24 in), while brook trout are in the 25-30 cm (10-12 in) range. The fishing in Little Trout Lake is generally better than in Butt Lake. There are 20 campsites on Butt Lake and another 11 on Little Trout Lake, including a few island sites.

Casey Lake (E3) is a small Algonquin interior lake that lies between Daisy and Rain Lakes. There are 3 beautiful campsites on the lake and fishing is usually fair for small brook trout. Spring can increase chances of success.

Coffee Lake (C4) is a small secluded brook trout lake that can be found by a short trail from a 4wd road. Fishing can be good at times for decent sized brook trout. If you follow the trail a little further, it leads to an unnamed lake that offers similar fishing as Coffee Lake. Brookies have been caught to 35 cm (14 in ) in these lakes.

Daisy Lake (E3) lies to the south of Hambone and Butt Lakes in the interior of Algonquin Park. There are 7 rustic campsites on the lake, with two of the sites lying on the lake's large island. Fishing is slow throughout the year other than in spring when success is generally fair. Lake trout and brook trout are found in the lake.

David and Mubwayaka Lake (E1) are two interior Algonquin lakes that offer fair fishing for brook trout in the 25-30 cm (10-12 in) range. Fishing can be slow. There are two wilderness campsites on each lake. The main access route to these lakes is from Butt Lake.

Dick Lake (D3) lies near Algonquin Park's western border and can be accessed via a rough road. Fishing can be good at times for brook trout in the 25+ cm (10 in) range. Trout have been caught to 35 cm (14 in) in this lake. Try ice fishing or early spring for better success.

Fox and Willie Lake (B6) are two secluded lakes that can be accessed via trail. A rough road comes close to Willie Lake and then a trail can be picked up from the north side of the lake that leads north to Fox Lake. Both lakes offer fair smallmouth bass fishing that can be good at times. Bass average 0.5-1.5kg (1-3.5 lbs) and can be found much bigger. Topwater lures and flies can provide great excitement. The lakes are surrounded by crown land and wilderness camping is possible.

Graphite Lake (B1) is a long, thin lake that lies near the western border of Algonquin Provincial Park. The lake offers fair fishing for natural lake and brook trout. Lakers can be found to 60+ cm (24 in), while brookies are found in the 25-30 cm (10-12 in) range. Fishing for both trout species is productive in winter and spring. The last few weeks of the season (in September) can also be surprisingly good.

Greenish and Hungry Lake (D7, C6) can both be accessed via 4wd roads. Fishing is generally fair but can be good for brook trout to 35 cm (14 in).

Hambone and Magnetewan Lake (D3) are found in Algonquin Park's western side. Magnetewan Lake is one of the more popular western interior access points to the park. Hambone Lake is one portage east of Magnetewan Lake. There are a few campsites on each lake that receive regular use throughout the year. Fishing in the lakes is slow other than in early spring. Both lakes are inhabited by brook trout, although Hambone Lake also has a population of lake trout.

Hart Lake (B7) is a small secluded lake that provides fair fishing for brook trout. Fishing can be good at times. Try small spinners or nymph patterns for increased success. The small unnamed lake directly to the east of Hart also hosts a population of brook trout. Hart Lake can be found via a 4wd road and a short trail.

Hot and Islet Lake (G4) are accessed mainly from Rain Lake. Smallmouth bass were introduced many years ago to these Algonquin lakes and today they provide good fishing opportunities for interior trippers. Bass average 0.5-1kg (1-2 lbs) but can be found much bigger. Hot Lake is a little small for interior campsites but Islet Lake has 7 canoeing sites and 5 backpacking sites to choose from.

Ink Lake (C5) is a small lake that is easily accessed off a dirt, road. The lake has been stocked with rainbow trout, although angling success is varied. Try small spinners or flies for results.

Little Patterson and Wilkins Lake (B3) are two brook trout lakes that continue to support a fair number of natural brook trout. Both lakes can be accessed by rough roads. Brookies average 25-30 cm (10-12 in) in size but can be found bigger. Camping is possible at the lakes.

McCraney Lake (F5) was once known as Moose Lake but its name was changed many years ago to coincide with the name of the township. McCraney is a good sized Algonquin lake that has 10 rustic campsites including one great island site at the lake's southern end. Fishing is fair for lake trout and brook trout. Lakers average 40-50 cm (16-20 in), while brookies can be found to 30 cm (12 in) in size.

Middle Shanty and Pine Lakes (B2) are both stocked with brook trout every few years. They provide good fishing for brookies in the 20-35 cm (8-14 in) range. Try a small white jig through the ice in winter. In spring, fly fishing is the most productive method of angling. Both lakes can be accessed by 4wd roads. Across the road from Middle Shanty Lake lies a small unnamed lake that also has a good population of brookies in it. There is also another, larger lake just south of there that holds nice sized brook trout.

**Moccasin Lake (G2)** lies along the path from Rain Lake to Misty Lake. This is a small Algonquin Park lake that has 2 exquisite wilderness campsites along its shoreline. Smallmouth bass were introduced to the lake some time ago and provide good fishing opportunities to today's visitors. Bass average 0.5-1kg (1-2 lbs).

**Morgan's Lake (C7)** is surrounded mainly by crown land and offers good fishing at times for smallmouth bass to 2kg (4.5 lbs). Brook trout are also found in the lake but in smaller numbers. The best time of year for brook trout success is in winter. Whitefish can provide for some good action as well.

**Nelson Lakes (E7)** are two crown land lakes that are found close to Algonquin Park's western side. Nelson Lake can be accessed via a road and offers fair fishing for brook trout. Fishing can be slow at times. Little Nelson Lake lies west of Tasso Lake. The lake is stocked every few years with brook trout that can grow to 35 cm (14 in). Fishing is generally fair in spring and through the ice.

**Nightfall Lake (F6)** can be accessed off a 4wd road just outside of Algonquin Provincial Park. The lake supports brook trout. Fishing is sometimes good, although can be slow at times.

**Peters Lake (A6)** has a few camps along its shoreline and is surrounded by crown land. Fishing is fair for smallmouth bass in the 0.5-1kg (1-2 lb) range and usually slow for brook trout. The lake can be found via dirt road. Try plastic jigs for nice sized smallmouth.

**Queer Lake (G1)** is a little further into the interior of Algonquin Park. The lake has 13 rustic campsites and offers good fishing in spring for nice sized trout. Both brook trout and lake trout inhabit the lake. Try near the mouth of Little Queer Creek for feeding trout.

**Rain and Sawyer Lake (E4, F3)** are popular Algonquin Park interior lakes. Rain Lake is one of four western access points to the interior and is busy at times. There are 18 interior campsites on Rain Lake and another 6 on Sawyer Lake. Fishing in both lakes for lake trout is usually slow. Smallmouth bass can be found in the lakes and fishing can be good at times. A small population of brook trout is also found in Sawyer Lake.

**Round Lake (D5)** can be found off Rain Lake Road en route to the Rain Lake Campground of Algonquin Park. Fishing is generally slow but does pick up in spring and fall. The brook trout are usually quite small in this lake.

**Spruce and Whitestone Lakes (A2)** are two small secluded lakes that offer fair to good fishing for brook trout. Spruce Lake continues to be inhabited by a natural strain of brook trout, while Whetstone Lake is stocked every few years with brookies. The trout in Whetstone seem to be larger. Just north of Whetstone Lake, there are two more unnamed lakes that offer decent fishing for nice sized brookies. The first lake is on the left across from Little Whetstone Lake. The other can be found at the end of the 4wd road north of Little Whetstone Lake.

**Tim Lake (C1)** lies along one of the more popular western access routes to the interior of Algonquin Park. There are 6 nice wilderness campsites on the lake. Three of the sites lie on the lake's middle island. Both brook trout and lake trout are found in Tim Lake. Brookies average 25-35 cm (10-14 in), while lakers average 45-50 cm (18-20 in). Fishing is fair for both species but can be slow at times. Try near creek inflows and outflows for brook trout.

**Twentyeight Lake (B4)** can be accessed by trail and is quite secluded. Fishing at this small lake is good in the winter and spring for nice sized brook trout. Fly fishing can be great on this lake in spring.

## Canoe Lake Area (Map 12)

The Canoe Lake area within Algonquin Provincial Park is perhaps the most historic and busy area of the park. The area is the most developed part of the park with cottages and vehicle campgrounds along a few lakes off the Hwy 60 corridor. The area offers numerous trails and easy canoe access to the interior of the park. The canoe routes north of Canoe Lake involve generally shorter portages, which is popular with canoe trippers. The area lakes are somewhat larger than in other areas of the park and are inhabited by mainly brook and lake trout.

**Bonita, Canoe and Tea Lake (C6, C7)** are three busy Algonquin Park lakes that lie along the Hwy 60 corridor. There are cottages on all three lakes, including a park campground on Tea Lake. The lakes continue to support a small population of lake trout, however, heavy angling pressure on the lakes could pose a serious threat to the trout's future in the lakes. Currently there are slot size restrictions on the lakes. Smallmouth bass are also found in the lakes and provide fair fishing for bass in the 0.5-1kg (1-2 lb) range throughout the year.

**Bruce and Owl Lake (E5, E4)** are located north of Source Lake in the park interior. Bruce Lake has one nice campsite available on its shore, while Owl offers three regularly used sites. Bruce Lake is stocked every few years with splake, while Owl continues to support a small lake trout population. Fishing in Bruce Lake is fair in the spring and can be decent in late fall. Splake can reach the 55+ cm (22 in) range. Fishing in Owl Lake is generally slow.

**Brule and Potter Lake (A3, B4)** lie along the old OA&PS (Ottawa Arnprior & Parry Sound) railway. There once was a supply depot on Brule Lake, which helped supply materials to logging camps in the park's interior. The ruins of the old depot can be explored at the north end of the lake. These Algonquin lakes are inhabited by lake trout and smallmouth bass. Fishing is fair for average sized lake trout, while angling for smallmouth bass can be good at times. Smallmouth can be found to 2kg (4.5 lbs) in both lakes. Brook trout are reportedly caught still in Potter Lake, although evidence is sketchy. The introduction of smallmouth bass reduced brook trout numbers dramatically. There are only 2 wilderness campsites on Brule Lake, while there are 5 sites on Potter Lake.

**Cache and Smoke Lake (G6, D7)** are two of the most developed lakes in Algonquin Park with several cottages along the shorelines. This results in significant pressure on natural resources. Both lakes were once lake trout lakes only but smallmouth bass were introduced many years ago. The lake trout are currently under duress and are showing signs of collapse. Slot size restrictions are in place on the lakes, however, practicing catch and release will help preserve these great fish.

**Canisbay and Source Lake (G5, E5)** are found along the Algonquin Park Hwy 60 corridor. There is a campground at Canisbay Lake and 15 paddle-in campsites. The Algonquin Park Education Centre is located on Source Lake. Lake trout are found in the two lakes but in small numbers. Smallmouth bass are the most productive sport fish on the lakes and offer fair fishing for bass that can reach 2kg (4.5 lbs).

**Claude and Grape Lake (E7)** are both found via portage from Smoke Lake. Claude Lake lies along a canoe route and is stocked every few years with splake. Splake are generally small in this lake but can be found exceeding 35 cm (14 in). Grape Lake is a little more out of the way and is stocked every few years with brook trout. The lake can be found by following the small feeder creek to the lake from Smoke Lake's eastern side. Fishing is generally fair for brook trout in the 20-30 cm (8-12 in) range.

**Delano and Hilliard Lake (G6)** are found a few portages south of Cache Lake. There is one rustic campsite at each lake, providing some seclusion during the Algonquin night. Hilliard Lake is stocked with splake every few years, which provides fair fishing for splake to 60 cm (24 in). Delano Lake continues to have a small population of lake trout in the lake, however, fishing is relatively slow.

**Fools and Hailstorm Lake (G2)** are two very secluded Algonquin Park lakes that are inhabited by both lake and brook trout. Unfortunately, the trip to these lakes would take more than one day from Opeongo Lake and there are no campsites available.

**Found, Ouse and Peck Lake (E6)** are three lakes that are found just off the Hwy 60 corridor of Algonquin Park. The lakes are stocked with splake every few years and fishing is fair in spring for small splake. The odd splake can be found exceeding 35 cm (14 in).

**Grant and Jake Lake (G6)** are two small lakes that can be found just south of Hwy 60. The Track and Tower Trail travels past Grant Lake, while Jake Lake can be walked to from the highway. Grant Lake is stocked with splake every few years and offers fair fishing in spring for splake to 40 cm (16 in). Smallmouth bass also inhabit the lake and provide fair fishing throughout the summer months. Jake Lake is stocked every few years with brook trout and fishing is fair for small brookies.

**Groundhog, Loft and Rainbow Lake (B4, C5)** are three interior lakes that are often overlooked by canoeists entering Canoe Lake. Out of the three lakes, there is only one canoe campsite, which is on Rainbow Lake. There are two backpacking sites on both Rainbow and Loft Lake. Fishing on the lakes is fair in the spring for brook trout in the 25-30 cm (10-12 in) range. Rainbow Lake is usually the better of the three lakes.

**Iris Lake (G3)** has a scenic campsite on its northern shore. The lake lies north of Linda Lake and offers generally fair fishing in spring for average sized brook trout. Try small spoons for cruising brookies.

**Jack Lake (G5)** is stocked every few years with splake and lies along the Hwy 60 Algonquin Park corridor. The Hemlock Bluff Trail provides access to the lake. Fishing for splake in the 35+ cm (14 in) range can be good in short spurts. Generally, the fishing is fair in spring.

**Joe Lakes and Tepee Lake (D4, C4)** are scenic lakes found north of Canoe Lake. The lakes offer several wilderness campsites. There is fair fishing for smallmouth bass on all three lakes. Bass average 0.5-1kg (1-2 lbs), although can be found bigger. Joe Lake offers slow fishing for average sized lake trout, while Little Joe Lake continues to support a small population of brook trout. Tepee Lake is inhabited by both lake trout and brook trout. Brookies are generally hard to find, while fishing for lake trout is fair for lakers in the 45-50 cm (18-20 in) range.

**Kenneth and Head Lake (G6)** are located south of Cache Lake. The lakes continue to support a natural strain of lake trout, which can reach 55 cm (22 in). Fishing is generally slow but can be fair at times in spring. Head Lake has 6 rustic canoeing campsites on its shoreline and another 4 backpacking sites. Kenneth is a good lake to find a little seclusion close to Hwy 60. There are 3 campsites on Kenneth Lake, which usually offers better angling success, especially in spring.

**Kirkwood and Phipps Lake (G7)** are found in the southern interior of Algonquin Park and offer fair fishing for lake trout in the 35-45 cm (14-18 in) range. There are two wilderness campsites on each lake.

**Linda and Polly Lake (F4)** are found north of Cannisbay Lake and provide good fishing at times for smallmouth bass to 2kg (4.5 lbs). Lake trout also inhabit Linda Lake. Fishing for lakers to 45 cm (18 in) is fair in early spring, just after ice off. Polly Lake has two rustic campsites available, while Linda Lake offers four, including a picturesque island site. The Minnesing Trail also travels around both lakes.

**Little Doe and Tom Thompson Lake (D4)** are two fine Algonquin interior lakes. Tom Thompson Lake used to be named Blackbear Lake until it was changed in honour of the great Canadian painter. The lakes offer fishing for smallmouth bass to 2kg (4.5 lbs) that can be found bigger. There are some reports of brook trout still caught in Little Doe Lake, however, smallmouth have displaced the species. Lake trout are also found in Tom Thompson Lake in decent numbers. Fishing can be good at times in spring for lakers to 50 cm (20 in).

**Little Island and Tanamakoon Lake (F6)** lie south of Hwy 60 and can only be accessed by canoe/portage. There is a small population of lake trout in both lakes. Brook trout also inhabit Little Island Lake, although fishing is slow. Smallmouth bass provide decent fishing in Tanamakoon Lake.

**McIntosh, Timberwolf and Misty Lake (A2, B2)** are three picturesque interior lakes. There are several prime campsites available on all three lakes, including excellent island sites. Fishing is best in spring on these lakes and is generally fair. McIntosh Lake offers fishing for lakers in the 55-65 cm (22-26 in) range, as well as brook trout to 35 cm (14 in). Timberwolf Lake sports sizes of up to 70 cm (28 in) for lake trout, while brook trout can be found to 40 cm (16 in) on Misty Lake.

**Namakootchie and Sam Lake (B7, C6)** are found along a similar portage route from Canoe Lake. The route experiences low use for being so close to Hwy 60 and offers a great park experience. Three rustic campsites can be found on Drummer Lake and another on Namakootchie Lake. Sam Lake doesn't have any campsites, although it has been stocked with splake. Fishing is fair in spring for generally small splake. Namakootchie Lake offers slow fishing for generally small lake trout and fair fishing in spring for brook trout.

**Otterslide Lakes (F1)** are two gorgeous interior park lakes that are located north of Burnt Island Lake. Fishing is good in spring for lake trout that can be found to 4kg (9 lbs). Trolling a silver spoon near shore can find cruising lakers. If you are fly fishing try a streamer with plenty of crystal flash. Otterslide Lake is an ideal camping lake and has 11 wilderness campsites. Little Otterslide also offers camping.

**Ragged Lake and Parkside Bay** can be easily accessed via a 240m (787 ft) portage from Smoke Lake, a main access point to the southern interior of Algonquin Park. There are numerous campsites located on both water bodies and they can be quite busy all season long. Fishing is slow for brook trout and fair in the spring for average sized lake trout. Smallmouth bass can be found in the 0.5-1+ kg (1-2 lb) range and fishing is generally fair throughout the warmer months.

**Scott Lake (C7)** can be found by following the creek from Bena Lake a short distance north. Brook trout inhabit the lake in pretty good numbers. Fishing can be good for 30 cm (12 in) brookies in spring. The last two weeks of September can also be productive. The lake is a designated catch and release lake.

**Sunbeam Lake (D2)** is an exquisite interior lake that has 8 great campsites available. Three of the rustic sites are located on picturesque islands. Fishing is fair to good at times for lake trout that average 1-2kg (2-4.5 lbs) and are occasionally found bigger. Brook trout also inhabit the lake in fair numbers and can grow to about 30-35 cm (12-14 in).

**West Harry Lake (A6)** offers a secluded campsite on the lake's western shore. There is a dam on the Big East River near the campsite. Brook trout are found in the lake, however, fishing is generally slow.

**Westward Lake (B7)** can be portaged to from the Whiskey Rapids Trail. Brook trout are found in the lake and fishing can be good at times for nice sized trout. Early spring or the last few weeks in September are the best time of year. The lake is a designated catch and release lake.

**White Trout Lake (D1)** is connected to Big Trout Lake and the fishing is very similar. The lake is quite scenic and provides 11 rustic campsites. An old depot farm from the early 1900's, can be explored at the lake's north shore. Grassy Bay at the lake's southern end, is an excellent wildlife viewing area. Moose are often spotted amid the marshy grasses.

## Opeongo Lake Area (Map 13)

Highway 60 travels through the Opeongo Lake area providing easy access to hiking trails and a few vehicle access campgrounds. The Highland Backpacking Trail can be found in this area, as well as the Leaf Lake Cross-Country Ski Trails. Lake and brook trout are the main sport fish species in area lakes, although smallmouth bass also inhabit a number of the lakes. The Algonquin Visitor Centre is a popular attraction that provides educational information on Algonquin Park and its history.

**Aubrey Lake (E7)** is found not far from the northern shore of Galeairy Lake across the old OA & PS railbed. The lake is quite small, although has a good population of smallmouth bass. Bass are generally small but can reach the 1kg (2 lb) range.

**Blackfox and Redfox Lake (B3)** are two interior lakes that do not see much canoeing traffic throughout the year. The only trippers who are willing to make the long trek to these lakes seem to be anglers. Blackfox Lake is stocked every few years with brook trout and provides good fishing for brook trout to 35 cm (14 in). Redfox Lake continues to support a natural brook trout population. Fishing is also good in this lake, especially in spring. Brook trout are on average a little smaller than in Blackfox Lake. Late September can also be productive on both lakes. . There is a seldom used wilderness campsite available on Redfox Lake.

**Bluff, Brewer Lake and Lake St. Anthony (F4)** are three Algonquin lakes that are easily accessed along the Hwy 60 corridor. Brewer Lake is the only lake that can be seen from the highway and is stocked with splake every few years. Splake average 25-35 cm (10-14 in) in size and fishing is fair, especially in spring. Lake St. Anthony is a small lake that can be accessed by portage from Brewer Lake. Bluff Lake is accessed by portage from Hwy 60. Both lakes are stocked every few years with brook trout and offer fair fishing for small brookies. Fishing can be good at times but fly fishing can increase success dramatically.

**Bud and Leaf Lake (F5)** are two small lakes that can be found via trail from Hwy 60 near the west gate of Algonquin Park. A portage from Hwy 60 leads directly to Bud Lake, which is stocked every few years with splake. Fishing is fair and can be good in spring and late September for splake to 40 cm (19 in). Leaf Lake can be found by following a small creek from Pinetree Lake. The lake is stocked with brook trout and offers fair fishing for small brookies. Fishing can be good at times.

**Clarke Lake (G6)** was once a natural brook trout lake. Today, smallmouth bass can also be found in the lake and provide fair fishing for bass to 1.5kg (3.5 lbs). Try floating minnow imitations or bass poppers for exciting top water action.

**Cloud, Coon and Fisher Lake (D5)** are three easily accessed lakes found along the road to the Coon Lake Campground. Cloud and Fisher Lakes are stocked every few years with brook trout, while Coon Lake is stocked with splake. Fishing is slow on Coon Lake but can be fair on Cloud and Fisher Lakes for small brookies.

**Costello and Little McAuley Lake (F4, G4)** are both located north of the Hwy 60 corridor. Costello Lake can be accessed from the Opeongo Lake Road and is stocked with splake but fishing is generally slow. Little McCauley Lake lies along an old stretch of railway bed and can be hiked or portaged to from Hwy 60. The lake is stocked every few years with brook trout and provides good fishing in spring for brookies in the 20-30 cm (8-12 in) range. Late September can also be productive.

**Farm Bay Lake (F7)** is a small lake that can only be found by following a small stream from Purcell Cove on Galeairy Lake. The lake has been stocked with brook trout and provides good fishing for small trout.

**Faya and Provoking Lake (A5)** are two lakes that are found along the Highland Backpacking Trail in Algonquin Park. Provoking Lake has been stocked with splake and is also inhabited by smallmouth bass. Fishing for splake and smallmouth bass is fair, although at times smallmouth can be very aggressive creating a good frenzy of action. Faya Lake is stocked with brook trout every few years. Fishing is fair in spring but can be quite slow. Fly fishing or a worm and bobber are proven methods on Faya Lake. There are 12 backpacking campsites available on Provoking Lake and one on Faya Lake.

**Fraser and Sylvia Lake (E6)** are two interior lakes found south of Hwy 60 along a low-use canoe route. Both lakes have a great interior campsite available, where you can have a whole lake to yourself. Fraser Lake supports a small lake trout population that is most active in early spring. Sylvia Lake offers fishing for both brook trout and lake trout, however, fishing is generally slow.

**Galeairy Lake (G7)** is one of the access points to Algonquin Park's southern panhandle. The lake is quite large and is inhabited by lake trout, smallmouth bass and largemouth bass. Bass fishing is fair throughout the lake for fish to 2.5kg (5.5 lbs). Activity can be good during overcast periods. Fishing for lake trout is slow most of the year, although picks up in late winter/early spring. Lakers can be found in excess of 75 cm (30 in) in this lake. Watch for slot size and special restrictions on the lake.

**Gem and Sandy Lake (E7)** are two small southern Algonquin lakes that are stocked every few years with brook trout. There is an established portage to Gem Lake from Pen Lake. Fishing in Gem Lake can be good at times for small brook trout, although the odd 30+ cm (12 in) brookie can be caught. A rustic trail leads to Sandy Lake but the going is tough. The lake also has good fishing at times for small brookies.

**Godda and Tattler Lake (G3, G2)** can be accessed from Booth Lake. Godda Lake is a few portages away from Booth Lake but makes a great camping location. Fishing is good for lake trout and brook trout. Lakers can be found to 55+ cm (22 in), while brookies can be caught up to 40 cm (16 in). Tattler Lake is really an extension of Booth Lake's western side. There is an old ranger cabin at the lake that can be rented if you reserve ahead. Fishing for smallmouth bass is good throughout the season and the odd brook trout is still found in the lake.

**Gordon and Rosepond Lake (D6)** lie along the Booth Rock Trail of Algonquin Park. Rosepond is a small lake that is stocked with splake every few years. Fishing is fair throughout the year for small splake. Gordon Lake is inhabited by smallmouth bass that can reach 2kg (4.5 lbs) in size. Fishing for smallmouth can be good during overcast periods.

**Harness and Lawrence Lake (A7)** lie in Algonquin Park, south of Hwy 60. Harness Lake can be reached via portage or the Highland Backpacking Trail. There are 6 canoeing sites on the lake and 5 backpacking sites on the lake. Both lakes offer fair fishing in spring or late September for small lake trout.

**Hartley, Little Minnow and Myra Lake (E3)** can each be reached by trail or portage from the southern portion of Opeongo Lake. Little Minnow and Myra Lake are stocked with brook trout every few years and provide fair fishing in spring. Brook trout average 20-25 cm (8-10 in), although are found bigger. Hartley Lake is stocked with splake that can grow to 40 cm (16 in). There are no campsites on these lakes.

**Hiram and Whitegull Lake (B3, B2)** are two secluded lakes that don't see too many visitors. Mainly anglers travel to the lakes from Hwy 60. There are two rustic campsites available and fishing is good on both lakes. Lake trout are found in both lakes to 55 cm (22 in) in size. Whitegull Lake also supports a population of brook trout. Most brookies are caught in the 25-30 cm (10-12 in) range.

**Kathlyn Lake (A4)** lies west of Sasajewun Lake. It can only be accessed by following the small creek to the lake or by orienteering. Lake trout inhabit the lake, although in low numbers. Fishing is slow.

**Kearney Lake (C5)** is found along the Hwy 60 corridor. There is a campground on the lake and fishing is generally slow for small lake trout. Smallmouth bass fishing can be productive at times that average 0.5kg (1 lb). Brook trout are also found in small numbers.

**Lake Of Two Rivers and Pog Lake (B5)** both support lake trout and smallmouth bass. Campgrounds are found on the lakes, which increases activity on the lakes. Fishing is slow for lake trout and fair for smallmouth bass. Bass average 0.5kg (1 lb) but can be found bigger. There are slot size restrictions on lake trout in Lake of Two Rivers.

**Langford and Marmot Lake (C1, D2)** can be reached by portage from Opeongo Lake's western shore. Marmot Lake is a small lake that is stocked with brook trout. Fishing can be good at times for small brook trout. Langford Lake is located at the end of a 1km portage from the North Arm of Opeongo Lake. The lake is stocked every few years with splake and provides for good fishing for small splake in the spring. Try a small nymph pattern or spinners on both lakes.

**Longairy Lake (G6)** lies outside of Algonquin Provincial Park's eastern boundary. The lake can be accessed by snowmobile or on foot from Hwy 60. Splake are stocked almost annually and provide for good fishing in winter/early spring. Splake average 25-35 cm (8-14 in) in size but can be found larger.

**Lunch and Milon Lake (G5)** are two small lakes that lie along Algonquin Park's border. The lakes are stocked with brook trout every few years. Access to the lakes is limited to snowmobile or on foot. Fishing can be good for brookies in the 25-35 cm (8-14 in) range.

**Opeongo Lake (D2)** is the largest lake in Algonquin Provincial Park and wind is often a problem. There are over 135 interior campsites scattered on Opeongo Lake. Lake trout, whitefish and smallmouth bass inhabit the lake. Lakers are found up to 80 cm (32 in) and smallmouth bass average 0.5-1kg (1-2 lbs) but can be caught to 1.5kg (3.5 lbs). Whitefish are quite aggressive at times and can be found cruising bays. They also put up a commendable fight. Fishing is usually slow for lake trout and fair for smallmouth bass.

**Pinetree Lake (F5)** offers fair fishing for generally small lake trout. Pinetree Lake can be found a few portages south of Hwy 60 and is a picturesque lake with 3 superb wilderness campsites.

**Rod & Gun Lake (A7)** is a small southern interior lake found just north of Lake Louisa. There are no campsites on the lake, however, fishing is fair in spring and late September for small brook trout.

**Rock and Whitefish Lake (D7, C6)** are two popular lakes that are easily accessed form the Hwy 60 corridor. Both lakes have cottages on their shoreline, although Rock Lake is more developed. There are organized campgrounds on the lakes as well as popular hiking/biking trails. Lake trout and smallmouth bass are found in each lake. Fishing for lake trout is slow, while smallmouth bass can be active at times. Dusk and dawn are the best times for smallmouth. There are also rustic campsites available on each of the lakes.

**Speckled Trout Lake (C6)** can only be accessed by canoe form the Rock Lake access point or by foot. The lake is stocked with splake and offers fair fishing in spring for average sized splake.

**Sunday and Sproule Lake (D4)** are stocked every few years with splake. The lakes are found close to Hwy 60 and are often busy. There are rustic campsites on both lakes. Fishing is fair in spring and late September for splake in the 30-35 cm (12-14 in) range.

## Madawaska Area Lakes (Map 14)

The small town of Madawaska is surrounded by an endless array of outdoor recreation activities. The Upper Madawaska River provides thrilling whitewater action in the spring. Fishing is good for trout as well as smallmouth bass and walleye in a few of the lakes. Canoer trippers use the Shall Lake access point, north of the town of Madawaska, as the starting point to the Algonquin interior.

**Alsever, Roundbush and Vireo Lake (F2, G1)** are three remote interior lakes that can only be accessed by portage and canoe. All three lakes offer good fishing for trout, especially in spring and late September. Alsever Lake is inhabited by lake trout and brook trout. 40+ cm (16 in) brook trout have been caught in Roundbush Lake. Vireo Lake is the most difficult lake to access and lake trout have been found in the 60+ cm (24 in) range. There are rustic campsites on all lakes.

**Bailey, Band and Boot Lake (A4)** are located on the southeast side of Algonquin Park and are accessed by canoe and portage from Booth Lake. The only campsites found on the lakes are the 2 sites on Boot Lake. The lakes are in a low-use area of Algonquin and fishing is good, especially in spring. Bailey and Band Lake are inhabited by brook trout, while Boot Lake offers both brook trout and lake trout. Brookies found in the lakes average 25-30 cm (10-12 in) in size but are often found bigger. Lake trout in Boot Lake have been caught to 55 cm (22 in). Band Lake is a little harder to get to than the other two lakes. You must follow the feeder stream from Boot Lake's northwest corner.

**Barns, Major and Wish Lake (C4, D4)** are stocked with brook trout every few years. Barns can be accessed by snowmobile or on foot and fishing is good at certain times of the year. Major Lake lies off a dirt road; therefore, it receives the most pressure. Fishing is fair in spring or through the ice. Wish Lake can only be accessed by trail and the southern part of the lake is private land. Fishing is good, especially in spring. Brook trout in these lakes average 20-30 cm (8-12 in).

**Billy Lake (C3)** can be driven to via a dirt road. The lake offers 6 campsites that surprisingly, see low use. The lake has been stocked with splake and fishing is fair for splake that average 30-35 cm (12-14 in) in size.

**Booth Lake (A2)** is a picturesque Algonquin lake. There are 18 rustic campsites available on the lake, including 6 sites scattered on a few of the islands of the lake. The McCarthy Creek and marsh that is found at the southern side of the lake, is a great wildlife viewing area. Fishing in Booth Lake is generally slow for lake trout and brook trout, however, smallmouth bass are quite active at times. Fishing can be good for smallmouth in the 0.5-1kg (1-2 lb) range. Try in the many bays of the lake or deep holes off rocky points.

**Bridle and Kitty Lake (B2)** are located close to the Shall Lake Algonquin access point. There are two interior campsites on Kitty Lake as well as an old ranger cabin, which can be rented. The cabin rental is a different and exciting Algonquin experience. Fishing on Kitty Lake is fair for smallmouth bass that average 0.5kg (1 lb). Brook trout continue to inhabit the lake, however, fishing is usually slow.

**Crevice and Moonbeam Lakes (C5)** are three brook trout lakes that are found off a 4wd road that follows the power line. The lakes are stocked every few years with brook trout. Brookies can reach 35 cm (14 in) in size and fishing is good through the ice and in spring. Late September can also be productive.

**Crotch, Farm and Shall Lake (D3, C3, E3)** are easily accessed from the Shall Lake access point. There are interior campsites on all three lakes, as well as designated paddle-in sites on Crotch Lake. Fishing is fair for small northern pike that are mostly found in the weedier sections of the lakes. Smallmouth bass are also found in these lakes and fishing can be good at times for bass that average 0.5-1kg (1-2 lb). Lake trout can still be found in the lakes, although fishing is usually slow. Lakers can be found to 55 cm (22 in) in size.

**Gliskning and Lobster Lake (A6)** are two semi-secluded lakes that are found close to the village of Whitney. Lobster Lake can be accessed via a 4wd road and provides good fishing at times for nice sized smallmouth bass. Lake trout are also stocked in the lake and offer fair fishing in winter or spring. Gliskning Lake continues to support a small natural lake trout population. Fishing is generally slow but picks up in winter and early spring. Lakers on both lakes can reach 70 cm (28 in).

**Green Lake (G7)** is located by trail found off a dirt road south of the village of Madawaska. The lake is stocked every few years with brook trout and fishing is fair for brookies that average 20-25 cm (8-10 in).

**Greengrass and McFee Lake (C6)** are two secluded lakes that can only be accessed by snowmobile or on foot through sometimes dense bush. Greengrass Lake is stocked with splake and offers good fishing for splake in the 25-35 cm (10-14 in) range. McFee Lake is stocked with brook trout and provides good fishing much of the year. The best times are in winter, spring and late September.

**Hardtack Lake (A5)** can be accessed by 4wd road and is stocked every few years with splake. Splake can be found to 55 cm (22 in).

**Headstone Lakes (A5)** are two lakes surrounded by crown land that are located close to Algonquin Park's West Gate. A rough 4wd road travels directly to Headstone Lake but West Headstone Lake can only be reached by snowmobile or on foot. Headstone Lake is inhabited by smallmouth bass and fishing is good for bass to 1.5kg (3.5 lbs). West Headstone Lake is stocked every few years with splake and offers good fishing at times. Ice fishing or trolling in spring are the most productive angling methods. Splake can reach 55 cm (22 in) in size.

**McCauley Lake (C6)** is a scenic Madawaska Highland lake that is accessible by dirt road. There are a few cottages along its shoreline but fishing is still good at times for smallmouth bass in the 1kg (2 lb) range. Brook trout and lake trout are also found in the lake. Brookies are hard to find, mainly due to competition with smallmouth bass. Lake trout fishing is fair for natural lake trout that can reach 55 cm (22 in). Any further development of the lake may jeopardize the lake trout population. Watch for special restrictions on the lake.

**McKaskill Lake (E1)** is a scenic Algonquin interior lake that has 7 nice campsites to choose from. An old ranger cabin is also found on the lakes, which can be rented on a per night basis. Fishing is good for nice sized brook trout and lake trout. Spring is the most productive time of year, however, the last few weeks of September can also be good. Try near any stream inflows for big brookies. Streamer patterns or small silver spoons are the flies or lures of choice.

**McNevin and Sea Lake (G4, E4)** are two smallmouth bass lakes found near Victoria Lake. Access is rough road. The lakes are surrounded by private land and there are cottages on the shorelines. Fishing is fair throughout the year but can be good at times. Bass are found to 2kg (4.5 lbs) in both lakes.

**Mole and Raja Lake (A3)** are two interior lakes that are located south of Booth Lake. Mole Lake offers good fishing for smallmouth bass to 1.5kg (3.5 lbs). Brook trout continue to inhabit the lake, although fishing success is only fair. Raja Lake has a healthy population of brook trout, which can grow to 35 cm (14 in). Fishing is good in spring and late September. Both lakes have campsites available.

**Oneside and Otherside Lake (D5)** are two secluded lakes. Although a dirt road passes near the lakes, you must walk or use an ATV to reach the lakes. There is a short trail from Oneside Lake that leads to Otherside Lake. Oneside Lake is stocked every few years with splake, while Otherside Lake is stocked with brook trout. Fishing is good at times in both lakes in winter or early spring. The splake in Oneside Lake are generally larger than the brookies in Otherside Lake.

**Poverty Lake (A7)** can be accessed by dirt road south of Whitney. Fishing for largemouth bass is fair for bass in the 0.5-1kg (1-2 lb) range. Rustic camping opportunities exist on the lake.

**Rapid Lake (A6)** is a widening of the Madawaska River found downstream from Whitney. Smallmouth bass and walleye are found in the lake. Fishing is fair for smallmouth and generally slow for walleye. Smallmouth can be found to 1.5kg (3.5 lbs) in the lake.

**Richard Lake (B4)** can be accessed by snowmobile or by canoe and portage from the interior of Algonquin Park. Fishing is good for stocked splake in the 40-50 cm (16-20 in) range.

**Round Island Lake (A1)** lies deep within the Algonquin interior and is quite difficult to access. This scenic lake offers 4 wilderness campsites to choose from. Fishing is good in this lake for lake trout that average 35-40 cm (14-16 in) in size but can be found to 70 cm (28 in) in size. Try trolling a little cleo or streamer pattern along the shoreline in spring. In summer, lakers retreat to the colder depths of the lake and are much harder to find.

**Ryan Lake (D1)** has 10 interior campsites on the lake and can be busy on summer long weekends. The lake is stocked every few years with splake that can be found to 50 cm (20 in). Fishing is fair in spring and late September. The lake was stocked with rainbow at one time.

**Shirley Lake (C1)** is a scenic Algonquin interior lake found north of the Shall Lake access point. There are 9 rustic campsites on the lake that are all quite nice. Fishing for lake trout to 65 cm (26 in) is slow throughout the year but picks up in early spring.

**Seesaw Lake (A5)** is a small secluded lake that is stocked every few years with brook trout. Brookies in the lake are small and can be quite active in late winter or early spring. The only access to the lake is on foot or by snowmobile.

**Trout and Tub Lake (G6)** are two hidden trout lakes that are stocked every few years with brook trout. The only access to the lakes is by snowmobile or on foot. Fishing is good through the ice and in spring for small trout.

**Tuya Lake (B6)** can be accessed by following the power line along the 4wd access road. The lake is stocked with brook trout and offers fair fishing for generally small trout. Try a small spinner or nymph patterns.

**Victoria Lake (F3)** is one of the larger lakes in the area. The lake lies amid the Algonquin Highlands near the border of the park. A road leads to the lake and there are several cottages along the shoreline. Fishing is good for smallmouth bass to 2kg (4.5 lbs) and fair for lake trout to 70+ cm (28 in). In summer, lake trout fishing is quite slow. Watch for slot size restrictions and special winter regulations. There is no camping available at the lake.

## Barry's Bay Area (Map 15)
Barry's Bay is a great outdoor recreation area with five provincial parks in the region to enjoy. Fishing in the area is quite good on both the larger and smaller lakes in the region. Barry's Bay is known for its picturesque highland scenery and is an ideal place to experience the magnificent display of fall colours. There are camping opportunities at provincial parks as well as on crown land around many of the lakes.

**Aylen Lake (B4)** is one of the largest lakes in the area and is a popular cottage destination lake. Fishing can be good for smallmouth bass to 2kg (4.5 lbs). There is also a natural strain of lake trout in the lake but fishing is slow most of the year. Lakers can reach 70 cm (28 in) in size. There is a public access point on the lake's southwestern shore. In summer, jigging off Big Green Island can be productive for smallmouth bass. Watch for special regulations on the lake.

**Balfour Lake (A3)** can be accessed by a 4wd road west of Aylen Lake. Fishing is good for smallmouth bass to 2kg (4.5 lbs) and fair for lake trout. Lake trout are stocked in the lake and can be found to 3kg (6.5 lbs) in size. Wilderness camping opportunities exist at the lake.

**Bark Lake (B7)** hosts the non-operating Bell Bay Provincial Park on its northern shoreline. There are also cottages on the lake, although a large portion of the lake's shoreline remains crown land. Fishing can be good for smallmouth bass in the 0.5-1kg (1-2 lb) range but bass can be caught to 2kg (4.5 lbs). Lake trout also inhabit the lake, however, the natural population is almost gone. The lake is stocked annually to provide a decent angling experience on this popular lake. Fishing for stocked lake trout is fair for trout that can exceed 80 cm (31 in).

**Basin Lake (D1)** is an interior Algonquin lake that can be accessed on a rough road. There is parking available at the southern end of the lake, which has 4 charming campsites, including one on a small island. Fishing is good at times for smallmouth bass to 1.5kg (3.5 lbs), which are occasionally found bigger. Northern pike are also found in the lake in the 1.5-2.5kg range. Fishing is best during overcast periods or in the evening. Remnants of the Basin Lake Depot can still be found at the lake. The depot was an important supply station for interior logging camps from the mid 1800's to 1913.

**Bear and Spectacle Lake (A6, B6)** have both been stocked with splake. Bear Lake can be accessed on foot or by snowmobile and a dirt road leads to Spectacle Lake. A few good sized splake have been caught in these lakes.

**Carson and Trout Lake (E7)** are separated by Hwy 60, west of the town of Barry's Bay. The lake's were originally natural lake trout lakes, however, over fishing brought the natural strain to extinction. Today, the lakes are stocked every few years with lake trout. Fishing is slow most of the time but can pick up in winter and early spring. Check special regulations for Carson Lake.

**Fish Lake (B6)** is a small trout lake that is stocked every few years with brook trout. The lake can be accessed on foot from a dirt road, not far from Hwy 60. Fishing is fair for brook trout to 25+ cm (10 in).

**Finger and Haskins Lake (C5, D5)** are two hidden trout lakes that are found south of Aylen Lake. Finger Lake can be accessed by snowmobile or on foot and is stocked every few years with brook trout. Fishing is fair for brookies to 30 cm (12 in) and is best in spring. Haskins Lake has been stocked with lake trout. Fishing for small lakers is good through the ice. There is a 4wd road that leads to the lake.

**Martineau Lake (D3)** reportedly supports a decent natural brook trout population but evidence of angling success is sketchy. The lake can be accessed via snowmobile trail and 4wd road.

**McDonald Lake (D2)** is a secluded trout lake that can be accessed by snowmobile or on foot from a rough 4wd road. The lake is stocked with brook trout every few years and offers good fishing for brookies to 30 cm (12 in). Jig a little cleo through the ice in winter for added success. Fly fishing can really increase your action in spring.

**Monkshood Lake (A4)** can be found by a long trail from Aylen Lake Road. The trail makes a good hike-in opportunity to a secluded lake. The lake is stocked every few years with splake and provides good fishing through the ice and in spring for nice sized splake.

**Mink Lake (A7)** is a small lake that lies off Bark Lake's southwestern shore. The easiest access is by following the outflow stream from Bark Lake. Fishing is fair for small natural brook trout on Mink Lake

**O'Neill Lake (B2)** can only be accessed by trail or portage from the north side of Aylen Lake. A small portion of the lake's northern shore lies within Algonquin Provincial Park. Interior camping permits must be obtained to stay at the 2 designated campsites on the lake. Fishing is good in spring for stocked splake to 50 cm (20 in).

**Paugh Lake (F4)** has a few cottages along its shoreline and offers fair fishing for lake trout and walleye. Lakers can be found to 70 cm (28 in), while walleye average 1-1.5kg (2-3.5 lbs). Fishing success for both species increases somewhat in winter. Lakers that are especially hard to find in summer. Most of the lake remains crown land and there is a public access point on the lake's eastern shore.

**Robitaille and Wilkins Lake (B2, A1)** are two remote Algonquin Park lakes that offer good fishing for trout. The lakes can only be accessed by canoe and portage from Aylen Lake. If you intend to go directly to Wilkins Lake, there is a cart trail near the north end of Aylen Lake that can be used. There are 6 wilderness campsites on both lakes, which are all quite nice. Lake trout are found in both lakes to 65+ cm (26 in) in size. Robitaille Lake is also inhabited by brook trout which can reach 35+ cm (14 in). Fishing can be quite good in spring or late September for both species. Moose are often spotted along the marshy shores of Robitaille Lake.

**Pine Lakes (G1)** offer good fishing at times for small northern pike. Pike do not usually exceed 2.5kg (5.5 lbs) and average 1-2kg (2-4.5 lbs). Upper Pine Lake is often better for pike. Lower Pine Lake can be found via 4wd road while Upper Pine Lake lies within Algonquin Park and can be accessed by travelling up the Pine River from Lower Pine Lake. There are no designated campsites on Upper Pine Lake.

**Walker Lake (G1)** can be accessed by snowmobile or on foot from a 4wd road. Fishing is good for stocked brook trout, which can reach 35 cm (14 in) in size in this lake.

## Round Lake Area (Map 16)
The Round Lake area is a popular cottage destination region and is a great place to spend the lazy days of summer. Round Lake and Golden Lake are the main attraction of the area, although there are a few smaller lakes that provide outdoor recreation opportunities. Walleye are the most sought after sport fish species in the area, however, other warm water sport fish species are also available in decent numbers.

**Acorn Lake (A1)** is a small lake that can be accessed on foot from the dirt road that follows the Bonnechere River. The lake is stocked almost annually with brook trout and fishing can be good at times for brookies in the 20-25 cm (8-10 in) range.

**Round Lake (C3)** is one of the larger lakes in the area and is a popular cottage destination lake. Bonnechere and Foy Provincial Parks can also be found on the lake. Fishing is fair for northern pike to 5kg (11 lbs). Smallmouth and largemouth bass inhabit the lake in fair numbers and fishing can be quite productive at times for bass to 2.5kg (5.5 lbs). Walleye and lake trout are also found in the lake. Fishing is fair for walleye to 3.5kg (8 lbs), while lake trout fishing is generally slow for natural lake trout that can exceed 80 cm (31 in) in size. Watch for slot size and special winter regulations.

**Golden Lake (G5)** is one of the larger lakes in the area. The lake is a popular cottage destination lake and offers fair fishing for bass. Smallmouth and largemouth bass are found in the lake to 2.5kg (5.5 lbs). Fishing for northern pike is also fair for northerns in the 2-3kg range. Walleye fishing is slow but can be fair at times for walleye that reach 3kg (6.5 lbs). Muskellunge are also present in Golden Lake. Fall is the best time of year to find elusive muskellunge.

**Silver Pond (E1)** is a small pond that is stocked with brook trout. Access to the pond is by 4wd road and fishing is fair for small brookies. Try a small spinner or nymph pattern for added success.

**Skard's Bay (E3)** is a small bay found down river from Round Lake. Most of the bays from Round Lake to Golden Lake have similar characteristics as this one. There is a public access point on the bay. Fishing is fair for northern pike and bass. Both smallmouth and largemouth bass are found in the bay to 2kg (4.5 lb). Walleye are also found in the bay, although in small numbers.

## Eganville Area (Map 17)

The Eganville area lies within the transition zone from cool highland waters to the warmer waters of the Ottawa Valley. Eganville is a small, scenic, valley town that offers a number of outdoor recreation possibilities, including fishing. Snowmobiling is one of the more popular recreation activities in the winter.

**Crooked Lake (B1)** can be accessed by a rough road and is surrounded by crown land. Fishing is fair for smallmouth and largemouth bass in the 0.5-1kg (1-2 lb) range. Walleye can be found in the lake along with small northern pike. Pike fishing is usually fair.

**Johnsons Lake (A3)** can be accessed by a rough dirt road. Smallmouth bass are found in fair numbers and grow to about 1.5kg (3.5 lbs). Brook trout are stocked in the lake every few years and provide fair fishing for brookies to 30 cm (12 in).

**Lake Dore (F4)** is a popular cottage destination lake that offers fair fishing for smallmouth and largemouth bass to 2.5kg (5.5 lbs). Crayfish imitation lures and flies are the tackle of choice to find larger smallmouth. Fishing for northern pike to 4kg (9 lbs) is also fair throughout the summer months. Try casting near shore in evening to find prowling pike. Walleye are also found in the lake, however, in small numbers. There is a public boat launch at the lake's northeastern side.

**Mink Lake (G5)** has many cottages along its shoreline as well as three public access points. Fishing is slow for generally small walleye and northern pike. Smallmouth bass are also found in the lake to 2kg (4.5 lbs). Fishing can be fair at times for smallmouth.

**Mud Lake (G1)** is part of the Muskrat River system. The murky lake is inhabited by northern pike and offers fair fishing for pike to 2.5kg (5.5 lbs). The main access point is found off Hwy 17.

**Silver Lake (B7)** is surrounded by private property and permission may be needed to access the lake. Smallmouth bass are found in the lake in fair numbers. Bass have been caught to 2kg (4.5 lbs) in this lake.

**Wilber Lake (D6)** is part of the Bonnechere River system and offers slow fishing for northern pike to 4kg (9 lbs). Smallmouth and largemouth bass are also found in the lake in fair numbers.

## Cobden Area Lakes (Map 18)

The Cobden Area is a historic small Ottawa Valley town that was one of the first settlements in the region. Muskrat Lake and the small chain of lakes south of it make up the historic canoe route of Samuel De Champlain. The route was a large detour around the violent rapids on the Ottawa River near Rocher Fendu. The lakes became a part of the historic voyageur transportation route from Quebec City to Lake Superior.

**Muskrat Lake (C2)** is a large lake found south of Pembroke and can be busy during the summer months. There are many cottages along the lake's shoreline as well as two public boat launches on the lake's southwestern shore. Lake trout are found in the lake along with northern pike and bass. Lake trout can be found to 80 cm (30 in) in size and fishing is usually slow. Fishing for northern pike, which average 3kg (6.5 lbs), is fair. Smallmouth and largemouth bass fishing is fair for bass to 2.5kg (5.5 lbs). Try minnow imitations for pike and bass.

**Olmstead Lake (F5)** is inhabited by smallmouth bass and northern pike. Fishing for both species is fair and is best during overcast periods. Northern pike can be found to 3kg (6.5 lbs), while smallmouth bass have been caught to 2kg (4.5 lbs). The lake is easily accessed by paved road and can be busy during summer months.

**Waites Lake (G2)** is a small lake found near Grant's Settlement, southeast of Beachburg. The lake continues to support a population of brook trout. Permission must be obtained to access the lake.

## South River/Trout Creek Area (Map 19)

South River and Trout Creek are two small Ontario towns that are the ideal location for outdoor recreation enthusiasts. Summer and winter recreation activities abound in the area. The region is set amid the Almaguin Highlands and provides access to Algonquin Provincial Park's western side. Fishing in the area is a popular attraction, with the main species being brook trout. Winter or spring are the most productive periods when fishing for brook trout, although late September can also be successful.

**Bacon Lake (C5)** lies next to the railway line from South River to Trout Creek. A dirt road leads to the railway, which can then be followed to the lake. Fishing is slow for natural lake trout, partly because the lake receives significant ice fishing pressure.

**Beautiful, Laurier and Seven Lake (C4)** are three secluded brook trout lakes. Beautiful Lake can be accessed by a rough 4wd road and Laurier Lake and Seven Lake can only be found by trail. A large portion of Beautiful Lake is private land but there is a crown land trail to the lake's eastern side. Beautiful Lake and Laurier Lake are both stocked with brook trout every few years. Fishing is often good for brook trout to 30+ cm (12+ cm). Seven Lake supports a natural brook trout fishery and fishing can be quite good for small brookies.

**Blue Lake (G4)** is a small lake found just south of Kawawaymog Lake. The lake supports a population of natural brook trout. Fishing is fair in spring and winter for brookies in the 20-30 cm (8-12 in) range but fishing can be quite slow. A dirt road passes by the lake.

**Butterfield and Paisley Lake (F6)** can both be easily accessed by a dirt road. Butterfield Lake has a small population of brook trout remaining in the lake, while Paisley Lake has been stocked with brook trout. Fishing is fair in Paisley Lake for generally small trout. Much of the shoreline of both lakes is private land.

**Capsell and Long Lake (G5)** are both stocked every few years with brook trout. The lakes can be accessed via a rough dirt road and offer good fishing at times for brookies to 35 cm (14 in). Fly fishing in spring can increase your success. Wilderness camping opportunities exist at the lakes.

**Corncob and Tower Lake (F4)** are two brook trout lakes that are found west of Kawawaymog Lake. Corncob Lake can be accessed on foot from a 4wd road, while a dirt road passes by Tower Lake. Fishing is generally fair in Corncob Lake but can be good at times. Tower lake is stocked every few years with brook trout and fishing for brookies to 30 cm (12 in) can be good at this lake.

**Cornick and Shaw Lake (G3)** are accessed by a dirt road and are surrounded by crown land. Shaw Lake has been stocked with rainbow trout and fishing can be good for rainbows to 35 cm (14 in). Cornick Lake supports a brook trout fishery that holds throughout the year.

**Deadhorse and Twin Lake (G5)** are two lakes that can only be accessed by trail from a dirt road. The lakes support populations of natural brook trout and fishing can be good in both lakes, especially in spring. Brookies have been caught exceeding 35 cm (14 in) in these lakes. Try a small silver spoon or nymph fly patterns.

**Dight Lake (E7)** is surrounded by private land and permission must be obtained to access the lake. Brook trout inhabit the lake in good numbers and have been found in excess of 30 cm (12 in).

**Forest Lake (D6)** is part of the South River system and has many cottages along its shoreline. Fishing is slow for brook trout that were stocked a number of years ago. Rainbow trout were also stocked at one time.

**Genesee Lake (E1)** can be accessed via a 4wd road east of the town of Trout Creek. Fishing can be good for brook trout to 35 cm (14 in). Try a small spoon through the ice or mayfly patterns in early spring.

**Hawe and Timpano Lake (D3)** lie southeast of the town of Trout Creek. Hawe Lake can be accessed by 4wd road, while Timpano Lake can only be accessed by snowmobile or on foot. A large portion of Hawe Lake is private land and permission may be needed to access the lake. Fishing is fair for usually small brook trout. Timpano Lake offers good fishing for similar sized brook trout.

**Hinsburger and Osborne Lake (F2)** are two natural brook trout lakes that can be found via a rough dirt road. Fishing is fair for brook trout to 35 cm (14 in). Try fly fishing in the spring for increased action.

**Kawasda and Tyne Lakes (G2)** are all accessible by a rough dirt road. There are a few camps on Tyne and Little Tyne Lake, however, Kawasda Lake is surrounded by crown land. Tyne Lake is stocked every few years with splake and provides good fishing for splake to 50 cm (20 in). Little Tyne Lake continues to support a natural brook trout population and fishing is fair for trout to 30 cm (12 in). Kawasda Lake is stocked every few years with brook trout. Brookies grow a little larger in Kawasda Lake and fishing can be quite good at times.

**Kawawaymog Lake (G4)** is one of the larger lakes in the area and serves as one of the western access points to Algonquin Provincial Park. There are a few cottages along the lakes shore, however, most of the shoreline is crown land. A dirt road provides access to much of the lake. Brook trout inhabit the lake and fishing is fair in spring for good sized brookies. Trolling small spoons is one of the preferred methods.

**Lambs and Little Beaver Lake (F3)** are two small secluded lakes that offer fishing for small brook trout. Lambs Lake lies at an intersection of bush roads, while Little Beaver Lake can only be accessed by trail. Lambs supports a natural brook trout population and fishing is generally fair. Little Beaver Lake is stocked with brook trout every few years and fishing can be quite good, especially in spring.

**Loxton and Smyth Lake (F3, E3)** both have a few cottages along their shorelines but are mostly surrounded by crown land. The lakes are accessible by dirt roads. Loxton Lake supports a natural brook trout population and fishing is fair in spring or through the ice for brookies to 35 cm (14 in). Smyth Lake is stocked every few years with rainbow trout, which provides for good fishing, especially in spring. Damselfly patterns can be effective at Smyth Lake. For spin casters try a small mepps spinner.

**Lynch Lake (D7)** can be accessed by a paved road east of the town of Sundridge. There are cottages on the lake, however, the eastern side of the lake remains crown land. Rainbow trout are stocked every few years and provide fair fishing opportunities in spring and late fall.

**Peyton Lakes (G7)** are two remote, picturesque lakes found amid the Almaguin Highlands. The only access to the lakes is by trail, which has helped immensely in maintaining the quality of the lakes. Almost all of the fishing on these lakes is done through the ice in winter. Snowmobiles make it much easier to access the lakes. Both lakes are inhabited by natural brook trout and offer quite good fishing at times. Brookies in the lakes are not very big but they do hit hard at times. Trout caught in the lakes average 20-35 cm (8-14 in) in size.

**Red Deer and Scheil Lake (C4)** are two scenic brook trout lakes found not far from Hwy 11. Both lakes are stocked with brook trout every few years. Scheil Lake is surrounded by private land, although the 4wd access road leads to a portion of shoreline that is crown land. Fishing is fair for trout to 35 cm (14 in). Red Deer Lake can be accessed by snowmobile or on foot from a 4wd road. The small lake is encompassed by crown and offers good fishing at times for similar sized brookies.

**Sausage Lake (D2)** has a few cottages on the lake and is easily accessed from a road. Brook trout inhabit the lake in fair numbers, however, fishing is usually slow. Trolling a small spoon in spring can be effective. For fly fishers, try a streamer or wooly bugger pattern.

**South River Area (B6)** is easily accessed by town roads. We have included the river here because beside the town is the size of a lake even though it is not officially a lake. Brook trout are still occasionally found in the reservoir and rainbow trout were stocked in the area at one time. Smallmouth bass are your best angling bet, with a fair population found in the 0.5-1kg (1-2 lb) range.

**Starvation Lake (F7)** is a small lake that can be accessed by trail from a dirt road. Smallmouth bass to 2kg (4.5 lbs) are found in the lake and fishing can be very good at times.

**Twelve Lake (E2)** is a small hidden lake set amid the Almaguin Highlands. The lake can only be accessed by trail, which helps reduce the fishing pressure on the lake. It has been stocked with brook trout and fishing can be good throughout the year. In spring or late September, fishing success increases, especially if fly fishing. For spin casters, try a small spinner in spring.

**Twentyseven Lake (F5)** can be accessed by 4wd road east of South River. The lake supports a natural brook trout fishery, which provides good fishing at times for nice sized trout. Ice fishing with a small spoon or white jig can be effective. Small spinners have been productive in spring. Damselfly nymphs have also created good action on this lake.

**Wendigo Lake (D4)** has been stocked with rainbow trout and fishing reports are positive. There are claims of good fishing for rainbows up to 35 cm (14 in) in size. The lake is easily accessed from the Forestry Tower Road.

## North Tea Lake Area (Map 20)

The North Tea Lake area is set amid the western highlands of Algonquin Provincial Park. The area is a popular access to the western interior of the park due to the endless amount of canoe route options. Brook trout are the main fish species that are found in the area, however, lake trout are also found in a number of interior park lakes. Fishing is best in these lakes in early spring or the last few weeks in September.

**Beaverpaw, Loontail and Vulture Lake (G6, G5)** are probably three of the most remote lakes in Algonquin Park. The lakes lie amid a designated Algonquin nature reserve area. There is no access to the lakes and there are no designated campsites. All three lakes are inhabited by brook trout.

**Biggar Lake (F3)** is a large interior lake. If winds are not a factor on North Tea Lake, Biggar Lake can be accessed within one day. There are over 20 rustic campsites on the picturesque Biggar Lake. Fishing is a major attraction for visitors in spring. Lake trout can be found in excess of 70 cm (28 in), while brook trout have been caught to 45 cm (18 in). Due to the size of the lake, angling success varies as it can be difficult to find fish. In general, the lake offers fair angling, which can be good at times. Try near creek mouths for foraging trout.

**Big Bob Lake (B7)** is a remote lake that is rarely visited. There are 3 wilderness campsites on the lake and fishing can be good in spring or late September for brook trout in the 20-30 cm (8-12 in) range.

**Birchcliffe and Calm Lake (G3)** are two secluded Algonquin lakes that take at least two days to access. There are 2 nice interior campsites on Birchcliffe Lake and an old ranger cabin. The cabin is in great shape and can be rented if prior arrangements are made. Fishing in Birchcliffe Lake can be very good for smallmouth bass that average 0.5-1kg (1-2 lbs) but have been caught in excess of 2kg (4.5 lbs). Calm Lake is a 1,395m portage south from Birchcliffe Lake. There are 2 rustic campsites found on this small, scenic lake. Small brook trout are found in good numbers in Calm Lake.

**Crystal Lakes (A7)** can only be accessed by snowmobile or on foot by trail. The trail can be picked up off the road near Wolf Lake. The first lake north from Wolf Lake is really the only lake officially named Crystal Lake. The other two lakes found due north from Crystal Lake are unnamed, however, offer similar fishing. These lakes are seldom visited in spring and summer months. Their inaccessibility has helped maintain a very good natural brook trout fishery. Be conscious of the fragility of these lakes and practice catch and release.

**Fassett and Shad Lake (A1)** are found on the north west corner of Algonquin Park. It is at least a two day trip from the nearest access point to reach these lakes. The scenery is magnificent and the fishing is good. Both lakes are inhabited by brook trout, while Fassett Lake also has lake trout. Brookies can be found to 35 cm (14 in). Lake trout in Fassett Lake have been caught in the 65 cm (26 in) range. There are wilderness campsites on both lakes. In summer, lake trout are difficult to find.

**Gibson Lake (F6)** is off the beaten path in the remote interior of Algonquin Park. There are 4 campsites on the lake and an old cabin that has seen better days. It is at least a two day trip to access the lake, where fishing is fair for brook trout to 30+ cm (12 in).

**Island and Wolf Lake (A7)** are two remote lakes that can be accessed by rough dirt road. Natural brook trout are found in both lakes to 35 cm (14 in) in size and fishing can be quite good occasionally. In spring, try a small spinner or nymph patterns. In summer, try near creek mouths.

**Kakasamic Lake (A2)** is located north of North Tea Lake. There are 3 rustic campsites found on this remote Algonquin lake. Brook trout fishing can be quite good in spring or late September. Bigger trout seem to hone in on the larger silver spoons or streamer patterns.

**Longbow and Rosebary Lake (F7)** are remote Algonquin lakes that are popular destinations due to their scenery and wildlife viewing opportunities. There are 9 interior campsites in total on the two lakes. Fishing is quite good in spring for decent sized brook and lake trout. Brookies average 25 cm (10 in) in these lakes and have been found a little bigger. Brook trout are frequently found near creek mouths and the outflow area of the small dam on Longbow Lake, while lake trout are almost impossible to find in summer. Access to the lakes is by the Tim River, which can be quite low during summer months. It is recommended to check conditions before your trip.

**Lorne, Lost Dog and Sisco Lake (B2, A3)** are three Algonquin lakes that can be accessed from North Tea Lake. It is possible to get all the way to Lorne Lake in one day's travel. All three lakes are inhabited by lake trout, while Lorn and Lost Dog Lakes also host brook trout. Lorne Lake has 6 campsites to choose from, including a great island site. Fishing can be good in spring, after ice off or in late September as the water begins to cool again. Lost Dog Lake is the easiest of the three to access and there are 4 campsites on the small lake. Fishing can be good in spring for both lake trout and brook trout. Sisco Lake has 2 interior campsites available along its rustic shoreline. Out of the three lakes fishing is the slowest in this lake.

**Manitou Lake (D1)** is one of the larger lakes within the interior of Algonquin Park. There are over 45 designated campsites, including some beautiful island and beach sites. Similar to North Tea Lake, wind can be a major hindrance to travel and to fishing success. Lake trout in excess of 3.5kg (8 lbs) have been caught in the lake, while brook trout have been found in the 40 cm (16+ cm) range. Fishing is generally fair in spring and quite slow through summer months.

**Meda Lake (E3)** can be found by orienteering about 1,000m from Biggar Lake. Brook trout abound in the lake. Due to its inaccessibility, the lake sees very few anglers.

**Mud, Trout and Stoney Lake (A7)** are three secluded brook trout lakes. Mud Lake can be accessed from a rough dirt road, whereas, the other two lakes can only be found by trail. Due to Mud Lake's accessibility it is the slowest of all three lakes, however, the fishing is still quite good. Natural brook trout are found in all three lakes as well as in a few of the small, unnamed, surrounding lakes. Be sure to practice catch and release to ensure the future quality of the lakes.

**North Tea Lake (B3)** is one of the more popular lakes on the west side of Algonquin Park. The large lake has over 70 interior campsites available, with a number of the sites on small secluded islands. The lake can be easily accessed within a day from Kawawaymog Lake. Wind on the big lake can play havoc with your canoeing progress and your fishing success. Some good sized lake trout are pulled from North Tea each year but the only good time to try and fish for lakers is in the spring. The water temperature of the lake is more uniform at this time, which allows lake trout to roam almost anywhere in search of food. In fact, big lakers have been caught by casting from shore in spring. Brook trout are more likely to be found near stream mouths or in the smaller bays of the lake. Large brook trout are also caught annually.

**Pat Lake (A3)** is a small, secluded natural brook trout lake. There is barely a trail to this lake, which helps keep it hidden and maintains the quality of the fishery. Brookies are small but plentiful. If you are looking for big trout, this is probably not the place for you. However, the scenery is unbeatable and the trip is rustic, making it a great experience.

**Three Mile Lake (F1)** can be accessed in about two days from the closest Algonquin interior access point. The lake is quite secluded and has 18 rustic campsites to choose from. Lake trout and brook trout inhabit the lake with spring being the most productive time. The lake is fairly big and holding areas are difficult to locate, which makes fishing more challenging. Try near creek mouths or near the narrows at the middle of the lake for added success. Lakers can reach 70 cm (28 in) in size. Brookies have been caught in the 40 cm (16 in) range.

**Wet Lake (A4)** can be found via a rough 4wd bush road. The lake offers good fishing at times for natural brook trout, especially in spring and late September. Further down the road from Wet Lake lies another similar lake that is unnamed. The lake is found just before the Algonquin Park border. You may have to walk the last 500m to the lake. Fly fishing is unbeatable on these lakes and your success will increase dramatically if you can match the hatch on one of these small lakes.

## Burntroot Lake Area (Map 21)
The Burntroot Lake area is deep within the interior of Algonquin Provincial Park. The area offers a mixture of large and small lakes that are connected by an excellent array of established canoe routes. Lake trout and brook trout are the main species in the area, however, a few lakes are inhabited by smallmouth bass. Unfortunately, smallmouth bass were introduced some time ago and have forced brook trout out of some of the lakes.

**Behan and Kelly Lake (A4)** are two secluded Algonquin interior lakes that do not have an established access route or any designated campsites. Any attempt to access the lakes must be completed in a day in order to follow Algonquin camping regulations. The lakes are inhabited by brook trout.

**Big Trout Lake (F7)** is one of the larger lakes of the Algonquin interior and received its name for the good sized lake trout that were abundant in the lake. Today, the large lakers that gave Big Trout Lake its name are all but a memory. Although the fishing can be good. There are over 30 rustic campsites on the lake, with many of them situated on picturesque islands. Allow at least two days to access the lake. Both lake trout and brook trout inhabit the lake but fishing is tough most of the time, due mainly to the size of the lake. The canoe limits your ability to cover water, although it helps preserve this beautiful environment. Lake trout can be found in the 65+ cm (26 in) range and brook trout can be caught to 40 cm (16 in). Brookies are often found near creek mouths or cruising shallow bays in spring.

**Bird Lake (G3)** is a very small lake located near the south end of Catfish Lake. There are no designated trails to the lake, however, ambitious canoeists can take a day trip to find the lake. It is about 500m due south from Catfish Lake's southeastern bay. Small brook trout are found in good numbers.

**Blue and Longer Lake (D7)** are two interior lakes that can be accessed by portage from Big Trout Lake. There are 3 campsites found on Longer Lake and one on Blue Lake. Both lakes offer good fishing in spring for average sized trout. Lake trout are found in both lakes and brook trout are also be found in Longer Lake. Lakers are difficult to catch in summer but can be aggressive feeders in spring or late September. Brook trout have been caught to 40 cm (16 in) on Longer Lake.

**Burntroot Lake (D5)** is the typical beautiful interior park lake. The large lake offers over 25 great interior campsites but fishing can be frustrating. The trout are hard to find, although perseverance is often rewarded. Lake trout have been caught exceeding 60 cm (24 in). Brook trout are also found in the lake and average 30-35 cm (12-14 in) in size. Try near creek mouths for feeding brookies. Trolling a small silver spoon is a reliable angling method for both trout species. As a side trip, check out the old depot farm at the southwest side of the lake. The depot began operation back in 1882 and supplied interior logging camps with necessities.

**Calumet and Cuckoo Lake (G4)** are two secluded lakes that are rarely visited. The lakes are found northwest of Hogan Lake. Calumet Lake has two campsites along its shoreline, while Cukoo Lake has one. The lakes are inhabited by brook trout, although lake trout are also found in Calumet Lake. The trout found in these lakes may not be as big as in other larger interior lakes but are plentiful in spring. Lake trout can be elusive at times.

**Carl Wilson Lake (F1)** is a fairly large interior lake that is very scenic. In fact, large portions of the lake's shoreline have been designated natural reserve areas. The reserve portions of the lake are excellent wildlife viewing areas and moose are often spotted in the marshy section to the south and the north of the lake. A number of birds and small, fur bearing animals also frequent the areas. There are 7 wilderness campsites on the lake. Lake trout and brook trout are found in the lake to good sizes. The dam area on the lake can be a decent holding area for trout.

**Catfish Lake (G3)** has numerous bays and inlets as well as several small islands that all make the lake awkward to navigate. At times you can find yourself questioning where you are on the lake. On one of the northern islands of the lake, the remains of an old alligator machine can be explored. The machine was used to haul log booms along lakes back in the late 1800's. There are 12 rustic campsites found on Catfish Lake, including many great island sites. Fishing in the lake can be good in spring or late September for lake trout and brook trout. Lakers can reach sizes of up to 70 cm (28 in). Brook trout average 25-30 cm (10-12 in) in size, although they can be found to 40+ cm (16 in).

**Coldspring and Kennedy Lake (A5)** lie south of the Nipissing River amid a designated nature preserve area of Algonquin Park. There are no access routes to the lakes or designated campsites making them virtually off limits to trippers. Both lakes are inhabited by brook trout.

**Devine Lake (A7)** is a small lake that is rarely visited. This is due in part to the brutal portages that lie to the east of the lake. An exquisite island campsite rewards the visitor. It has been said that the same site used to be a favourite among poachers in the park. Back in the early 1900's the site was used to hide from rangers. Fishing in the lake can be quite good in early spring. On average, brook trout in the lake are not very big; however, they can be found exceeding 30 cm (12 in).

**Erables and Maple Lake (A1)** are two very scenic large Algonquin interior lakes. The lakes can be accessed within a day from the Kiosk access point. There are 7 wilderness campsites on Maple Lake and another 12 on Erables Lake. Both lakes offer island campsites. Along with the scenery, the fishing is another good reason to visit the lakes. In spring, lake trout fishing can be good at times for lakers that can exceed 75 cm (30 in) in size. Brook trout are also found in Maple Lake to 40 cm (16 in). Fishing is best in spring but picks up again in late September. Trout can be quite elusive during summer months.

**Glacier, Gull and Varley Lake (G1)** are three small brook trout lakes that are found en route from Cedar Lake to Carl Wilson Lake. All three lakes are a nice place to spend some time and there is a campsite on Gull and Varley Lakes. Fishing is often good in spring for brook trout to 35+ cm.

**Hayes and Perley Lake (E4)** are both found northeast of Burntroot Lake. Hayes Lake is a small, out of the way lake that does not see much traffic during a year. It does offer one campsite which allows visitors to have the lake to themselves. Brook trout are found in the lake in good numbers. Brook trout can be caught to 40 cm (16 in) in Hayes Lake. Perley Lake is part of the Petawawa River system, just before the river begins to quicken. There is one campsite on this elongated lake and fishing is generally fair for average sixed brook trout.

**Hemlock Lake (G6)** is a small secluded interior lake that is often overlooked by canoe trippers in the park. There are no campsites on the lake but the fishing can be quite good for brook trout to 35+ cm (14 in). It is recommended to set up camp at Merchant Lake to the south and travel to Hemlock Lake for a day trip.

**Lake La Muir (F6)** lies deep within the interior of Algonquin Park. Fishing on the lake is good for both brook trout and lake trout during late September. Lake trout have often been caught in excess of 55 cm (22 in) and can reach sizes in excess of 70 cm (28 in). Brook trout average 30-40 cm (12-16 in) in size but are found bigger. There are 8 wilderness campsites found on this picturesque lake.

**Luckless and Lynx Lake (F3)** can be reached to the south of the Nipissing River or from the west side of Catfish Lake. If you wish to spend time on the lakes there are 2 campsites found on each lake. Brook trout are found in both lakes in good numbers and average sized lake trout are also found in Lynx Lake. Fishing is good in spring on both lakes. Brook trout can reach 40 cm (16 in) in size.

**Merchant Lake (G7)** is found north of Happy Isle Lake. Fishing on the lake can be good at times for lake trout to 60+ cm (24 in) and brook trout in the 30-35 cm (12-14 in) range. Both brookies and lake trout have been found bigger. Seven rustic campsites are found well situated along the shore of this beautiful lake. For fly fishers, try a nymph near the weedy shoreline areas for cruising brook trout.

**Minnehaha Lake (C6)** is a very remote interior lake that lies in a nature reserve of the park. There is no formal access or campsites on the lake, which holds brook trout.

**Mouse Lake (C1)** once went by the name Moose Lake. The lake has 6 nice interior campsites along its shoreline. In early morning, moose are often spotted near the eastern shoreline of the lake. Brook trout are found in Mouse Lake and in good numbers. Fishing for brookies to 35+ cm (14 in) can be good at times. Of course, the heat of summer reduced success dramatically.

**Nadine and Osler Lakes (C3, B3)** are wedged between the Nipissing River and Erables Lake. All three lakes are inhabited by brook trout. Spring time offers good fishing for nice sized brook trout, which reach 35 cm (14 in) in size. There are 4 rustic campsites on Nadine Lake, 4 on Osler and 3 more on Little Osler. Each of the lakes is a short day trip from one another. If your angling success is slow at one of the lakes, take a journey to another.

**North Cuckoo and Plumb Lake (F3, E3)** are two secluded Algonquin lakes that are found on some of the lesser beaten paths. The lakes lie between Burntroot and Catfish Lakes on of the way route detours. There is a campsite on the lake but fishing is quite good for nice sized brook trout. The trout are a little easier to find on North Cuckoo Lake, although they seem to be a little bigger in Plumb Lake.

**North Raven Lake (A2)** is a small interior lake that does not see as much traffic as other lakes in this part of the park. This is due mainly to the fact that there are numerous small portages required to access the lake. The lake is at least a two day trip from the nearest access point. There are 4 pretty campsites on the lake and fishing is often good in spring for average sized lake trout. The small size of this lake is ideal for the fly fishing enthusiast who wishes to match their skill with Algonquin lakers. Little cleos are a productive spin cast lure.

**Ravenau Lake (G1)** can be easily accessed in a day from the Cedar Lake interior access point. There is a great campsite on the lake's shore or, alternatively, you can also stay at Lantern Lake to the south. Fishing at Ravaneau Lake is fair for brook trout in the 25-30 cm (10-12 in) range. In spring, fishing success increases.

**Robinson and Whiskeyjack Lake (D4)** lie deep within the Algonquin Park interior. At least 3 days are needed to access the lakes, which limits the visitors to this area. There are campsites found on both lakes. Small lake trout are found in both lakes and good sized brook trout are also found in Whiskeyjack Lake. Fishing for trout can be quite good in spring or late September.

## Cedar Lake Area (Map 22)
Cedar Lake is site of one of Algonquin Park's northern interior access points. The area is dotted by some of the largest lakes in the park, including Hogan Lake and Lake Lavieille. Fishing in the area is mainly for lake trout and brook trout. Some of the larger, northern lakes offer warm water sport fish species such as walleye. Cedar Lake is also the starting point to whitewater routes on the mighty Petawawa River.

**Cedar Lake (A1)** is one of the largest lakes in Algonquin Park and is a designated interior access point. The village of Brent is located on the lake's north shore, along with the Brent Campground. There are also over 25 canoe access campsites scattered about the lake. Wind can be a major problem to canoe travel. Fishing in the lake is generally slow for walleye and lake trout, while smallmouth bass offer the best opportunity at angling success. Fishing can be good at times for smallmouth that average 0.5-1.5kg (1-3.5 lbs) but have been caught in the 2.5kg (5.5 lb) range. Brook trout also inhabit the lake, although are tough to find. Creek inflows are the best spot to find feeding trout. The Nipissing and Petawawa River inflows are good bets for most fish species. Walleye can reach 3kg (6.5 lbs) and lake trout 3.5kg (8 lbs).

**Chickaree Lake (A7)** is reached by a short portage from Merchant Lake. The small lake has no designated campsites, although makes a perfect day trip from Merchant Lake. Small lake trout are found in the lake in decent numbers.

**Cinderella Lake (B3)** is a remote interior lake that is very difficult to get to. Brook trout inhabit the lake.

**Crow Lakes (B5, B6)** are two secluded lakes that offer quite good fishing for trout, especially in spring. Brook trout are found in both lakes and lake trout are also found in Big Crow Lake. Brookies have been reportedly caught in the 50 cm (20 in) range but average about 30 cm (12 in). There are 10 rustic campsites on Big Crow Lake and another 3 on Little Crow Lake. An old ranger cabin is also found on Big Crow Lake. The cabin is well equipped and makes an excellent place to spend a few nights, if rented. Near the Big Crow Lake Dam, there is a trail that leads into a magnificent stand of virgin White Pines. The side trip along the trail is highly recommended.

**Farncomb Lake (F4)** is a small lake that can be reached by a short portage near the north end of Lake Lavieille. There are no campsites on the lake, although fishing is quite good for brook trout to 40+ cm (16 in). Spring fishing can be even better. The lake is rarely visited.

**Happy Isle Lake (A7)** is located west of Opeongo Lake and offers lake trout and smallmouth bass. Smallmouth bass are found in good numbers in the lake and fishing can be quite good at times for bass to 2kg (4.5 lbs). Some larger bass have been caught in the lake, although they are difficult to find. Lake trout can reach 65+ cm (26 in) and fishing is good at times in spring. 14 rustic campsites are found on the lake, with 3 of the sites lying on an island in the middle of the lake. The Happy Isle Creek is a frequent moose viewing area.

**Hogan Lake (A5)** is one of the larger interior lakes and offers 10 beautiful campsites. Even with a shuttle up Opeongo Lake, you should allow two days to reach Hogan Lake. The southern portion of the lake is a vast marshland area, which provides good opportunities to spot Algonquin moose. Both lake trout and brook trout are found in the lake. Anglers are often rewarded with nice sized trout, especially in spring. Brookies average 30 cm (12 in). Parks Bay is a popular area for finding good numbers of trout.

**Lake Lavieille (G4)** is one of the largest Algonquin interior lakes. The trip to get to Levieille Lake is challenging but worth while as the lake has a long history as a great lake trout lake. The size of the lake makes it a challenging lake to fish. Even in spring, some days can be brutally slow, while other days activity is fierce. Lavieille's reputation as "the spot to be", brings many anglers after the spring thaw. Crow Bay is a popular spot for lake trout, although there are just as good or better spots on the lake. Don't be afraid to spend some time exploring this beautiful water body. Brook trout are found in the lake to sizes of up to 40+ cm (16 in), while lake trout can reach 60+ cm (24 in) in size. Whitefish are a welcomed surprise in the lake. Many an angler has thought they had a big lake trout only to be fooled by a scrappy whitefish. The silver spoon lure is designated as the 'old reliable' on this lake. There are 25 interior campsites on the lake.

**Menona Lake (E1)** lies along an underused portage route from the Petawawa River to Radiant Lake. Menona Lake makes a great camping location as the lake is very scenic. It is found in the transition area of the park, where the highland becomes lowland. Fishing can be quite good for brook trout, especially in spring. Menona Lake has been known to even produce into the early summer period.

**Narrowbag Lake (A2)** is a part of the Petawawa River system and is located at the north end of Catfish Lake. The lake is quite beautiful and there is a nice campsite on the lake's northern shore. Brook trout are found in decent numbers in the lake and have been caught to 35+ cm (14 in). Although fishing success is best in spring, late September can bring surprising success.

**Nepawin and Redrock Lake (B7)** can be reached from Opeongo Lake's northwest corner. Redrock Lake is much larger than Nepawin Lake and offers 7 rustic campsites to choose from. Nepawin Lake can be found via an 810m portage from Redrock Lake and makes an ideal day trip. Both lakes have quite good fishing for both lake trout and brook trout. The trout are larger in Redrock Lake but more plentiful in Nepawin Lake. The long narrow bay on Redrock Lake is a good area to find cruising trout. Lakers can reach 65+ cm (26 in) on Redrock Lake, while brook trout in both lakes average 30+ cm (12 in).

**Philip Lake (C3)** lies deep in the Algonquin interior and was created by the damming of the Little Madawaska River. Brook trout can be found congregating near the inflow and outflow areas of the river and fishing can be quite good, especially in spring. In summer, angling success for trout is slow, similar to most lakes. Due to the water movement in the lake, fishing can pick up dramatically in September. Brook trout average 25-30 cm (10-12in) and can be found in the 40+ cm (16 in) range. 4 wilderness campsites are found on the lake.

**Plover Lake (G1)** lies east of Radiant Lake off the Petawawa River. There are no campsites on the lake, although there are 2 sites on the Petawawa River just before the lake. The flow on the river is slow enough to paddle to the lake and back to the campsites. Smallmouth bass and walleye are found in the lake. Smallmouth bass are plentiful in the 0.5-1kg (1-2 lb) range and fishing is fair for nice sized walleye.

**Proulx Lake (C7)** can be easily reached within one day if you choose to take a water taxi to the top of Opeongo Lake. 12 interior campsites are scattered along the lake's shoreline. The north portion of the lake is quite marshy and leads to the Crow River, a known viewing area for moose. Fishing in Proulx Lake can be good in spring for brookies to 45+ cm.

**Radiant Lake (F1)** went by the name 'Trout Lake' until the early 1900's. After the railway was built through the park, many of the lakes where stations were located, adopted their station name. Hence was the case for 'Radiant Lake'. The old railbed can be found on the southern shore of the lake, as well as remnants of the Radiant settlement on the western shore. The grave site of early loggers/visitors is marked at the southeast end of the lake. Scattered along the shore are also 9 rustic campsites. Lake trout, brook trout, smallmouth bass and walleye are all found in Radiant Lake. Fishing is generally fair for lake trout and walleye while smallmouth bass fishing can be very good at times. Unfortunately, brook trout are often tough to find. Walleye can reach 2.5kg (5.5 lbs), while smallmouth bass have been caught to 2kg (4.5 lbs).

**Thomas Lake (F6)** is a remote interior Algonquin lake that is a part of the headwater of the Thomas Creek, which flows into Lake Lavieille's southwestern bay. There are no campsites at the lake and no organized Canoe Route access. Brook trout inhabit the lake.

**Wright Lake (F7)** is located along the Canoe Route from the East Arm of Opeongo Lake to Dickson Lake. Lake trout and smallmouth bass inhabit the lake which is often overlooked by trippers who are more concerned with getting to Dickson Lake. The picturesque lake has a great campsite on its northern shore. Lake trout are usually small and smallmouth bass average 0.5-1kg (1-2 lbs). Fishing can be good for bass and is fair for lake trout in spring.

## Lake Traverse Area (Map 23)

Lake Travers is the main starting point of whitewater canoe trips on the Petawawa River. The area is set amid a transition zone of Algonquin Park from highlands to lowlands. Trout are still the predominant species in the area, however, a number of water bodies also sport warm water fish such as smallmouth bass.

**Alluring, Animoosh and Cat Lake (C7)** are located east of Dickson Lake. Animoosh Lake is the only lake of the three that is actually on an established canoe route. From Animoosh, you can take a day trip through the bush to find Alluring and Cat Lake. It is not hard to find the lakes, although you should have good orienteering skills and be prepared for rough travel. These lakes are rarely visited. Fishing in all three lakes is quite good for brook trout in the 40+ cm (16 in) range. Lake trout also inhabit Alluring Lake in good numbers. Animoosh Lake is a designated catch and release lake.

**Barron Lake (G5)** can be accessed by portage from Greenleaf Lake and lies in a nature reserve area, which protects an important Algonquin watershed. Smallmouth bass and brook trout are found in the lake. Fishing for brook trout is fair for decent sized fish, while fishing for smallmouth bass can be very good at times. Brook trout have been caught in excess of 35 cm (14 in) and smallmouth bass can reach 2kg (4.5 lbs) in size. 6 wilderness campsites are found on the lake.

**Dickson Lakes (A7)** attract many anglers in spring who come in search of the lakes' renowned trout. Both lakes offer good fishing for lake trout and brook trout. Brook trout have been found to 50 cm (20 in) in size while good sized lake trout are also found in Dickson Lake. The trout in Little Dickson Lake are somewhat smaller. Both lakes are picturesque and are truly the essence of the Algonquin environment. 12 wilderness campsites are located on Dickson Lake and another 3 can be found on Little Dickson. A number of the campsites are private island sites. In summer and fall, it is hard to find anyone else on these lakes. The grueling portage into Dickson Lake keeps the bulk of canoe trippers away. Dickson Lake is also home to some of the oldest known Red Pine trees in Algonquin Park. These towering giants are found on the lake's eastern shore and are a sight to see. The big pines are over 340 years old!

**Eustache Lake (C3)** is rarely visited by canoe trippers and is found west of Lake Travers. The route to the lake entails travelling up the Petawawa River (a challenge in itself!) to the grueling 2,650m (8,694 ft) portage to the lake. However, the trip to the lake has its rewards. Eustache Lake is the deepest lake in Algonquin Park at 90+m (295 ft) and is wonderfully clear. The lake is also surrounded by magnificent cliffs that reach as high as 25m (82 ft) in some areas. Three fantastic campsites are found on the east side of the lake and all offer an incredible view. Fishing in the lake can be good in spring for nice sized brook trout and lake trout.

**Francis Lake (A2)** is part of the Petawawa River system and lies down river from Radiant Lake. The only way to access the lake is to travel the stretch of the Petawawa River to the lake. Brook trout and smallmouth bass are found in the lake. Brookies are hard to find but bass are plentiful. Scrappy smallmouth offer very good fishing in some areas of the lake. An old railbed lines along the northern part of the lake and 6 rustic campsites are scattered along the lake's shore.

**Lake Travers (E2)** marks the transition from highland lakes in Algonquin Park's western side to the lowlands of the eastern portion of the park. Warm water fish species are found in Lake Travers, including smallmouth bass, walleye and muskellunge. Fishing for walleye and musky is generally slow, while smallmouth bass action can be very good at times. Smallmouth have been found in the lake to 2.5kg (5.5 lbs). Access to the lake is by road from the Sand Lake Gate. The Algonquin Radio Observatory is found on the lake, as well as 22 interior campsites.

**Little Crooked Lake (B6)** is located northeast of Dickson Lake at the end of a challenging portage. There are only two campsites on the lake and plenty of room between them. Little Crooked Lake is the home of some of the last remaining pure strains of Algonquin Park brook trout. For this reason, the lake has been designated a catch and release lake to help preserve the natural strain. Be sure to check and abide by all regulations.

**McNorton Lake (D5)** is a small, remote lake found north of White Partridge Lake. There was an old portage trail off White Partridge Creek to the lake, however, it is heavily overgrown and virtually non-existent. Brook trout inhabit the lake.

**North Branch and Sundassa Lake (E6, C6)** can both be found via portage from the much larger White Partridge Lake. These lakes see low canoe traffic throughout the year due to their remoteness. North Branch Lake lies to the east of White Partridge Lake, while Sundassa lies to the west. There are 4 interior campsites on North Branch Lake. Fishing in the lakes can productive throughout the year, especially in spring. Book trout average 25-35 cm (8-14 in).

**White Partridge Lake (C6)** is a large Algonquin interior lake that is difficult to access. There are a number of long portages involved en route to this lake. Fishing in the lake is quite good for lake trout and brook trout. Brook trout can be found to 45 cm (18 in), while lake trout can reach 65 cm (26 in) in size. There are 6 interior campsites scattered along the shore of the lake.

## Grand Lake Area (Map 24)

The Grand Lake Area is the site of the Achray interior access point to Algonquin Park. There are many interior canoe routes, including the trip to the magnificent Barron Canyon. Fish species in the area is a mix of trout and smallmouth bass.

**Carcajou Lake (B5)** can be accessed within one long day from the Achray access point. The section of the route between Wenda Lake and Carcajou Lake is very marshy and water levels fluctuate throughout the year creating havoc on would be paddlers. There are 4 scenic campsites on the north shore of Carcajou Lake. Fishing is good in spring for lake trout and brook trout. Lakers can exceed 50 cm (20 in) in size, while brook trout have been found to 40 cm (16 in) in size. Try fly fishing with a nymph or small streamer pattern for brookies. Little cleos also work well for cruising trout.

**Clemow Lake (A3)** is located west of the much larger Grand Lake. The old Canadian National Railway can be found on the lake's north shore and is a staunch reminder of human activity within Algonquin Park. Opposite the railbed, there are 4 interior campsites. Fishing in the lake is good for smallmouth bass to 2kg (4.5 lbs) and fair for lake trout to 60+ cm (24 in) in size.

**Clover Lake (F7)** is found along a less traveled canoe route in Algonquin's southeast side. The lake can be reached within a day from the Achray access point but an early start is needed. There are 5 excellent campsites on the lake's shore and a number of smaller lakes can be reached within one or two portages. Fishing on the lake is quite good for nice sized brook trout. Spring is the most productive time of year, however, seasoned anglers will be able to find trout year round on this lake.

**Foys Lake (B7)** can be reached by vehicle down the rough Basin Lake Road. Fishing is fair on Foys Lake for brook trout and lake trout. Brookies can be found to 35 cm (14 in) in size and lakers have been caught to 45+ cm (18 in). There are 3 interior campsites found on the lake.

**Grand Lake (D5)** is a designated access point to the eastern side of Algonquin Park. The Achray Campground and the Eastern Pines Backpacking Trail can also be found here. The old Canadian National Railway travels along the entire length of Grand Lake and crosses the lake south of Kennedy Bay. There are 19 rustic campsites on the lake, with the bulk of the sites found near the southern part of the lake. A few sites are also located in beautiful Carcajou Bay, the backdrop to the famous 'Jack Pine' Tom Thompson painting. Lake trout and smallmouth bass inhabit the lake. Fishing is generally slow for lake trout and is often good for smallmouth bass. Smallmouth bass average 0.5-1kg (1-2 lbs) and can reach 2.5kg (5.5 lbs) in size. Brook trout are also found in the lake but fishing is slow.

**Greenleaf Lake (A4)** is set amid a designated park nature reserve, which helps protect an important Algonquin watershed. Impressive cliffs tower over the lake, which are home to the Algonquin Wood Fern. The fern is extremely rare and found in only one other part of the world. 3 wilderness campsites are found on the lake and all offer picturesque views of the lake. Fishing in the lake is fair for lake trout and can be good at times in spring. Smallmouth bass that average 0.5-1kg (1-2 lbs) are found in good numbers in the lake.

**Length Lake (G5)** is a small lake that is often crossed en route to or from the Barron Canyon. There are 2 interior campsites on the lake and the lake has been stocked with brook trout. Currently, fishing is fair in spring for small brook trout.

**Opalescent Lake (G4)** lies along the main route to the Barron Canyon. The lake makes an ideal base camp lake for further exploration of the Canyon and area. There are six campsites found along the lake's shoreline. Fishing is quite good at times for smallmouth bass that average 0.5-1.5kg.

**Rouge and St.Frances Lake (G5)** can be accessed from St. Andrews Lake at the Achray side of the Park. There are no campsites on Rouge Lake, however, there is a nice site on St. Frances Lake. Brook trout are found in both lakes, although in small numbers. Fishing can be fair at times in spring when trout are most active. St. Frances Lake also has a population of smallmouth bass. Fishing for these smallmouth can be very good at times for bass to 2kg (4.5 lbs).

**Smith and Whitson Lake (G1)** are part of the Petawawa River system. A total of 15 interior campsites can be found on the lakes, with many sites set amid beautiful stands of Silver Maple. Small walleye and muskellunge are found in the two lakes. Fishing is usually slow for small fish.

**St. Andrews Lake (G5)** has 8 scenic campsites scattered along its shoreline. The lake's easy accessibility, can make it a popular destination during summer long weekends. Lake trout and brook trout inhabit the lake, although fishing is usually slow.

## Sand Lake Gate, Pembroke and Westmeath Areas (Maps 25, 26, 27)

This region is a part of the beautiful Ottawa Valley and has long been dependant on resource based industries. Today, the region is becoming more and more of an outdoor recreation playground. Winter and summer recreation opportunities abound, including fishing. The Ottawa River (Allumette Lake) is the most popular area for fishing and offers plenty of great angling action. A wide variety of sport fish are found on this majestic river.

**Allumette Lakes (26/C4, 27/B7)** is really the Ottawa River, although due to its size, it was named as a lake. Lower and Upper Allumette Lakes offer similar fisheries. Almost every warm water sport fish species is found in this big water body. Channel catfish, perch, whitefish, cisco, suckers, sturgeon and even ancient gar are all found in the Allumette Lakes. The main sport fish species in the lakes are northern pike, smallmouth bass and walleye. To locate these species, you have to look for structure in the lakes. One advantage that anglers have, is that there is a strong current in the lakes, which helps to predict the areas where fish are holding. Currents often attract species such as walleye, while slower bays and inlets are often holding areas for bass and pike. Walleye fishing in the Allumette Lakes can be very good for walleye to 5kg (11 lbs). Jigging is the preferred method, although casting crankbaits can also be effective. Smallmouth bass are found in the lakes to 2.5kg (5.5 lbs) but there are yearly reports of larger fish. Look for rocky bottoms when trying to locate smallmouth holding areas. Once you find a spot, it is not unheard of to catch your limit in minutes! Northern pike cruise the shallower, weedy bays and inlets in search of minnows. Once you find a quite bay, cast into the shallows or along weed lines. Pike can be found over 6kg (13 lbs).

**Beechnut and Big Trout Lake (25/C7, D7)** can both be accessed by a rough dirt road near Algonquin Park's southeast border. The lakes are stocked every few years with brook trout and offer good fishing at times in winter or spring. Brookies average 25 cm (10 in). Fly fishing can increase your success on these lakes.

**Clear Lake (25/A1)** is stocked every few years with brook trout. The lake is most heavily fished in the winter when access can be easily obtained by snowmobile. There is also an unnamed lake northeast of Clear Lake that is stocked with brook trout. This lake lies off a 4wd road. Clear Lake is often the better fishing lake of the two, due to the difficult access. Brookies average 25-30 cm (10-12 in) in both lakes.

**Cork Lake (25/A5)** is part of a small series of lakes that is found south of the Barron Canyon in Algonquin Park. The lake is a day trip from the canyon, which makes it an attractive camping location. There are 3 wilderness campsites on the lake and fishing is very good at times for smallmouth bass in the 0.5-1kg (1-2 lb) range.

**Flat Iron Lake (25/F7)** can be reached by snowmobile or on foot and is stocked every few years with splake. Splake can be found to 35+ cm (14 in) in size. The best fishing is in winter through the ice or in spring, just after ice off. A small white jig can be deadly through the ice.

**Ignace Lake (25/B4)** is passed along the road en route to McManus Lake. Fishing can be good at times for average smallmouth bass.

**McManus Lake (25/A2)** is the site of one of Algonquin Park's eastern interior access points. Actually, the access point is used more as a pick up area for Petawawa River trippers. For people wishing to spend a night on McManus Lake, there are 5 rustic campsites to choose from. Walleye and muskellunge are found in the lake, although fishing for both species is often slow. Be sure not to venture east from McManus Lake, this is Canadian Forces Base Petawawa territory and part of a live firing range!

**Norm's Lake (25/C5)** is a small eastern Algonquin lake. The lake sees low use and can be reached via portage from Sec or Wet Lake. Small brook trout inhabit the lake in fair numbers and fishing can be good at times in spring, just after ice off.

**Sand Lake (25/E6)** is inhabited by natural brook trout, although fishing is usually slow. The good road access to the lake has brought a lot of pressure to the lake. Brookies in the lake are small and are best caught on a small nymph fly. The lake lies off the south side of Achray Road, about 9km east of Algonquin Park.

**Sec Lake (25/C6)** contains a wide range of sport fish species for visitors to enjoy. The lake can be busy during summer long weekends but is often deserted during the week. Lake trout, brook trout, northern pike and smallmouth bass are all found in this lake. Fishing is slow for lake trout and brook trout; therefore northern pike and smallmouth bass provide most of the action on this lake. The majority of pike are small but scrappy while smallmouth bass can reach 2kg (4.5 lbs). The access road leads right to the lake and there are 16 campsites on the lake. For a day trip, take a tour into Little Sec or Log Canoe Lake.

**Wee Trout Lake (25/C5)** can be reached by trail from Achray Road about 1.2km before the road enters Algonquin Park. The lake is stocked often with brookies and provides good fishing for brook trout to 30 cm (12 in). Try a small spinners or a bead head nymph pattern.

**Wet Lake (25/B6)** can be easily accessed by trail from the Sec Lake access point. There is an interior campsite at the lake, although it receives little use. The trail and camping area can be muddy well into July. Smallmouth bass fishing is very good on the lake for bass in the 0.5-1.5kg (1-3.5 lb) range. Try jigging off the rock ledges. Watch for snapping turtles, which are common in the lake.

**Wylie Lake (25/C2)** is located within the Petawawa Research Forest and permission must be obtained from the forestpersonnel in order to fish the lake. The lake is stocked with splake, which are most active in winter and spring. The splake in this lake can reach decent sizes.

## Powassan Area Lakes (Map 28)

The Powassan area lies just south of North Bay. The area topography is characteristic of the lowlands of the Lake Nipissing drainage. Fishing is popular in the larger lakes in the region, such as Trout Lake, although there are also a number of smaller lakes that provide good angling opportunities. The area can be busy in summer with cottagers and tourists but it is easy to find your own secluded location. Walleye and lake trout are the sport fish of choice in the near north and are found in decent numbers throughout the region. Be sure to practice catch and release whenever possible.

**Bigfish, Moosegrass and Werewolf Lake (G1)** are three secluded lakes found north of Turtle Lake on the Mattawa River system. The only access to the lakes is by canoe on the Mattawa River or by rustic portage. Small northern pike and walleye are found in all three lakes and fishing is often good. Smallmouth bass are found in Bigfish Lake and Werewolf Lake, while largemouth bass inhabit Moongrass Lake all in good numbers. Muskellunge are also found in both Moongrass and Werewolf Lake, however, fishing is generally slow.

**Collander Bay (B3)** is a part of the world renowned Lake Nipissing. The bay can be reached from several public and private boat launch locations along its shoreline. Several different sport fish species can be found in the bay, including northern pike, walleye, smallmouth bass, muskellunge and whitefish. Northern pike can be found to 5kg (11 lbs) and fishing is good in many areas. Look for weed lines in quite bays for lurking northerns. Walleye fishing in the bay is also quite good in areas. The prized sport fish can reach sizes of up to 3+ kg (6.5 lbs). Jigging can be an effective method for finding walleye during winter and ice off periods. Smallmouth bass are often overlooked on Lake Nipissing and Collander Bay. Bass provide very good fishing opportunities in the lake and can reach sizes of up to 2.5kg (5.5 lbs). Look for bottom structure, such as rocks. The skill of muskellunge fishing is not lost on Collander Bay. If you have the know how, fishing for musky can be good at times. Every year there are big muskellunge taken form the bay.

**Dreany Lake (B1)** is found off the Trans-Canada Hwy east of Dugas Bay. Northern pike inhabit the lake and fishing is slow for small pike.

**Graham Lake (F7)** can be accessed by dirt road and offers good fishing for northern pike and bass. Northerns can be caught in the 4+ kg (9 lb) range, while smallmouth and largemouth bass reach sizes of up to 2kg (4.5 lbs). Try a floating rapala for great top water action.

**Lake Nosbonsing (F4)** offers anglers a wide range of fish species. The lake is quite large and continues to produce some decent fishing opportunities. Fishing is fair for walleye to 3kg (6.5 lbs) and northern pike in the 2-3kg range. A good holding area for walleye and pike is near the mouth of the Kaibushkong River. Both smallmouth and largemouth bass inhabit the lake and fishing can be good at times for bass that average 0.5-1kg (1-2 lbs). Muskellunge are found in the lake, although fishing is usually slow. Pacific and Atlantic salmon (Ouananiche) have been stocked in the lake and have been caught to 2.5kg (5.5 lbs). Brook trout, brown trout, lake trout and splake are also found in the lake but in small numbers. Sturgeon are natural to Lake Nosbonsing but heavy fishing has reduced their numbers dramatically. Be sure to check the special regulations for this lake.

**Long and Loren Lake (E1, F1)** can only be accessed by portage from the south shore of the Mattawa River. Due to the lakes' difficult access, fishing is usually good in both lakes. Smallmouth and largemouth bass are found in Long Lake and can reach good sizes. Loren Lake is inhabited by smallmouth bass and small northern pike.

**Mink Lake (F4)** is a small lake that is found off Southshore Road south of Lake Nosbonsing. Largemouth bass inhabit the lake in fair numbers and fishing is best during overcast periods or during dusk. Top water lures and flies can be productive.

**Reservoir Lake (A1)** is found near the town of Powassan. Fishing in the lake is fair for decent sized walleye and northern pike, although smallmouth bass provide the most action. Bass can reach 2 + kg (4.5 lbs) in size and fishing can be good at times.

**Trout Lake (C1)** is almost as popular as Lake Nipissing and is found east of the City of North Bay. There are many homes and cottages on the lake, which can increase boating traffic during summer months. A wide variety of sport fish species are present in Trout Lake. The most sought after species are lake trout and walleye. Fishing for lakers and walleye is fair, although can be slow much of the time. Lake trout average 40+ cm (16 in) and walleye average 0.5-1kg (1-2 lbs). Ouananiche, a strain of Atlantic salmon, offer fair fishing throughout the year. Ouananiche are usually quite small, although are caught up to 2.5kg (5.5 lbs) occasionally. Both smallmouth and largemouth bass are found in the lake in good numbers. Bass average 0.5-1kg and are often found bigger. Northern pike fishing is generally fair. Pike are best found in the sleepy bays of the lake during dusk. Some good sized pike are taken out of Trout Lake annually. One of the more elusive species in Trout Lake is the mighty muskellunge. Unseasoned musky hunters have a difficult time finding this predator.

**Wasi Lake (F5)** is found south of Lake Nosbonsing. There are several access points to the lake that can be found via roads. Wasi Lake is a popular lake in summer and several cottages line the lake's shoreline. Fishing is fair at times for walleye and can be good for smallmouth bass, which reach sizes of up to 2kg (4.5 lbs) on the lake. Look for underwater rock structure for smallmouth bass and walleye.

## Samuel De Champlain Park Area (Map 29)

This area offers easy access to a number of different recreation areas, including the north side of Algonquin Provincial Park. The rolling highlands meet the Mattawa River lowlands in this region. Fishing is one of the major pastimes in both summer and winter months. A wide range of sport fish species can be found from lake trout to the mighty muskellunge.

**Bay and Ukalet Lake (D5)** can be accessed by snowmobile or on foot via a rough trail or orienteering. The lakes are mainly fished in winter and provide good fishing for brook trout to 35+ cm (14 in). If you are ambitious enough to access the lakes during spring, you can be well rewarded. Wilderness camping opportunities exist at the lakes.

**Boullion and Moore Lake (E1, F1)** are part of the Mattawa River system. Moore Lake lies within Samuel De Champlain Provincial Park, while Boullion Lake is found within the Mattawa River Provincial Park boundaries. Both lakes offer decent fishing for smallmouth bass and small northern pike. The odd big pike can be found in the lakes. Walleye and muskellunge fishing is generally slow for small fish. Both lakes are easily accessed by roads.

**Burbot and Crooked Chute Lake (F2)** are both found off Hwy 603 south of Hwy 17 and receive significant angling pressure during the year. Fishing is fair at times for generally small northern pike. Try a floating rapala for active northerns.

**Curly Lake (E6)** can be accessed by following the abandoned Canadian National Rail Line near the Amable Du Fond River. Fishing at the lake is good at times for nice sized brook trout but winter angling pressure has reduced the quality of this lake.

**Froggy Lake (A1)** is a small lake found north of Hwy 17, just west of Pine Lake Road. The lake is stocked every few years with brook trout and fishing is fair in spring or during the winter.

**Guilmette Lake (C6)** is a good sized lake that can be reached by a rough dirt road. Natural lake trout were once found in the lake, however, over fishing has brought the natural stock to collapse. Splake are now the predominant species of the lake and are often mistaken with lake trout. Splake reach good sizes in the lake and provide good fishing opportunities in winter and spring.

**James and Wright Lake (D1)** are two small lakes that lie north of Pimsi Bay of the Mattawa River. Access to the lakes is limited to rustic portage routes that may be overgrown. Fishing can be quite good in both lakes. Smallmouth bass are found in James Lake and largemouth bass in Wright Lake. Minnow imitation lures and flies are effective on both lakes. Bass average 0.5-1kg (1-2 lbs) but are found bigger.

**Johnston Lakes (D2)** can be reached by rustic portage from Smith Lake. Alternatively, you can portage from Hwy 630 to Upper Johnston Lake along the railway tracks. Both lakes offer good fishing for smallmouth bass in the 0.5-1kg (1-2 lb) range. Northern pike and largemouth bass are also found in Upper Johnston Lake. Northern pike are small, although some 2.5+ kg (5.5 lb) pike are caught annually. Along with smallmouth bass, brook trout inhabit Johnston Lake. Brookies are tough to find most of the time.

**Kioshkokwi Lake (F7)** is a large Algonquin lake that is located at the northern part of the park. The lake's name in native Algonkin means 'lake of many gulls', which is recognizably true. From Hwy 17, Hwy 630 travels directly to the lake. The Kiosk Campground, an old ranger cabin and 25 interior campsites provide a variety of camping alternatives. Fishing on the lake is usually slow for both brook trout and lake trout. Perseverance often pays off for nice lake trout, which are caught in excess of 70 cm (28 in).

**La Chapelle and Sheedy Lake (A1)** can be accessed by rustic portage from Kabuskong Bay or by travelling on foot through bush from Pine Lake Road. Smallmouth bass, northern pike and walleye are found in both lakes. Walleye and northern pike are generally small and fishing is fair for both species. Smallmouth bass can provide good action for anglers. Try jigging for smallmouth and walleye. Floating rapalas can be a good choice for cruising northern pike.

**Lake Talon (B1)** is part of the Mattawa River Provincial Park. There are a number of campsites and cottages located on the lake. Park campsites are user maintained, so be sure to leave your site clean when done camping. Fishing on the lake is fair for lake trout and walleye. Lakers can reach sizes in excess of 65 cm (26 in), while walleye can be found to 4+ kg (9 lbs). Smallmouth and largemouth bass are often overlooked and provide for some very good fishing. Bass average 0.5-1kg, although can be caught to 2.5kg (5.5 lbs). Try off one of the many islands on the lake when looking for good bass holding areas. Northern pike and muskellunge can also be caught in Lake Talon. Good sized northerns can be found in the lake during dusk periods. Muskellunge are much more elusive, although some nice sized musky are caught annually. Autumn is the best time of year to find lunker muskellunge. The big predator travels into the slow bays of the lake in search of lethargic bait fish.

**Lauder Lake (G5)** lies within Algonquin Park's northern boundary and offers four secluded campsites. Fishing is fair for good sized lake trout and brook trout. The stream found at the southern part of the lake often attracts good numbers of brook trout. Brookies sit in front to the stream in search of dislodged nymphs and other food fare. The lake can be easily accessed within one day from at Kioshkokwi Lake.

**Little Clear, Long and Turtle Lake (B5, C5)** are three small trout lakes that are all easily accessed off a dirt road. The lakes are each stocked almost annually and offer good fishing at times. Brookies are small but have been caught to 35+ cm (14 in).

**Little Mink Lake (G7)** is a small interior Algonquin lake that can be reached via portage from Kioshkokwi Lake. Brook trout are found in the lake and fishing is fair in spring, after ice off but slows significantly as summer approaches.

**Little Twin Lakes (B5)** are two small trout lakes that are found northwest of Little Clear Lake. A rough 4wd road travels close to the lakes. Fishing can be good in the lakes for small natural brook trout.

**Long Lake (G1)** is a small lake found within Samuel De Champlain Provincial Park. The lake is stocked annually with brook trout since the lake receives significant angling pressure throughout the year. Fishing is fair at time in spring for small brookies.

**Pine Lake (A1)** lies within the boundaries of the Mattawa River Provincial Park. Access to the lake is by the Pine Lake Road from Hwy 17. Fishing is fair for smaller northern pike, although larger pike can be found in the lake. Smallmouth bass are present in good numbers and average 0.5-1kg (1-2 lbs). Muskellunge are also found.

**Smith Lake (E2)** is easily accessed off Hwy 630. There are a few cottages on the lake and the Eau Claire Gorge Conservation Area helps protect a portion of the lake's shoreline. Smallmouth bass, walleye and northern pike are all found in the lake. Fishing for walleye is usually slow, while fishing for northern pike is often decent. Northerns are not very big but average 1-2kgs (2-4.5 lbs). Smallmouth bass fishing can be good at times for smallmouth in the 0.5-1.5kg (1-3.5 lb) range.

**Sparks Lake (C4)** can be reached by rustic trail from Boundary Road. Fishing is fair for natural brook trout in the 20-30 cm (8-12 in) range. Fly fishing is often productive, or try small spinners or spoons.

**Wee Harry Lake (G5)** is a small lake located just outside of Algonquin Park's northern boundary. The lake can be accessed from Bronson Lake by trail. Natural brook trout inhabit the lake and fishing is fair throughout the winter and in spring. Brookies have been caught to 30+ cm (12 in) in this lake. A canoe is a definite necessity.

## Mattawa Area (Map 30)

Mattawa is a small historic town that lies at the confluence of the Mattawa and Ottawa Rivers. The scenery ranges from the lowland of the Ottawa Valley to the picturesque Laurentian Mountains on the Quebec side of the Ottawa River. The area is well known for its fishing and year round outdoor recreation opportunities. Lake trout and brook trout are found in most of the lakes in the area, although a few water bodies hold walleye and other warm water sport fish species.

**Aura Lee and Bug Lake (F7, G7)** can both be found by portage from Cedar Lake's northeastern corner in the Algonquin interior. Fishing is generally fair for brook trout in the 20-30 cm (8-12 in) range. There are 2 campsites located on each of these small lakes.

**Cauchon Lakes and Mink Lake (C7, A7)** are three interior lakes that can be reached within a day's travel. The old Canadian National Railway can be found along all three shorelines and was once a busy railroad. Today, it is hard to imagine these beautiful lakes with a full fledged railway passing through! Lake trout and brook trout inhabit the lakes in fair numbers and fishing can be decent at times during spring when trout cruise near the surface of the lakes. During this time trout are most aggressive and readily feed on hatching insects and nymphs. Rustic campsites are found on all three lakes.

**Club and Waterclear Lake (B7)** are two interior brook trout lakes that offer fair fishing for average sized brookies in spring. There are 3 campsites found on each lake. An old cabin lies on Club Lake's northern shore, which can be explored. Look for moose around the lakes marshy areas.

**Earl's and Taggart Lake (B1)** are two small lakes that can be accessed off Hwy 17, west of Mattawa. Earl's Lake receives a lot of local angling pressure and fishing is often slow for walleye. Largemouth bass are more plentiful and fishing is often fair for bass in the 0.5-1kg (1-2 lb) range. Taggart Lake also holds largemouth bass, which reach 1.5kg (3.5 lbs) and bigger.

**Fork and Sears Lake (C5)** are two small trout lakes found north of the Brain Lake access point of Algonquin Park. Fork Lake is easily accessed off a rough dirt road and is stocked annually with brook trout. Fishing can be good through the ice or in spring for brookies in the 25+ cm (10 in) range. Sears Lake can be found by snowmobile or on foot along a rustic trail from the Brain Lake access road. Natural brook trout are found in the lake in fair numbers. Sizes range from 20-30 cm.

**Gouinlock Lake (D7)** is a scenic Algonquin lake that can be found via portage from the south shore of Little Cauchon Lake. There are 2 great campsites on the lake and fishing is good in spring for nice sized lake trout and brook trout. Lakers can be caught exceeding 40 cm (16 in) and brook trout average 25-35 cm (10-14 in) in size.

**Hurdman Lake (F7)** is a long lake that is located north west of Cedar Lake in Algonquin Park. The lake can be accessed within a day from either Cedar Lake or the Brain Lake access point. 2 rarely used campsites are found on the lake's northern shore. Fishing in the lake is good at times for nice sized brook trout. Try fishing near creek inflows for feeding brookies. Large bead head nymph patterns can work well.

**Laurel and Loxley Lake (E7)** lie northwest of Cedar Lake and can be accessed within a day. Laurela Lake has 5 wilderness campsites to choose from and offers generally slow fishing for lake trout and walleye. Loxley Lake is a little more secluded than Laurel Lake. The southern shore of the lake has been designated a nature reserve area and 3 campsites lie along the lake's shoreline. Fishing is fair for lake trout and brook trout, which have been caught in excess of 40 cm (16 in), although average 25-30 cm (10-12 in).

**Papineau Lake (B4)** is one of the larger lakes in this area and can be found via a dirt road from Mattawa. The lake receives significant angling pressure and its original lake trout stocks are now extinct. A stocked species of lake trout now inhabits the lake along with former strains of the original species. Fishing can be good at times in winter and spring. Whitefish are also a good catch in Papineau Lake and are often more plentiful than lake trout. Lakers and whitefish reach sizes of 65+ cm (26 in). The Papineau Lake Conservation Area also lies on the lake and provides camping opportunities for visitors.

**Thompson Lake (A5)** is found along Algonquin Park's northern boundary. Park permits are not required to park at the lake. A rough dirt road leads directly to the lake where fishing is fair at times for brook trout that can reach sizes of up to 40+ cm (16 in).

**West Aumond Lake (G4)** is a secluded walleye lake that can be accessed via a rough 4wd road. The lake receives most of its pressure in winter by ice fishing anglers. Fishing in the lake is fair but can be slow at times. Walleye average 0.5-1kg (1-2 lbs).

**Whiteburch Lake (A7)** is an interior Algonquin lake that can be easily accessed within a day from Kioshkokwi Lake. There are 4 rustic campsites on the lake that are fairly close to each other. Lake trout are found in the lake and fishing can be fair for small lakers in spring.

## Deux-Rivieres Area (Map 31)
The Deux-Rivieres area is a fairly remote region that lies between the northern side of Algonquin Provincial Park and the Laurentian Mountains of Quebec. Both crown land and park camping is available in the region. Brook trout and lake trout inhabit most of the cool lakes in the area, although a wide range of sport fish species can be found in the Ottawa River. Be sure to practice catch and release whenever possible to help maintain the quality fishing of the area.

**Allen and North Depot Lake (F6, F7)** are popular lakes just after the spring thaw. Lake trout and brook trout are found in both lakes and in good numbers. Lakers are not as big as in the more southern park lakes, however, there are reports of 60+ cm (24 in) lake trout taken annually. Brookies can also reach good sizes and have been found in the 40+ (16 in) range. There are plenty of campsites on the two lakes. The one concern on these lakes is the misuse of the park environment. Every year cans and other garbage is left behind on the lakes. Be sure to practice low impact camping and please help remove any rubish you come across.

**Big George Lake (E7)** lies along a detour from the Canoe Route along the Petawawa River to Radiant Lake. There are two scenic campsites on the lake, including a beautiful island site. The lake holds good numbers of brook trout, which are most active in spring, after ice off.

**Big Poplar Lake (B3)** is a remote walleye lake that can be found with a snowmobile or on foot through some thick bush. Due to the access, the lake is most often fished in the most in winter. Walleye are not big but average 0.5-1kg (1-2 lbs). If you are ambitious enough, the open water season on the lake can provide great success.

**Bissett and Weasel Lake (G6, G7)** are two secluded Algonquin lakes that can only be accessed by canoe and portage along the Bissett Creek. Water levels on the creek can be very low during late summer, which could impede travel greatly. Both lakes offer good fishing for nice sized brook trout. The trout are a little easier to find in Weasel Lake, due mainly to its smaller size. Wilderness campsites are located on both lakes.

**Claradeer and Deermeadow Lake (F5, F6)** both lie near a rough dirt road. Short trails can take you to the lakes, which are inhabited by natural brook trout to 40+ cm (16 in). Try a silver spoon or a streamer pattern in spring.

**Clara Lake (G3)** can be found by snowmobile or on foot through some thick bush. The lake holds brook trout that can reach 40 cm (16 in) in size. Fishing is fair, although can be good at times. Try small white jigs through the ice or fly fishing in spring.

**Ghost Lake (C7)** is a small, secluded Algonquin lake that lies north of Cedar Lake. A long portage leads from Pan Lake and to Brent Road. 2 exquisite interior campsites are found on the lake and fishing can be quite good for small brook trout. Spring is always the best time of year for brookies, however, late September can also be surprising.

**Gilmour and Tecumseh Lake (A7)** can be reached by portage from the Brent Road. The lakes lie in the bottom of the Brent Crater and have a heavy limestone base. The crater is believed to be the result of the ancient meteorite that hit the area. The limestone is so rich that Gilmour Lake is the only lake in the park that is not affected by acid rain. The site is designated as a nature reserve to help preserve the geological importance of the area. Fishing in the lakes is fair for decent sized brook trout. Lake trout are also found in Gilmour Lake. There are three interior campsites found on each of the lakes.

**Greenbough Lake (E3)** is often overlooked due to the fact that only small smallmouth bass inhabit the lake. The lake can be accessed be 4wd road south of the village of Deux-Rivieres. The lake is fairly large and the fishing is often very good. Smallmouth bass in this lake have been found to 2.5kg (5.5 lbs). Wilderness camping opportunities exist.

**Mums Lake (D4)** can be reached by a rough 4wd road, which has played a part in decreasing the fishing quality of the lake. Brook trout are found in the lake in fair numbers, although fishing can be slow at times. Trout have been caught in the 35+ cm (14 in) range.

**Little North River Lake (B5)** is one of the larger lakes in the area. Access to the lake is by travelling up the North River from the access point. Park permits may be required to park your vehicle at the access, although are not needed to camp at the lake. Fishing is good at times during the spring for nice sized brook trout. A few 40+ cm (16 in) brook trout are reportedly caught in the lake each year. A small spoon or streamer pattern is the preferred lure on the lake.

**Merganser and North River Lake (D6)** are popular spots during the spring fishing run that encompasses Algonquin Park. The lakes are accessed by travelling down the North River from the access point off Brent Road. Only a 90m (295 ft) portage separates North River and Merganser Lake. Fishing on North River Lake is fair in spring for Lake trout to 45+ cm (18 in) and brook trout to 35+ cm (14 in). The inflow and outflow areas of the North River often hold good numbers of feeding trout. Merganser Lake is inhabited by brook trout and the fishing quality is similar to the North River Lake. Moose are often spotted on the stretch of the North River between North River Lake and Allan Lake. Campsites are found on both lakes.

**Rana Lake (A7)** can be found not far off the Brent Road about 6km into Algonquin Park. Fishing is fair at the lake for usually small brook trout. Try a small bead head nymphs fly pattern or a shiny spinner.

**Wabamimi Lake (E7)** is a secluded interior lake that experiences much lower use compared to other lakes in the Cedar Lake area. The lake can be accessed in a day and there are 2 perfect campsites located on the lake. Fishing can be quite good for nice sized brook trout.

**Windigo Lake (F5)** is a fairly big lake that doubles as an access point to Algonquin Provincial Park. A road leads to the lake, which offers fair fishing for lake trout and brook trout. Lakers are caught in the 45-55 cm (18-22 in) range, while brookies average 25-35 cm (10-14 in) in size. Fishing from shore is possible in spring, although a canoe is an asset. There are wilderness camping opportunities at the lake.

## Bissett Creek Area (Map 32)
A few rustic canoe routes can be accessed in the Bissett Creek area, including a couple challenging Algonquin Park canoe routes. Fishing in the area is mainly for lake and brook trout, although splake have been stocked in a few lakes. Purposely or inadvertently, smallmouth and largemouth bass have been introduced to a number of natural trout lakes. Fishing for natural trout has declined rapidly since these introductions. Be sure to report any incidents to authorities to prevent future trout lakes from being irreversibly damaged.

**Adelaird and Billys Lake (G2)** are located north of Hwy 17, before the village of Bissett Creek. Both lakes can be accessed by a dirt road and offer generally slow fishing for brook trout. Adelaird Lake has been stocked with brook trout and usually has better fishing.

**Big Bissett Lake (C5)** is one of Algonquin Park's northern access points and is accessed by the rough Bissett Creek Road from Hwy 17. Algonquin Park permits are required to camp on the lake. Big Bissett is stocked every few years with brook trout and fishing is fair for brookies that can reach 40 cm (16 in) in size. Largemouth bass were introduced into the lake several years ago. Fishing is good at times for bass up to 2.5kg.

**Campground and Quartz Lake (C4, D4)** are two small, remote lakes. Both lakes offer good fishing for small natural brook trout. Access to the lakes is by rustic trail through heavy bush. Fly fishers will be delighted with the action on these lakes.

**Chateau and Grants Lake (F6)** are two brook trout lakes that are found near Algonquin Park's northern border. A rough road leads to the park boundary where trails can be found to the lakes. Fishing is good at times, especially in spring. Brook trout average 20-30 cm (8-12 in) but have been found bigger in the lakes.

**Christopher Robin and Piglet Lake (E5)** are named after popular Winnie the Pooh Cartoon Characters. The two trout lakes are easily accessible by snowmobile. A rough 4wd road travels to Piglet Lake, although you must proceed on foot to Christopher Robin Lake. Lake trout are found in Piglet Lake and brook trout in Christopher Robin Lake. Fishing can be good at times but is generally fair. Angling pressure on Piglet Lake has forced new regulations to be instilled on the lake. The lake is now part of a winter/spring fishing sanctuary to help preserve ailing natural lake trout stocks.

**Cliff and Cranberry Lake (C5)** are two secluded lakes that offer slow to fair fishing for small brook trout. Cranberry Lake can be accessed by a dirt road, while Cliff Lake must be walked to. Due to the more remote access, Cliff Lake usually has better action.

**Fitz, Gerald and Reed Lake (A7)** are three beautiful interior Algonquin lakes that can only be reached by canoe down the scenic Bissett Creek. Moose and beavers are often spotted on the creek. Reed Lake, the first lake you come to, is a good place to base camp. Short portages separate the other lakes. Fishing is good on all three lakes for nice sized brook trout to 40cm (16 in).

**Gardiner and Rattail Lake (A3, A4)** are two seclude brook trout lakes. A 4wd road passes near Gardiner Lake and Rattail Lake can be accessed by rustic portage from Waterloo Lake. Brook trout are found in both lakes to 40 cm (16 in) in size.

**Genak Lake (D3)** lies south of Hwy 17 and receives heavy winter angling pressure. Due to this, the brook trout population is fragile and fishing on the lake is usually slow for small brook trout.

**Gibson Lakes (A2)** are easily accessed off Hwy 17, west of the village of Bissett Creek, yet are rarely visited. Gibson Lake offers fair fishing for smallmouth that average 0.5-1kg (1-2 lbs) as well as a nice picnic area on the lake. Big Gibson Lake can be found via a rough dirt road and offers fair fishing for northern pike and smallmouth bass. Lake trout are stocked in the lake every few years.

**Horseshoe and Marys Lake (G5)** are two natural brook trout lakes that can receive a lot of pressure in winter. They are easily accessed on snowmobile, while in the spring and summer they can be hiked to. Fishing is fair for brook trout to 30+ cm (12 in).

**Little Lake (C6)** can be found via 4wd road and lies on the Algonquin Park border. Splake are stocked in the lake annually. Fishing is good through the ice and in spring for splake in the 30-35 cm (12-14 in) range. Small spoons work well through the ice.

**Lost Coin and Otterpaw Lake (D7, C7)** are two remote Algonquin lakes that can be accessed by cart trails into the park's interior. The main barrier to getting to these lakes is a 7km trek from the park boundary. Hence, both lakes are rarely visited and offer good fishing for nice sized brook trout. There are no designated campsites on the lakes, however, there is an old ranger cabin on Lost Coin Lake. The cabin is comfortably equipped and can be rented by the night.

**Mag Lake (F5)** is a very small lake that is often overlooked. A short hike can take you to the lake and fishing in the lake is good for small but plentiful, brook trout. Fly anglers can have great success on this lake. Spin casters should try small spinners.

**Morin Lake (C2)** is a small lake that can be found by snowmobile from Hwy 17 or on foot through some dense bush. Small brook trout inhabit the lake and fishing is fair early in the spring.

**Mousseau and Valiant Lake (D3)** can be accessed by 4wd road or snowmobile. Mousseau Lake is stocked every few years with splake that can be found in the 40+ cm (16 in) range. Valiant Lake is stocked with lake trout every few years and fishing for lakers in the 40-50 cm (16-20 in) range can be good at times. Ice fishing is the most successful method of angling on both lakes.

**North Rouge Lake (F7)** has three rustic campsites along the lake's shoreline. The secluded lake is within Algonquin Park's interior and offers good fishing for nice sized brook trout. Brookies have been caught to 40 cm (16 in) in this lake. Access to the lake requires a rugged 1,895m (6,217 ft) portage.

**Oval Lake (G6)** lies close to Algonquin Park's northern border and can be accessed by trail from a 4wd road. Fishing can be good for brook trout to 35+ cm (14 in). Spring fishing is best, although late September can also be productive.

**Owl Lake (G4)** is a small, secluded lake that is stocked annually with brook trout. Fishing is quite good at this lake for small but plentiful brookies. If you catch a recently stocked trout (yearling), be sure to return it unharmed.

**Pooh, Puffball and Tigger Lake (F5, G5)** are another three lakes in the area that have been named after Winnie the Pooh Cartoon Characters. The lakes have all been stocked with rainbow trout. Fishing reports are good for small rainbows, especially when using flies or small lures. Spring is the best period, although these rainbows can be active into summer.

**Shingle Lakes (B3)** are two secluded lakes that can be accessed by a 4wd road and then short trails. Natural strains of brook trout remain in the lake and fishing can be good at times in winter and early spring. Late September can also be surprisingly productive. Be sure to limit your catch of the natural trout to ensure a future quality fishery.

**Waterloo Lake (A4)** is one of the largest lakes in the area. A rough 4wd road leads to the lake, however, most of the fishing on this lake comes during winter. Lake trout and brook trout are found in the lake in fair numbers. Along with ice fishing, spring angling is productive. Lakers can reach 45+ cm (18 in) in the lake and brook trout average 25-35 cm (10-14 in). The natural lake trout population has shown signs of stress and it is imperative to practice catch and release to maintain a quality fishery. Watch for special slot size restrictions and winter regulations. Wilderness camping opportunities exist at the lake.

## Driftwood Park and Deep River Areas (Maps 33, 34)

This area offers anglers many small trout lakes as well as wide variety of sport fish in the Ottawa River. Algonquin and Driftwood Provincial Parks are nearby, although crown land camping opportunities do exist on a number of the lakes in the area. Ice fishing is popular on the lakes outside of Algonquin Provincial Park. Be sure to limit your catch to help maintain the quality of the angling in this region.

**Conway Lake (33/C4)** is a very small lake that can be found via a 4wd road from Hwy 17. Natural brook trout are found in the lake, although in small numbers. Over fishing has hindered the lakes productivity.

**Beaver and Otter Lake (33/B6)** can be found via 4wd roads and provide fair to good fishing for natural brook trout. Brookies can reach 35 cm (14 in) in size, although heavy winter angling pressure often hinders the growth of the trout in these lakes. Be conscious and help preserve these beautiful trout.

**Devon and Garreau Lake (33/B5)** can be found by a rough 4wd road or trail. Devon Lake is stocked every few years with brook trout and offers good fishing in the winter and spring. Garreau Lake relies on natural reproduction and heavy fishing pressure has affected this small lake. Fishing is fair for generally small brook trout.

**Dunlop, McKenna and Sweezy Lake (33/A4, B4)** are three secluded brook trout lakes that offer fair to good fishing in the winter and spring. A 4wd road leads to McKenna Lake and short trails join the other lakes from there. Brook trout are usually small, although have been found in the 30+ cm (12 in) range.

**Findlay, Mill and Parkline Lake (33/D6)** are located near Algonquin Park's boundary. All three lakes are stocked every few years with brook trout and fishing can be good for trout in the 35+ cm (14 in) range. Fly fishing is effective as well as small spinners or spoons.

**Harvey and Wylie Lake (33/F5)** are both stocked every few years with brook trout. The lakes are accessible by rough roads and are popular ice fishing lakes. Fishing is fair for brookies that reach 30+ (12 in).

Head, Rat and Trout Lake (33/C6) are three trout lakes that can be accessed by 4wd roads. Trout Lake is stocked annually with brook trout and offers the best angling opportunity. Head and Rat Lake are smaller lakes with fewer trout. Brookies in Trout Lake average 20-30 cm.

Heart Lake (33/G5) can be reached by a 4wd road or trail. Fishing for smallmouth bass is good for bass that average 0.5-1.5kg. Northern pike are also found in the lake and fishing is fair for hammer head sized pike. Big pike are harder to come by but are caught yearly.

James Lakes (34/B7) are a chain of three lakes that offer good fishing for smallmouth bass. Bass can be found to 1.5kg (3.5 lbs) and are most aggressive during overcast periods. Northern pike are found in the lake in fair numbers, although are usually small. Muskellunge also inhabit the lake but only in small numbers. There is a public access point located at the southern end of First James Lake.

Jennings Lake (33/D5) is a small brook trout lake that is fished heavily in winter. A short trail leads to the lake from a dirt road. Fishing is fair for brook trout that average 20-30 cm (8-12 in) in size. Spring fly fishing can be productive.

Kellys Lake (33/G6) lies within Algonquin Provincial Park and can only be reached by orienteering through dense bush. There are no designated campsites on the lake, therefore, any trip to the lake would have to be a day trip. Fishing can be very good at the lake for smallmouth bass to 2kg (4.5 lbs).

Lee and Mossberry Lake (33/G5) are two brook trout lakes that receive significant angling pressure in the winter. Brook trout fishing is currently slow to fair. If more fish are released instead of becoming table fare, the lake could become a good fishing lake again.

McSourley Lake (33/A2) is stocked annually with lake trout and can be found via a dirt road west of Driftwood Provincial Park. Fishing is fair in winter and spring for trout to 45+ cm (18 in).

Menet Lake (33/B4) is easily reached by a road. The lake is stocked annually with splake, which provide for fair fishing for splake to 40+ cm (16 in). White jigs through the ice can be effective.

Oliver Lake (33/B4) is a very small lake that is stocked every few years with brook trout. Fishing is often good for small trout. Small flies and lure presentations are the key to this lake. The lake can be accessed on foot from Dunlop Lake.

Patersons, Sand and Woods Lake (33/E6) lie near Algonquin Park's boundary and are accessible by foot. All three lakes are quite small and fishing is only fair for brook trout to 30 cm (12 in). Heavy winter angling pressure has depleted these lakes. Be sure to limit your catch.

Perch and Smith Lake (33/B3) are two small lakes that can be found via roads. Perch Lake is stocked with splake and provides for fair fishing for small splake. Smith lake is stocked with rainbow trout, which can be quite elusive at times. Small spinners can be productive or try small nymph fly patterns in spring.

Roney Lake (33/F4) is a small lake that holds a good population of smallmouth bass. Fishing is good for bass in the 0.5-1kg (1-2 lb) range. Spinners or minnow imitation lures work well.

Way Lake (33/F4) is a small lake that lies next to the railway tracks. Brook trout are found in the lake, although in small numbers. Winter angling harvests has hindered the production of the lake.

# Stream Fishing

The Algonquin Region is renowned for the hundreds of lakes that lie within its beautiful highlands. As a result, the cool streams of the region are often overlooked as angling opportunities. Unknown to many anglers, these streams present some of the best angling in the entire region! The most common species you will find in Algonquin Region streams is the brook trout. Brookies flourish in cool, spring fed streams and it is not uncommon to catch your limit in less than an hour. The trout are small compared to trout that reside in lakes, although they are plentiful.

The small stream environment is one of the main challenges when fishing for stream trout. The angler always has logs, rocks and trees to tend with. On larger rivers, the use of a boat can increase results dramatically. The harder to get to areas can then be fished with little difficulty. Regardless, there is no better feeling than catching a bright spotted brook trout from a creek or river.

When fishing trout in creeks and rivers, nymph fly patterns work best, although the old reliable hook and worm will always provide results. Trout can be found in larger pools but are more often found at the front and back of pools where there is faster water. Shallow, fast water sections are also good trout holding areas. Trout will sit behind rocks and boulders waiting for dislodged insects to float by. Look for cover, such as logs or overhangs, to find bigger trout.

For warm water species, the rivers are often wider and deeper, although the tactics are similar to that of lakes. The same tackle used in lakes is also effective in rivers, although the fishing is often more difficult due to shore cover. Look for areas with overhangs or thick vegetation and let your lure or fly pass close by. The predators will be hiding in the cover and will often strike out at a well presented bait.

The seasons for stream fishing vary between species and location. Trout season in most areas, including Algonquin Park, is from the last Saturday in April to September 30. In some regions outside the park the season begins January 1. For warm water species resident in rivers, the normal fishing seasons apply.

Walleye and muskellunge enter the streams in early spring and can continue spawning into May. Fishing is closed on many warm water rivers during this time to ensure a productive spawning season occurs.

When stream fishing for small trout, it is recommended to de-barb your hooks to reduce injury to the fish. This will help ensure the trout survives after release to be caught another day.

### Amable Du Fond River (Map 29/F4)
The Amable Du Fond River is a hidden gem of the northern Algonquin Region. The river flows from Smith Lake near the Mattawa River to Kioshkokwi Lake in Algonquin Park. The river is reasonably wide in most areas and is easily accessible by roads. For fly anglers, the Amable Du Fond can compare to some of the best inland rivers in the country. Brook trout and rainbow trout are found throughout the system and in very good numbers. Nymph action is constant all year, although mayfly and caddis flies can produce results at the right times. Rainbow often outsize brook trout. Trout average 20-25 cm (8-10 in) in the river but are found in excess of 0.5 kg (1 lb)!

### Aylen River (Map 14/F1, Map 15/A2)
The Aylen River has two distinct sections. The upper section lies north of Aylen Lake into Algonquin Provincial Park. Inside the park, the river is rarely fished and provides some good fishing opportunities for brook trout to 30cm (12 in). The other section of the river flows out of Aylen Lake to the Opeongo River. This small stretch of river is frequented by anglers who expereince fair fishing for smallmouth bass. The bass are not big but are they are caught to 1 kg (2 lbs).

### Aumond Creek (Map 31/A2)
This small stream flows from the Ottawa River to Big Poplar and Aumond Lakes. The sections closer to Hwy 17 receive most of the angling pressure throughout the year but still provide good angling opportunities. Generally, the further you venture from the highway, the better the fishing. There are a number of nice, deep pools along this creek, especially in the sections closer to Big Poplar Lake. Some 25+ cm (10 in) trout have been caught in the larger pools. The creek's native trout species is the brook trout, however, previously stocked rainbow trout can also be found in the creek. Much of the creek is road accessible.

### Barron River (Map 25/D5, 25/B4)
Flows from the east side of Algonquin Park to the Ottawa River. The northern side of the river, outside of the park is Canadian Forces Base Petawawa Property and trespassing is strictly prohibited. Fishing in the river is good in sections for

smallmouth bass. The fishing gets better the further you venture from the town of Petawawa. Smallmouth Bass are caught to 1 kg (2 lbs). Muskellunge can also be caught in the river and can be found to 120cm (48 in).

### Big East River (11/E7, 12/B5)

The Big East River flows from the west side of Algonquin Park past Arrowhead Provincial Park and onto Lake Vernon. Natural Brook trout can be found in the sections of the river within the park and before Arrowhead Provincial Park. Brookies have been stocked on occasion in areas closer to Lake Vernon. Fishing is fair for small brookies west of Arrowhead Provincial Park and is good east of the park. Trout in the creek average 20-30 cm (10-12 in) in size.

### Bissett Creek (32/C4)

Bissett Creek is a meandering creek that flows from the Ottawa River to Reed Lake inside Algonquin Park. Fishing is best south of Hwy 17 but can be productive throughout the creek as small brook trout are found in good numbers. There are a few fast flowing areas outside of Algonquin Park that hold some bigger brook trout. The creek is road accessible most of the way to the park but the ideal way to fish this creek is to travel the Bissett Creek Canoe Route. That way you won't miss any of the good holes along the creek.

### Black Donald Creek (9/A6)

Black Donald Creek is a small creek that is fairly remote as it flows south into Black Donald Lake. The creek runs through the rolling Madawaska Highlands, which provides a scenic backdrop. Portions of the creek are accessible by 4wd road, although there are a number of areas that cannot be found by vehicle. This helps preserve the quality of the creek fishing. Brook trout are found in the creek and in very good numbers. Trout are generally small but can reach 25 cm (10 in) in size.

### Blueseal Creek (Map 29/A3)

Blueseal Creek flows into the Mattawa River and offers some remote areas that can only be found on foot. The fishing in the southern portion of the creek can be very good, whereas the sections closer to Hwy 17 receive the most pressure. Closer to the highway, roads lead to the creek while the southern, more remote, areas are accessible by 4wd roads in a number of places. Brook trout and rainbow trout are found in the creek and are usually small.

### Bonnechere River (Map 16, 17, 18) w, bs, np

The Bonnechere River can be productive in a few sections and is best fished by boat or canoe in most areas. Walleye are found in fair numbers in the river near Round and Golden Lakes. There is a good population of smallmouth bass throughout the river. Bass are not very big but are caught in the 1 kg (2 lb) range. Small northern pike also inhabit the river and fishing is usually fair. Walleye spawn in the river in spring and no fishing is permitted at that time. Check the regulations to verify exact dates.

### Crow River (23/B3)

The Crow River is found deep within the Algonquin Park interior. Most of the fishing on the river is done on the section between Big Crow Lake and Lake Lavieille. There are a number of fast water sections and big pools on the river that hold good sized brook trout. Fly fishing is very productive on the river, although small spinners also work well. Bead head nymph patters are usually the most effective fly on the river.

### Depot Creek (Map 29/A6, 28/G5)

Depot Creek is a small stream found east of Wasi Lake. Much of the stream is accessible by roads, although there are a few areas that can only be accessed on foot. Fishing in the stream is good for small brook trout. A worm on a small hook is usually quite effective. Try a small spinner to attract larger trout.

### Little Madawaska River (22/D3)

This is a remote Algonquin river that offers some good fishing for brook trout. Large brookies have been found to 30 cm (12 in) in the river but average about 20 cm (8 in). Flies work very well on this river. Try behind any one of the small dams that are found along the river.

### McGillvray Creek (Map 19/C1, 28/C1)

This small creek is found south of the town of Powassan. The creek flows under Hwy 11 and is accessible by dirt roads. Small brook trout are found in the creek that average 18-20 cm (7-8 in) in size. Fishing is fair, although can be good at times. During light showers the trout in this creek can be very aggressive. Overcast periods also increase angling success. Try a small bead head nymph pattern or a small worm.

### Mattawa River (Map 28/E1, 29/D1, 30/A1)

The Mattawa River flows from Trout Lake near North Bay to the Ottawa River at the town of Mattawa. A large portion of the river is part of the Mattawa River Provincial Park. The park is designated as a Canadian Heritage River and was one of Ontario's first waterway parks. Samuel De Champlain Provincial Park can also be found on the river located between North Bay and Mattawa. There are many access points to the river that parallels Hwy 17. If you are planning on drift fishing, some sections of the river are difficult to navigate due to fast water, although most of the river is quite slow. Overall, the fishing quality of the river is quite good for a wide variety of sport fish species. Smallmouth bass to 2 kg (4.5 lbs) are found in good numbers. Largemouth bass are also present in a number of areas. Walleye is the most sought after species on the river and fishing can be good at times. Some 4+ kg (9 lb) walleye have been caught in the river. One of the best locations for finding bass and walleye is near the confluence of the Ottawa and Mattawa Rivers. Night fishing can also increase production. Northern pike and muskellunge are two large predators that also inhabit the river. Muskellunge are much harder to find than their cousin, the northern pike. Small northerns provide good fishing opportunities and there are some big pike caught annually. Bright coloured crankbaits are a good lure to effectively catch bass, walleye and pike.

### Nipissing River (20/F6, 21/D2)

This Algonquin Park river is located deep in the interior of the park. The river flows from the west side of the park all the way to Cedar Lake on the park's northern side. The portion of the river west of the Highview Cabin is rarely traveled. Fishing for brook trout is very good in some areas along this remote section. From the Highview Cabin north to High Falls, the fishing is good and can be very good at times. Brookies average 20 cm (8 in) in size but are found bigger at times. Fly fishing will increase your success significantly but worms and or small spinners can produce well. Bead head nymphs are a good fly selection.

### Ottawa River (Maps 26, 27, 30, 31, 32, 33, 34)

The Ottawa River has played an integral role in the development of Canada and the Ottawa Valley. The river was a major transportation route for early settlers and for the log drives that helped shape the early economy of Canada. Today, the log drives are history, although the river continues to play a large role. Tourism on the river is flourishing with guided rafting tours, fishing lodges and other recreation based businesses. The public can access the river from several locations for free or modest fees.

The Algonquin Region portion of the Ottawa River can offer some very good fishing opportunities. Smallmouth bass are abundant. Once you locate a good holding area, fishing can be very good for nice sized bass. Smallmouth have been caught in the 2+ kg (4.5 lb) range. Northern pike are one of the largest predators in the river. Fishing is good at times for pike that can be found exceeding 6 kg (13 lbs). Look in the slower back bays for cruising northerns. Walleye fishing also be good for walleye that average 0.5-1.5 kg (1-3.5 lbs). Walleye are caught annually in the 4+ kg (9 lb) range. Walleye travel in loose schools; therefore, still jigging is an effective angling method. Once you find walleye, you should be able to catch a number of fish before they move on. Lake trout are found in the upper regions of the river near Mattawa. The trout are stocked periodically to improve angling opportunities, although fishing is still quite slow. Check for slot size restrictions on lake trout. Muskellunge inhabit the river in several areas and fishing is usually slow. Most musky are caught incidentally by anglers fishing for other species. Ardent muskellunge anglers boast that the river is a good area for musky. Several other exciting fish species inhabit the river, including sturgeon and whitefish. Fishing for sturgeon is always slow, however, schools of whitefish can provide non stop action. It is recommended to release any caught sturgeon so that the population remains stable.

Note: Some areas of the river contain very strong currents and whitewater. It is recommended to consult local outfitters before you venture out on the river. Be sure to check regulations before fishing.

### Oxtongue River (Map 2/F3, 12/C4)

The Oxtongue flows from the west side of Algonquin Provincial Park to Lake Of Bays. Both brook trout and rainbow trout have been stocked in the Oxtongue River section closer to Lake Of Bays. The portion of the river in and around Algonquin Park offers natural brook trout. Fishing for small rainbows and brook trout is fair in the area closer to Lake of Bays and fishing for brookies in the Algonquin section can be good at times for small trout.

## Pautois Creek (Map 29/G2, 30/A3)

This small creek is easily accessible by roads not far from Hwy 17. Small brook trout inhabit the creek in fair numbers and fishing is generally fair, although can be good during overcast periods. Small nymph fly patterns work well or try the old reliable hook and worm.

## Petawawa River (Lower) (Map 22/E1, 23/C2, 32/G7)

The lower section of the Petawawa River, found in Algonquin Park, flows from Cedar Lake to McManus Lake. Smallmouth bass are prevalent throughout this portion of the river and provide for good fishing at times. Bass average 0.5-1 kg (1-2 lbs) but can be found bigger. Northern pike and muskellunge are also found in sections of the river. Fishing for pike is fair for generally small pike, while muskellunge fishing is slow. Northern Pike have been found in excess of 4 kg (9 lbs) in some of the larger holes of the river. Note: This section of the river is regarded as a whitewater river and can be inherently dangerous.

## Petawawa River (Upper) (11/F2, 12/C1)

The upper portion of Algonquin Park's Petawawa River is a slow meandering river most of the time. The river flows from the west side of the park to Cedar Lake in the park's northern side. Brook trout inhabit the river almost all the way to Cedar Lake. Fishing is good in some sections but can be fair at times. Brookies are small, although can be caught to 25 cm (10 in) in some areas. Fly fishing with nymphs is effective.

## Robitaille Creek (Map 15/C1)

The Robitaille Creek flows between the Bonnechere River near Depot Lake and Robitaille Lake. The creek is very remote and the only access to it would be by canoe from the Bonnechere River or Robitaille Lake. The creek rarely sees an angler and offers very good fishing for small brook trout. Worms are effective as bait, although fly fishing with nymphs also works well.

## Sharpes Creek (Map 29/B3)

Sharpes Creek is a small stream that passes under Hwy 17 from Lake Talon. Small brook trout and rainbow trout inhabit the creek in good numbers. Fishing is fair in the sections closer to Hwy 17, although the further you get from the highway the better the fishing. Trout average 20 cm (8 in) in size but can be found bigger. Small silver spinners can attract bigger trout. Much of the creek is accessible by dirt roads.

## Shirley Creek (Map 14/B1)

This small Algonquin creek is located north of Shirley Lake in the park interior. The creek is not on an established Canoe Route, however, a canoe can be used in some sections. The foliage around the creek can be dense providing for good brook trout habitat. Fishing for brookies is good and can be very good at times. Similar to most trout creeks, the trout in Shirley Creek are small. Brookies have been caught to 25 cm (10 in) in size.

## South Madawaska River (Map 4/E2)

Some of Algonquin Park's rivers are the most productive trout waterbodies in the park. The trout are generally smaller than in lakes but the challenge of landing a wild brookie thrashing through brush and other obstacles can be exhilarating. The Madawaska River offers good year round fishing for brook trout in the 20-35 cm (8-14 in) range. Worms are always productive, however fly fishing can be unbelievably efficient in finding nice sized trout. Nymph patterns are a recommended choice for fly anglers.

*Trout are the predominant species found in the Algonquin Region. Small spinners and spoons can be an effective lure when fishing for trout in lakes. Spinners and spoons create a silver or gold flash that imitates a minnow in distress. This attracts cruising trout that are looking for and easy meal. Other variations of spinners that can be productive include the Deadly Dick and various small Mepps patterns. For spoons, the Little Cleo is the spoon of choice.*

*Fly fishing is continually growing in popularity throughout North America. Trout are the most sought after sport fish species by fly anglers, however, bass are quickly becoming a preferred target. The most popular and productive fly pattern used by fly fishers is the "nymph". The nymph is the larvae form of insects, such as the caddis fly and the damselfly. A common pattern that is a good all round imitator is the beadhead nymph. This is a nymph pattern that has a gold, silver or brass bead as a head. The bead acts as a great attractant for aggressive trout.*

### Metric Conversion Table

| | |
|---|---|
| 1 kg | 2.205 lbs |
| 1 cm | 0.3937 in |
| 1 km | 0.621 mi |
| 1 m | 3.2808 ft |
| 1 ha | 2.47 acre |
| 1 lb | 0.454 kg |
| 1 in | 2.54 cm |
| 1 mi | 1.609 km |
| 1 ft | 30.48 cm |
| 1 acre | 0.4047 ha |
| 4047.0 m² | 1 acre |
| 1 m² | 0.000247 acre |

## South River (19/A4, 20/B6)

The South River offers anglers a variety of different habitats and sport fish species. In sections closer to Powassan and north of the town of South River, smallmouth bass, northern pike and walleye can be found. Fishing is fair for smallmouth bass and small northern pike. Bass average 0.5-1 kg (1-2 lbs) but are found larger. Walleye are the most popular species on the river and fishing is often slow. In the sections of the river east of the town of South River, brook trout can be found. Fishing is fair for small brook trout, although gets better as you get closer to Algonquin Park. Brook trout average 15-20 cm (6-8 in) in size. Much of the river, other than the portions within Algonquin Park, can be accessed by dirt roads.

## Tim River (12/A1, 20/E7)

The Tim River is a slow meandering river that flows from the west side of Algonquin Park to Big Trout Lake. Much of the river can be traveled by canoe and provides good fishing in some areas. Sections closer to the Tim River access point are more heavily fished and success is slower than in more remote areas. The section of the river between Rosebary Lake and Big Trout Lake is less traveled and offers the best angling opportunities. Brook trout inhabit the Tim River and are generally small, although are found to 30 cm (12 in) occasionally. Try in the larger pools for big brookies.

## Trout Creek (Map 19/C3)

Trout Creek flows near Hwy 11 and is easily accessed by roads throughout. Fishing is fair for small brook trout that are best caught on small nymph fly patterns. Bead head patterns help brighten the fly and attract aggressive trout. Worms are always effective. Try a small spinner and a worm to find bigger trout.

## Wasi River (28/D5)

The Wasi River flows from Killrush Lake through Wasi Lake and on into Collander Bay. Smallmouth bass and walleye are found in most areas of the river, especially in the section from Collander Bay to Wasi Lake. Fishing can be good for smallmouth bass in the 0.5+ kg (1 lb) range. Walleye spawn in the river in spring and are often in the river during the open season period. Some big walleye are caught each year and fishing can be good at times. Brook trout and rainbow trout are found in the river in the sections closer to Algonquin Park. Fishing for small trout is good and can be quite good at times. Flies or worms always produce results.

## White Partridge Creek (Map 23/C4)

The White Partridge Creek flows from the north end of White Partridge Lake to the Crow River. The creek is navigable by canoe and offers very good fishing at times. Brook trout inhabit the creek and average 20 cm (8 in) in size and some good sized trout are caught annually. The creek receives little angling pressure throughout the year and is a real pleasure to paddle but low water conditions in late summer can impede travel.

## York River (Map 4/F6)

The York River is another river of Algonquin Provincial Park that is often overlooked. The upper sections of the river rarely see a lure or fly and only local residents fish the lower section of the river. Fishing is generally good throughout the year on the river for brook trout that average 20-30 cm (8-12 in) in size.

# Algonquin Region Mapkey

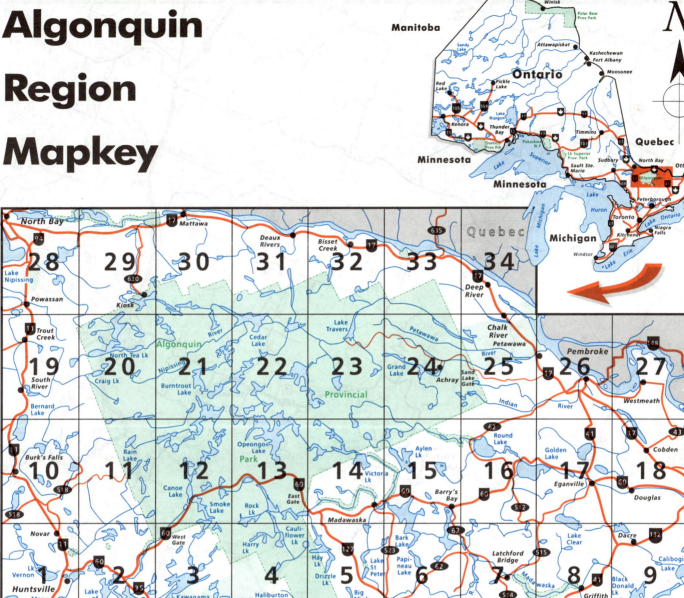

## Legend for the Maps

Scale 1:125,000

2km   0km   3km

1 km = 0.6214 mi.

### Recreational Activities:

Boat Launch ........................................................
Campsite / Limited Facilities ...............................
Campsite / Trailer Park ......................................
Campsite (trail / water access only) ....................
Cross Country Skiing ..........................................
Downhill Skiing ..................................................
Fishing ...............................................................
Float Plane .........................................................
Golf Course ........................................................
Hiking Trail ........................................................
Horseback Riding ...............................................
Mountain Biking .................................................
Motorbiking / ATV .............................................
Paddling (canoe-kayak) ......................................
Picnic Site ..........................................................
Public Access / Cartop Boat Launch ...................
Canoe Access Put-in / Take-out ..........................
Snowmobiling .....................................................

### Miscellaneous:

Airport/Airstrip ..................................................
Cabin/Lodge/Resort ...........................................
Deactivated Road ...............................................
Gate ...................................................................
Highways ...........................................................
   Trans-Canada ..............................................
   Secondary Hwy ...........................................
Interchange ........................................................
Lookout ..............................................................
Microwave Tower ...............................................
Mine Site (abandoned) .......................................
Parking ...............................................................
Point of Interest ................................................
Private Road (Restricted Access) ........................
Ranger Station ....................................................
Town, Village, etc ..............................................
Travel Information ..............................................
Viewpoint ...........................................................
Waterfalls ...........................................................

### Line Definition:

Highways ............................................................
Secondary Highway .............................................
County Roads ......................................................
2wd Roads / Side Roads ......................................
4wd / Unclassified Roads ....................................
Trails ..................................................................
Snowmobile Trails (winter use only) ...................
Routes ................................................................
Paddling Routes ..................................................
Powerlines ..........................................................
Pipelines .............................................................
Railways .............................................................
Park Boundaries .................................................
Ferry Route ........................................................

Provincial Parks     Wilderness Area     City

Restricted Area / Private Property     Quebec     First Nations Territory

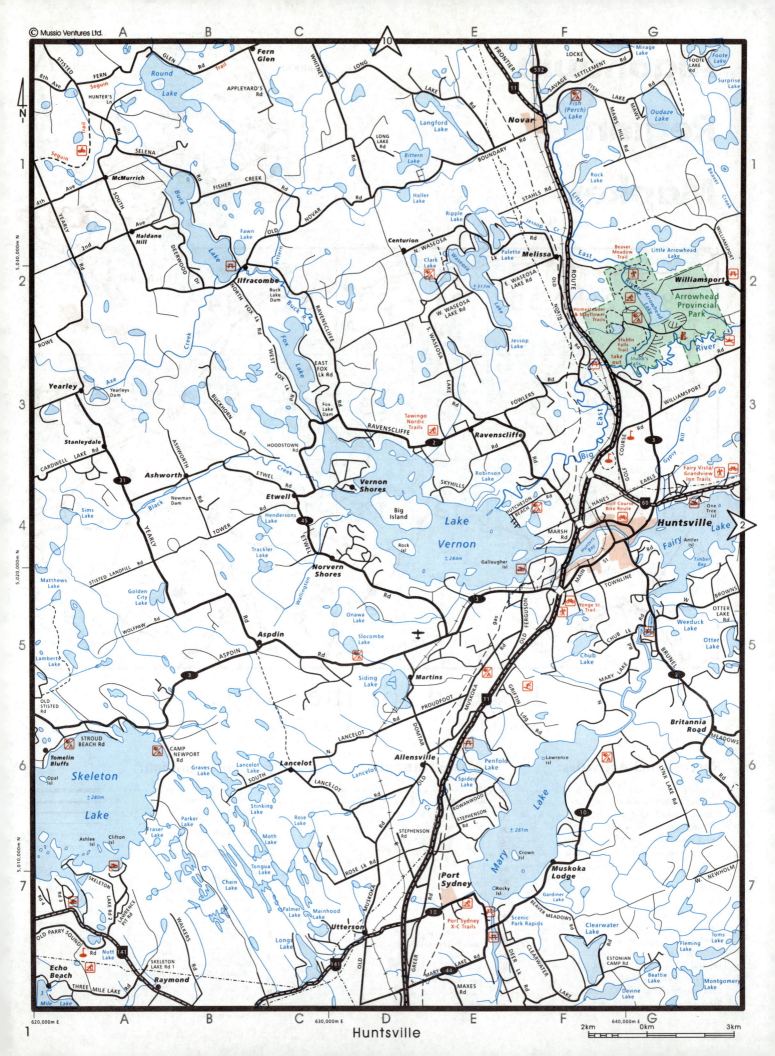

Huntsville

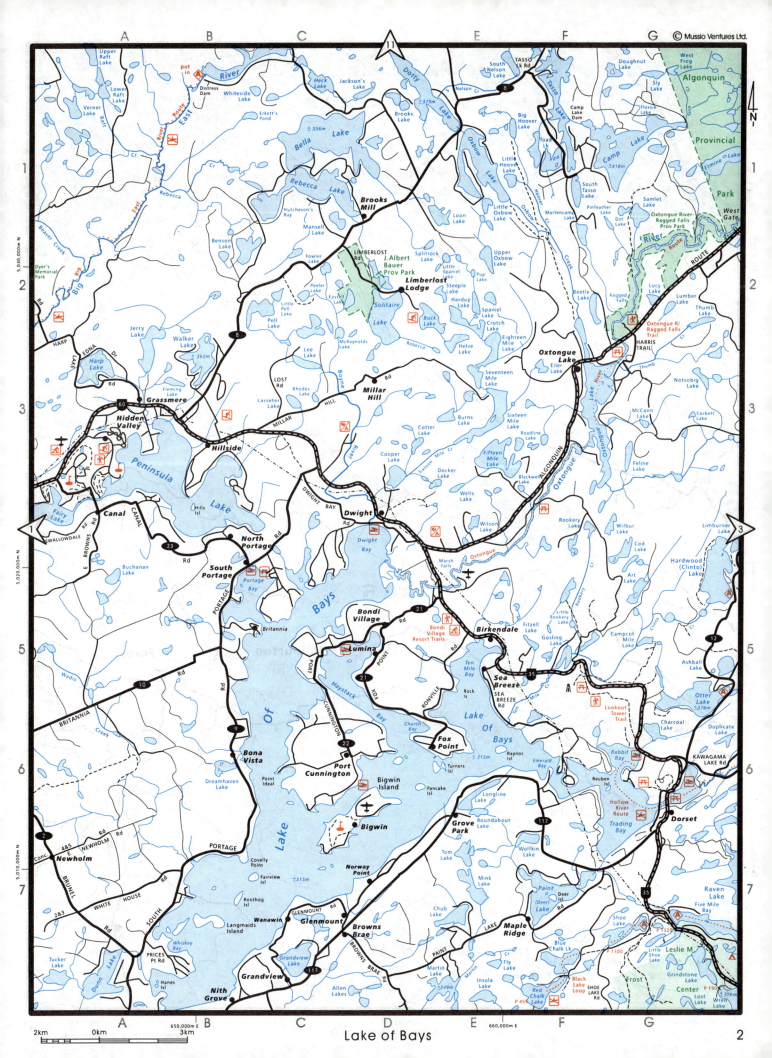

Lake of Bays

2

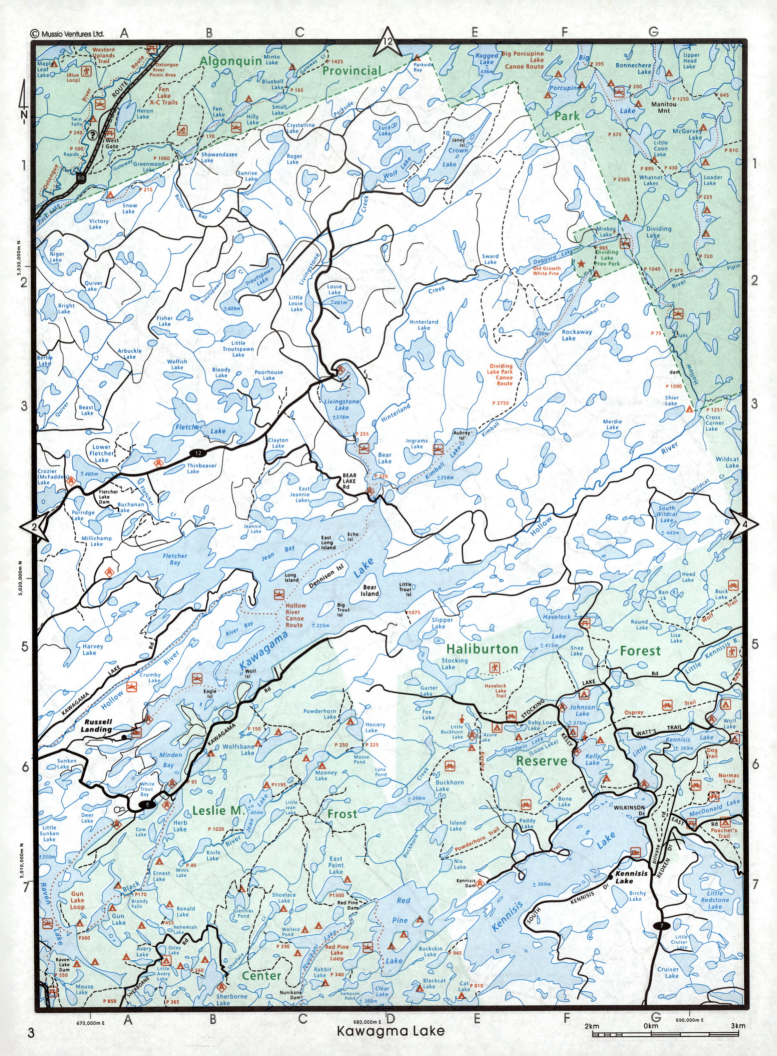

Kawagma Lake

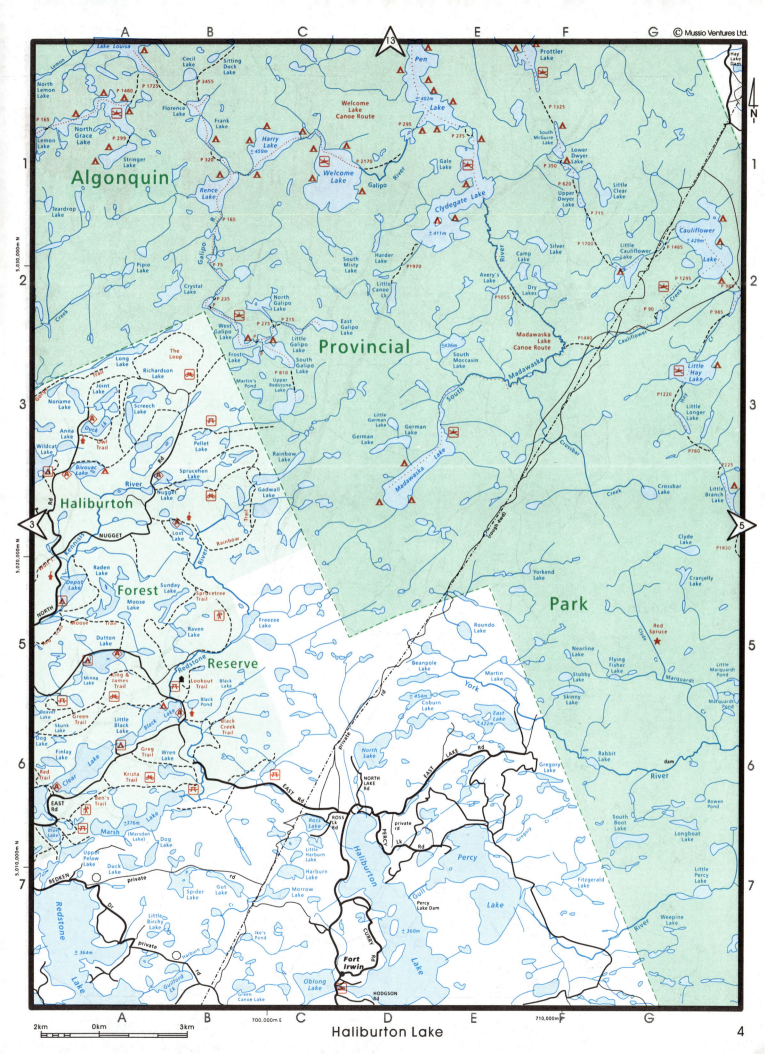

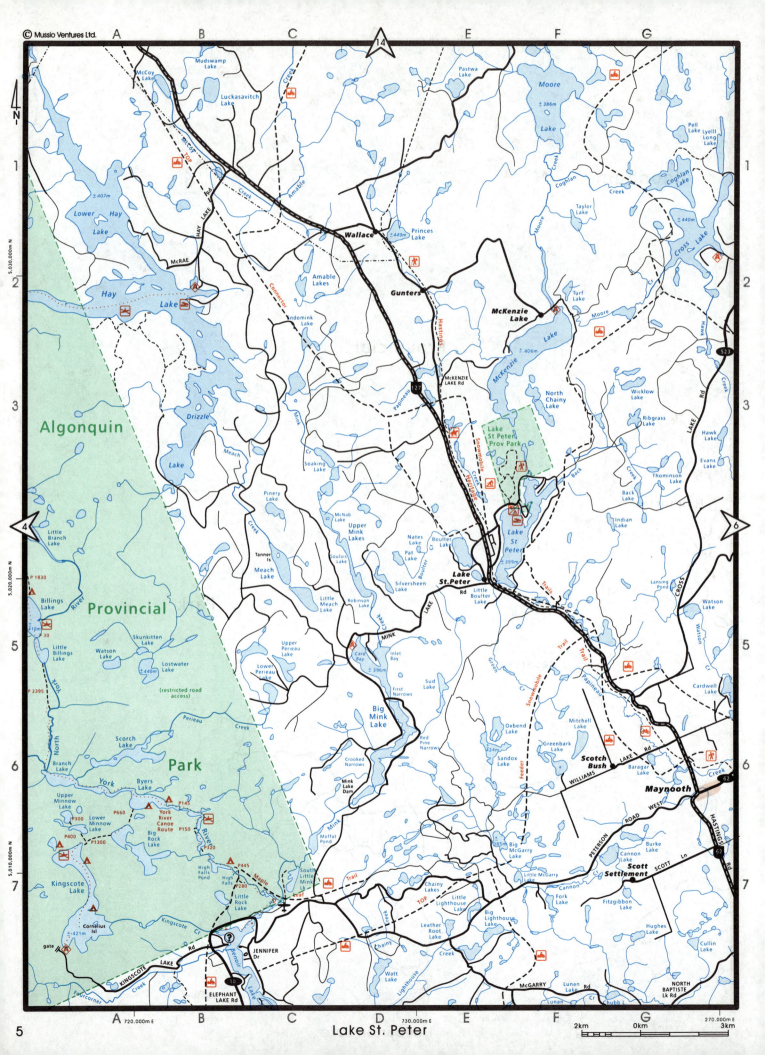

© Mussio Ventures Ltd.

Lake St. Peter

2km 0km 3km

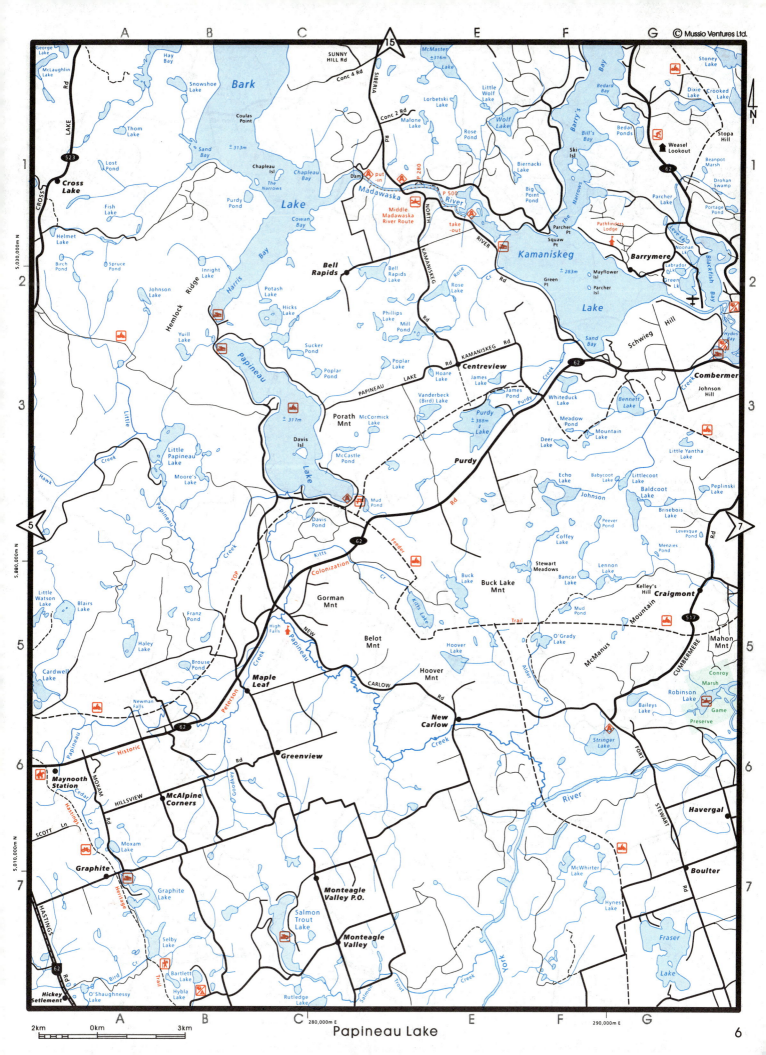

Papineau Lake

6

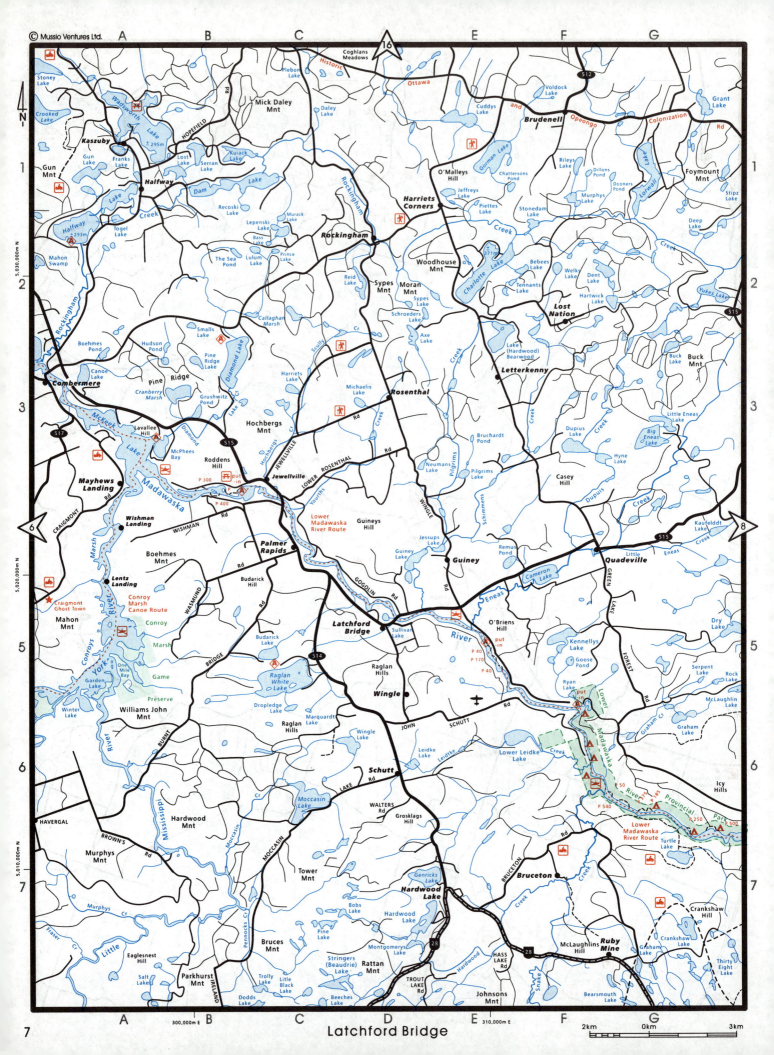

Latchford Bridge

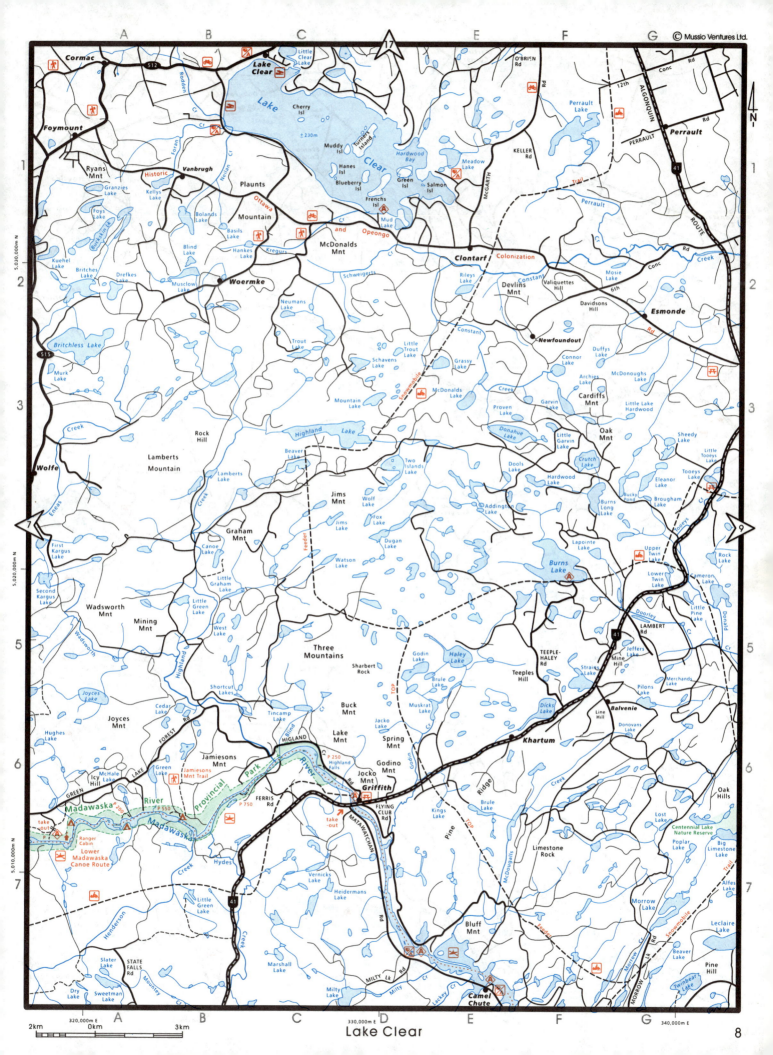

Lake Clear

8

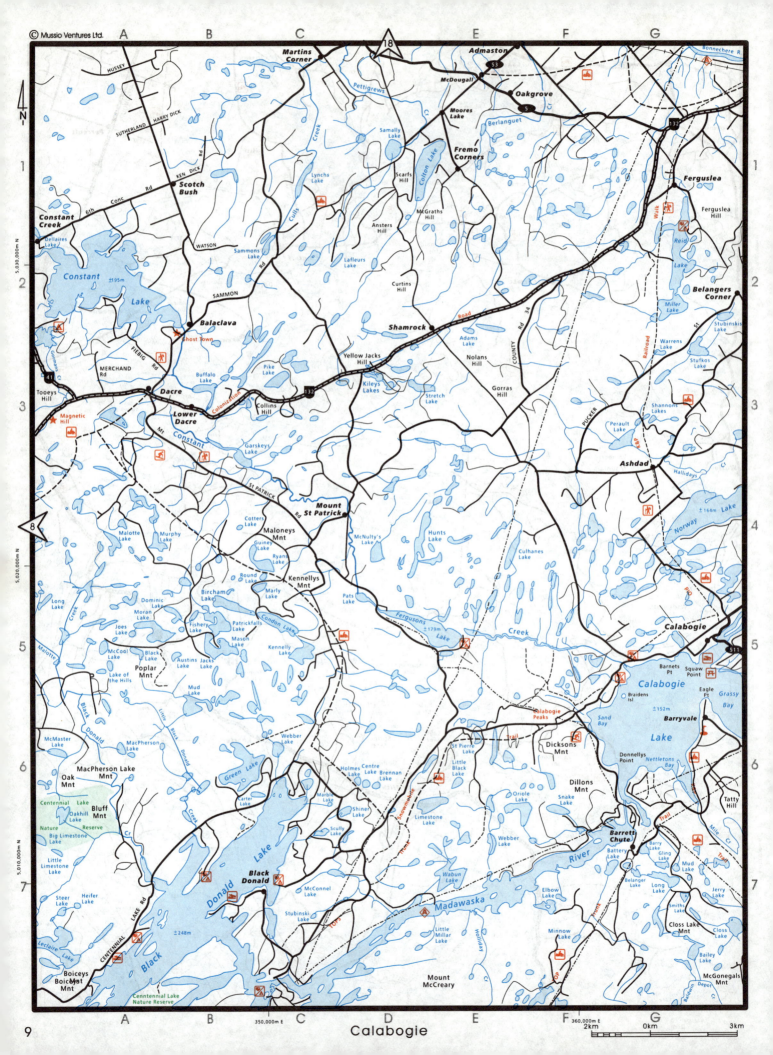

Calabogie

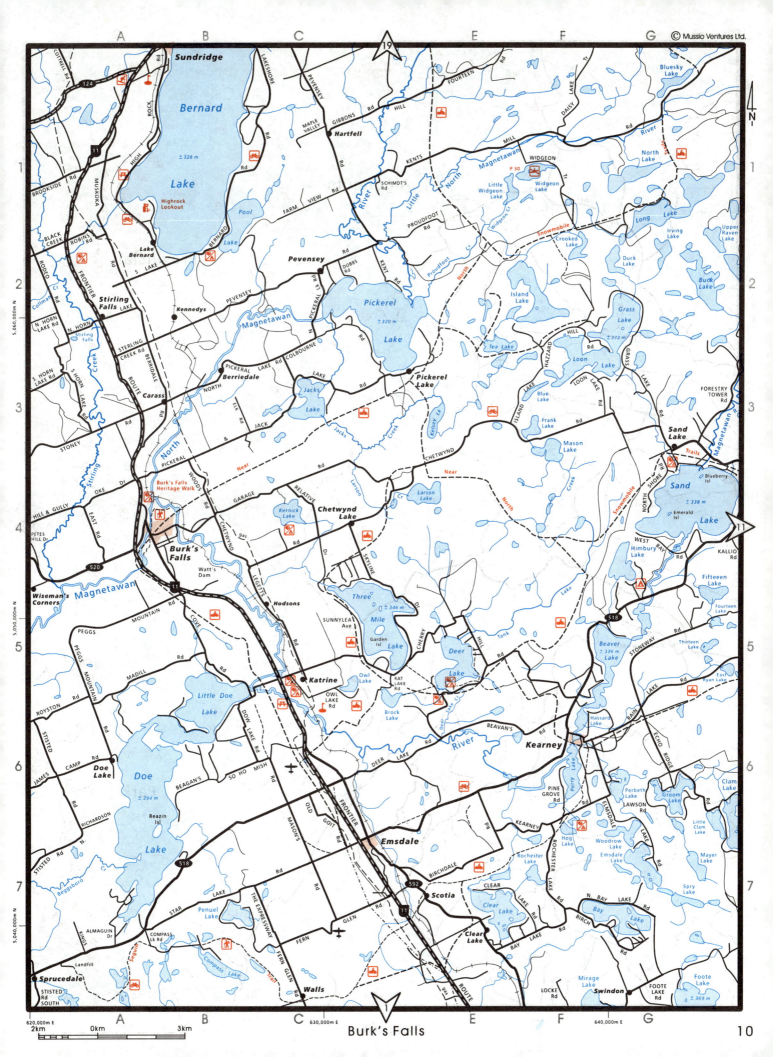

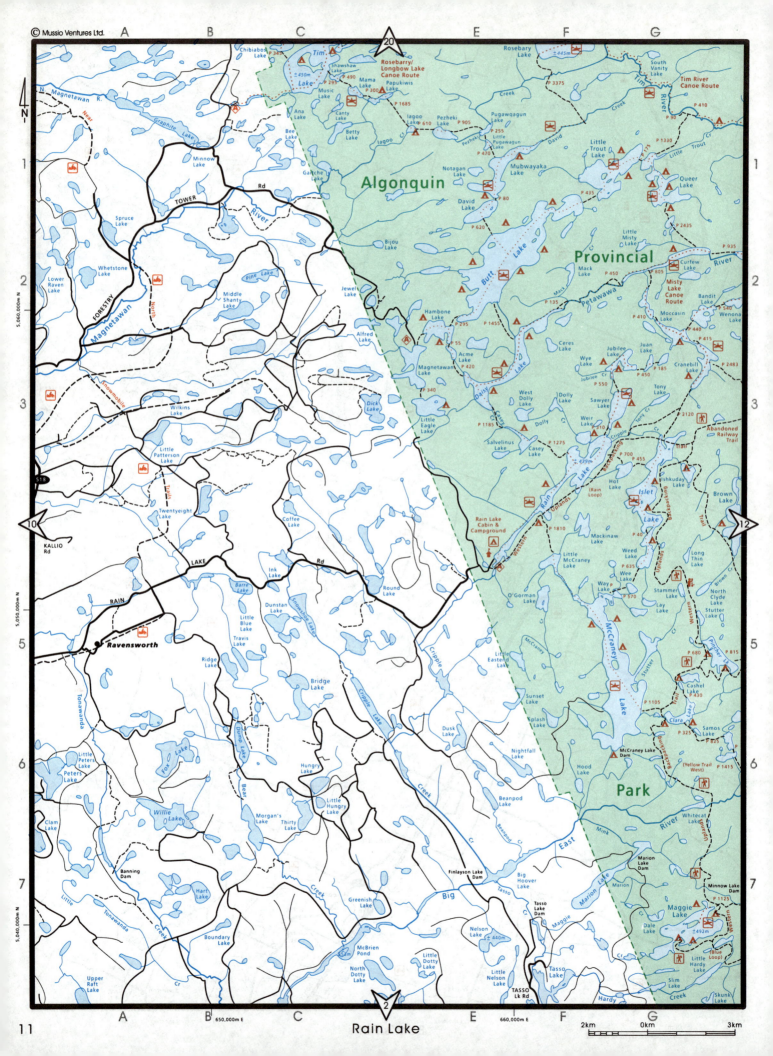

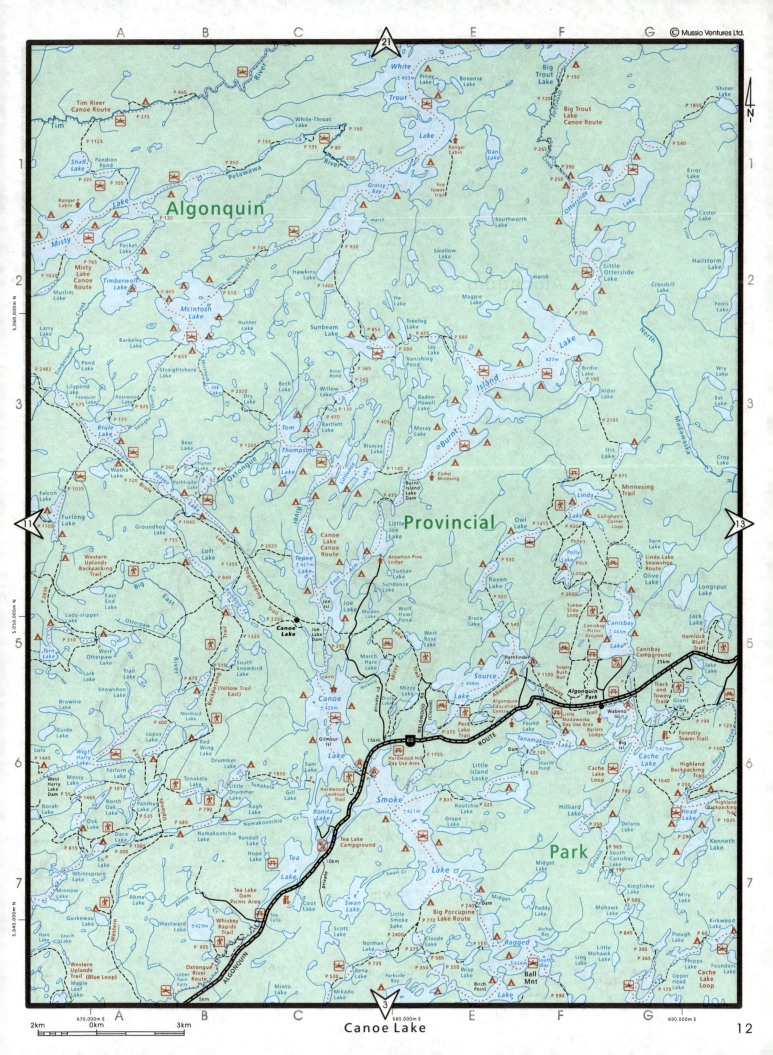

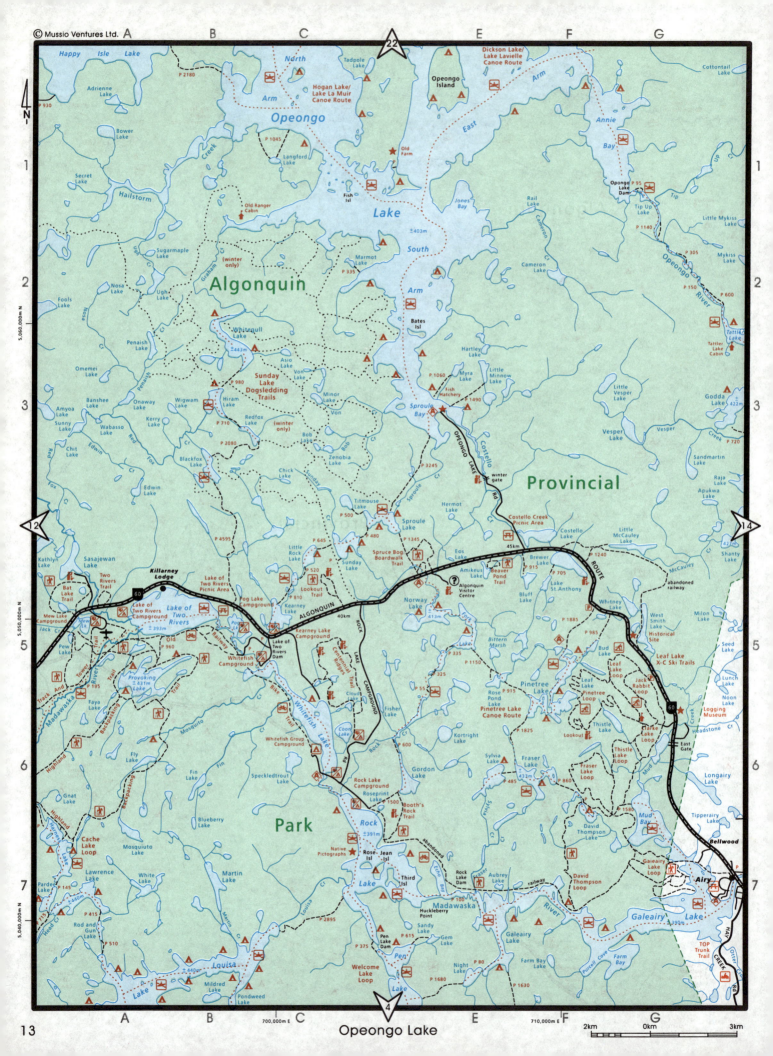

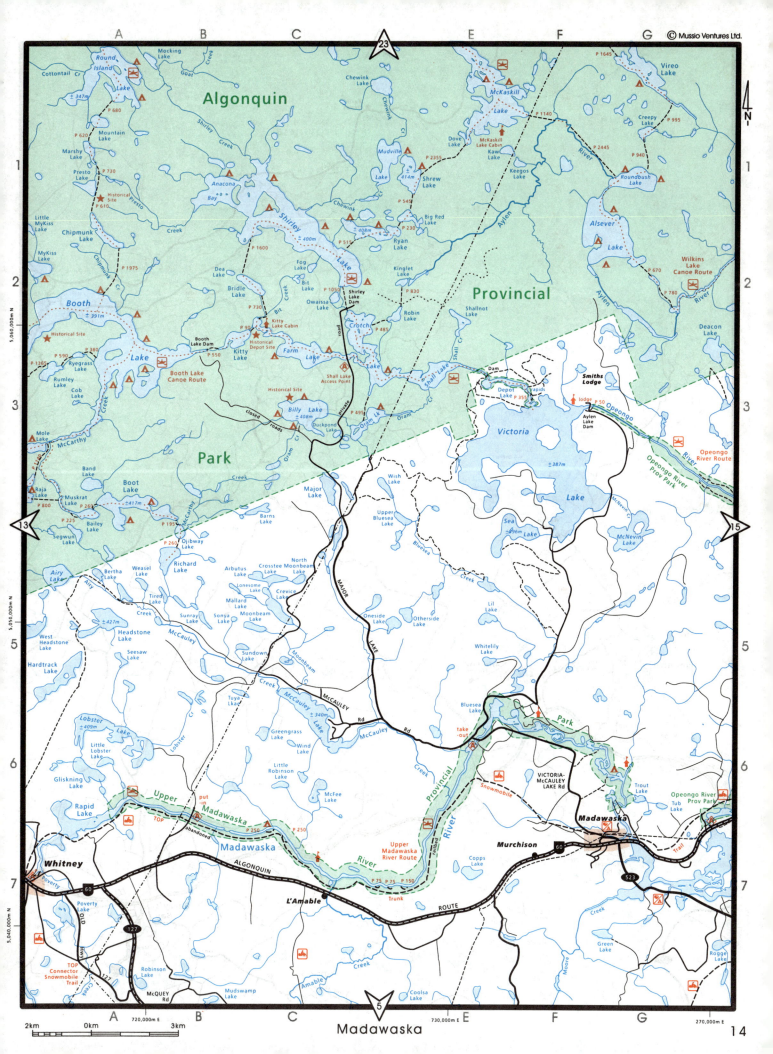

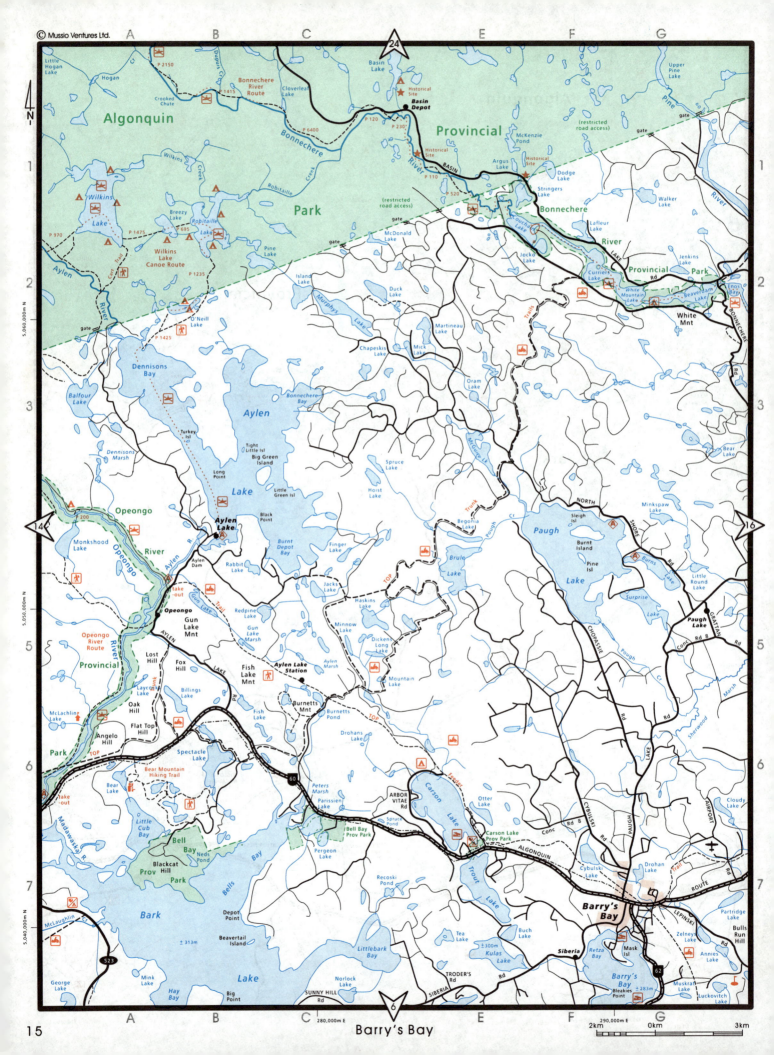

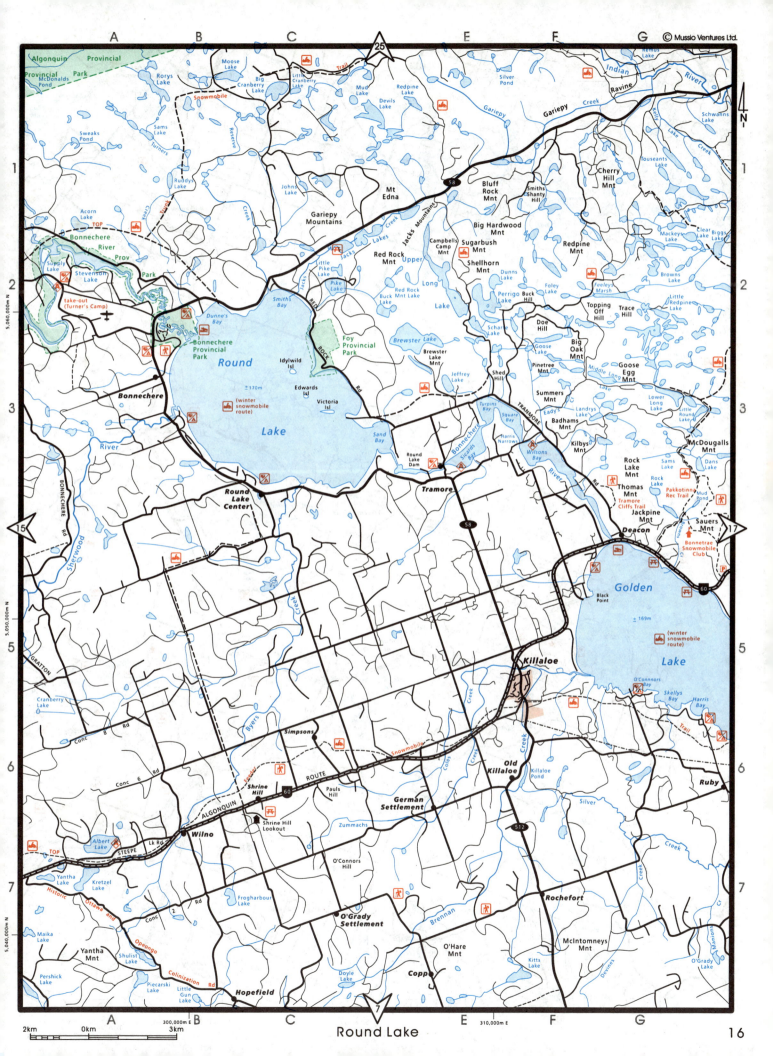

Algonquin Provincial Park
Provincial
McDonalds
Pond

Rorys Lake
Moose Lake
Big Cranberry Lake
Little Cranberry Lake

Sweaks Pond
Sams Lake
Turners
Reserve

Acorn Lake
TOP
Bonnechere River Prov
Park

Supply Lake
Stevenson Lake
take-out (Turner's Camp)

Johns Lake
Mt Edna
Gariepy Mountains

Ruddys Lake

Bonnechere

River

BONNECHERE Rd

GRATTON

Sherwood Rd

Cranberry Lake

Conc 8 Rd

Byers Creek

Conc 6 Rd

Simpsons

Shrine Hill

ROUTE
60
Pauls Hill

ALGONQUIN

Wilno
STEEPE
Lk Rd.

Albert Lake

Yantha Lake
Kretzel Lake

Maika Lake

Historic Ottawa and Opeongo

Yantha Mnt
Shulist Lake

Pershick Lake
Piecarski Lake
Little Gun Lake

Hopefield

Frogharbour Lake

Conc 2 Rd

O'Grady Settlement

Doyle Lake

Coppe

Mud Lake
Devils Lake
Redpine Lake

Jacks Lake

Smiths Bay

Little Pike Lake
Pike Lake

Dunne's Bay

Round

Lake

Idylwild Isl
Edwards (s)
Victoria Isl

±170m
(winter snowmobile route)

Bonnechere Provincial Park

Bonnechere

Round Lake Center

RED ROCK Rd

Foy Provincial Park

Sand Bay

Red Rock Mnt
Upper

Red Rock Buck Mnt Lake

Brewster Lake

Brewster Lake Mnt

Jeffrey Lake

Shed Hill

Round Lake Dam

Tramore

Scovds Bay

Turpins Bay

Square Bay

Harris Narrows

Bonnechere River

TRANMORE

Wilsons Bay

Campbells Camp Mnt
Sugarbush Mnt
Shellhorn Mnt

Dunns Lake

Scharie Lake

Perrigo Buck Lake
Buck Hill

Foley Lake

Goose Lake

Pinetree Mnt

Summers Mnt

Eady

Badhams Mnt

Landrys Lake

Kilbys Mnt

Rock Lake Mnt

Thomas Mnt

Tramore Cliffs Trail

Jackpine Mnt

Deacon

Bonnetrae Snowmobile Club

Golden

Lake

±169m
(winter snowmobile route)

Black Point

Killaloe

Old Killaloe

Killaloe Pond

512

German Settlement

Zummachs

O'Connors Hill

Brennan

O'Hare Mnt

Kitts Lake

Coles Creek

Silver Creek

Rochefort

McIntomneys Mnt

Indian River

Gariepy Creek

Gariepy

Silver Pond

Bluff Rock Mnt

Smiths Shanty Hill

Big Hardwood Mnt

Redpine Mnt

Cherry Hill Mnt

Touseants Lake

Mackeys Lake

Browns Lake

Little Redpine Lake

Topping Off Hill

Trace Hill

Doe Hill

Big Oak Mnt

Goose Egg Mnt

Middle Long Lake

Lower Long Lake

Little Round Lake

McDougalls Mnt

Sams Lake

Dans Hill

Rock Lake

Pakkotinna Rec Trail

Mud Pond

Sauers Mnt

60

Ruby

Remus Lake

Kelly Creek

Schwanns Lake

Clear Lake

Biggs Lake

O'Connors Bay

Skellys Bay

Harris Bay

Snowmobile Trail

Devines Creek

Manowin Creek

O'Grady Lake

Jacks Mountains

Long Lake

2km  0km  3km
300,000m E          310,000m E

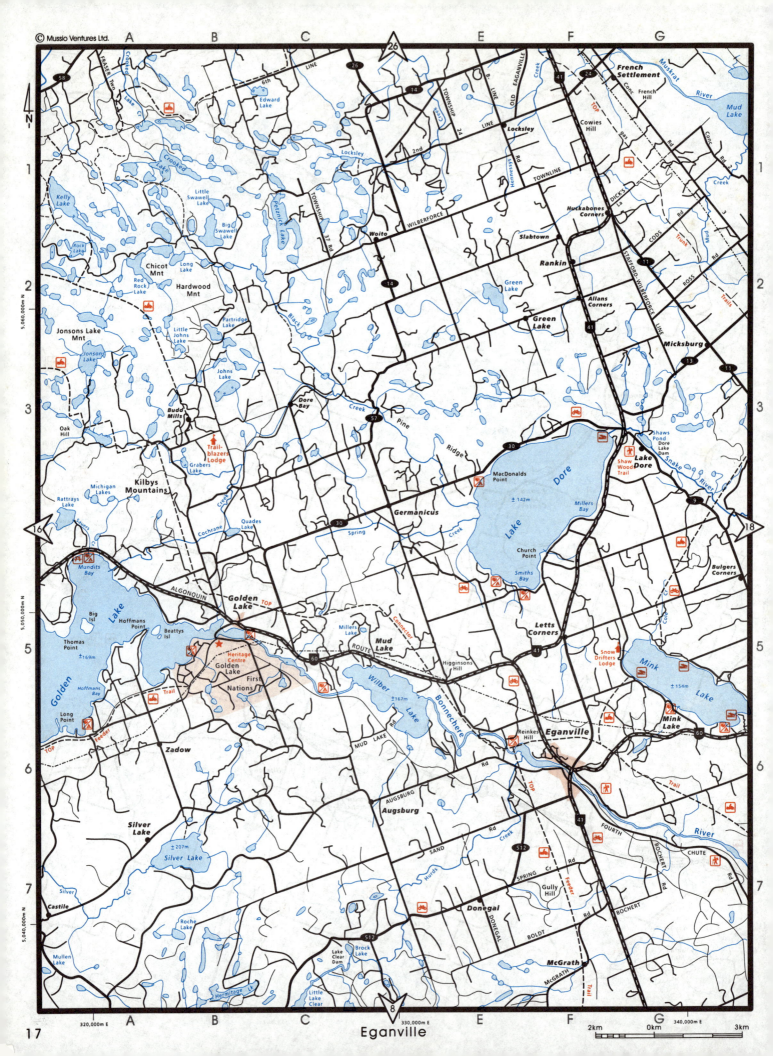

© Mussio Ventures Ltd.

A  B  C  D  E  F  G

58

N

**Kelly Lake**

**Crooked Lake**

**Little Swawell Lake**

**Big Swawell Lake**

**Edward Lake**

**6th**  **LINE**

26

14

**TOWNSHIP 24**

**Locksley**

**Cowies Hill**

**OLD EGANVILLE**

41  24

**French Settlement**

**French Hill**

**Muskrat River**

**Mud Lake**

**Rock Lake**

**Chicot Mnt**

**Red Rock Lake**

**Long Lake**

**Hardwood Mnt**

**Petzrick Lake**

**TOWNSHIP 37 Rd**

**Locksley**

**2nd**

WILBERFORCE

**Woito**

14

**Slabtown**

**Rankin**

**Green Lake**

**Allans Corners**

**Huckabones Corners**

**DICK'S La**

**STAFFORD-WILBERFORCE LINE**

11

**CODS Rd**

**ROSS Rd**

**Trunk Trails**

**Creek**

**Jonsons Lake Mnt**

**Jonsons Lake**

**Partridge Lake**

**Little Johns Lake**

**Johns Lake**

**Black Creek**

**Dore Bay**

**Pine Creek**

57

**Ridge**

**Green Lake**

41

**Micksburg**

13

11

**Oak Hill**

**Budd Mills**

**Trailblazers Lodge**

**Grabers Lake**

**Kilbys Mountains**

**Creek**

**Quades Lake**

**Cochrane**

**Germanicus**

**Spring Creek**

30

**MacDonalds Point**

±142m

**Lake Dore**

**Millers Bay**

**Shaws Pond Dore Lake Dam**

**Shaw Wood Trail**

**Lake Dore**

**Snake River**

9

**Michigan Lakes**

**Rattrays Lake**

**Sauers Cr**

16

**Mundits Bay**

ALGONQUIN

**Golden Lake**  TOP

**Spring**

**Church Point**

**Smiths Bay**

**Letts Corners**

41

**Bulgers Corners**

18

**Big Isl**

**Hoffmans Point**

**Beattys Isl**

**Golden Lake**

**Heritage Centre**

**Golden Lake First Nations**

**Millers Lake**

**Connector**

**Mud Lake**

60

ROUTE

**Higginsons Hill**

**Snow Drifters Lodge**

**Mink Lake**

±154m

**Thomas Point**

±169m

**Hoffmans Bay**

**Trail**

**Wilber Lake**

±167m

**Bonnechere**

**Reinkes Hill**

**Eganville**

**Mink Lake**

60

**Long Point**

**Feeder**

TOP

**Zadow**

**MUD LAKE Rd**

**AUGSBURG Rd**

**Augsburg**

**Creek**

**Fourth**

**River**

**BOCHERT Rd**

**CHUTE**

**Silver Lake**

±207m

**Silver Lake**

**SAND Creek**

**Hurds Creek**

512

**Spring Cr Rd**

**Gully Hill**

**Feeder**

41

**BOCHERT Rd**

**Silver**

**Castile**

**Mullen Lake**

**Roche Lake**

**DONEGAL Rd**

**Donegal**

**BOLDT Rd**

**McGrath**

**McGRATH**

**Trail**

**Lake Clear Dam**

**Brock Lake**

**Little Lake Clear**

512

**Hermitage Lk**

8

5,060,000m N

5,050,000m N

5,040,000m N

320,000m E  330,000m E  340,000m E

**Eganville**

2km  0km  3km

17

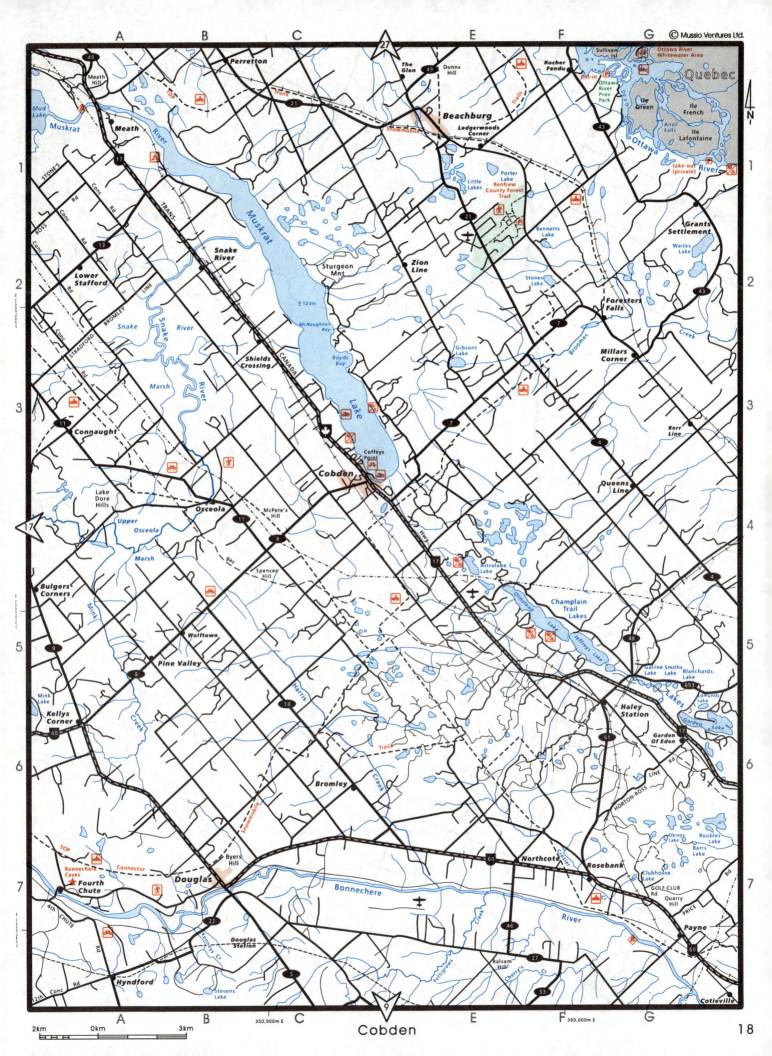

Cobden

18

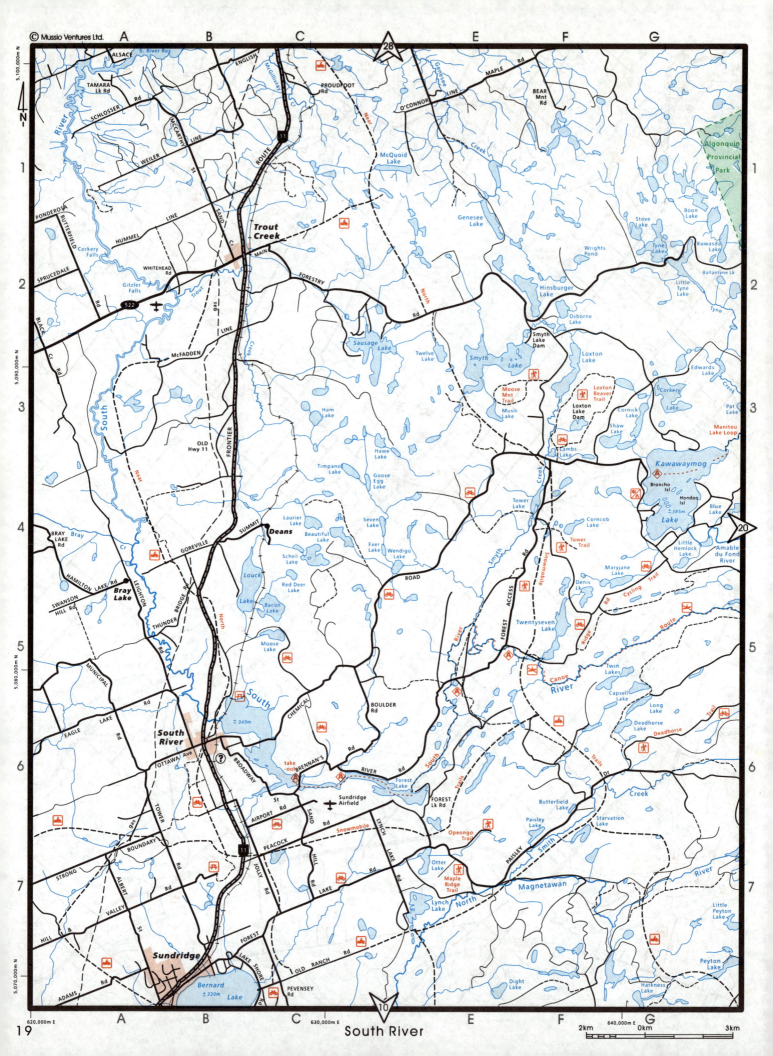

South River

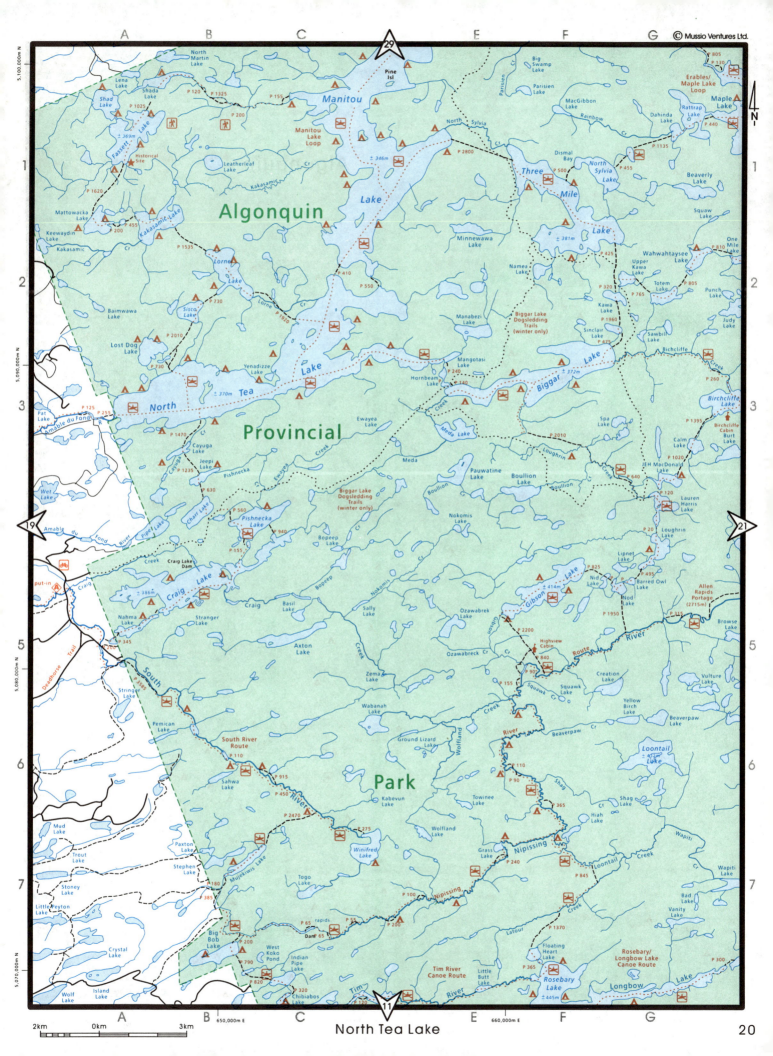

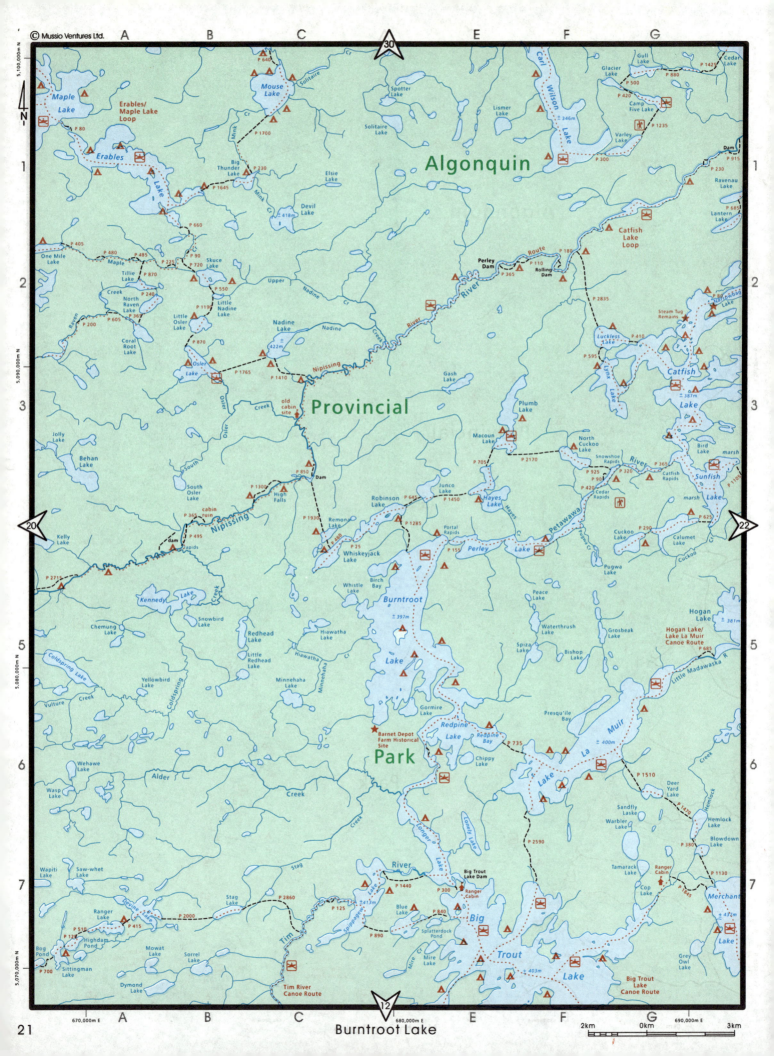

© Mussio Ventures Ltd.

**Algonquin**

**Provincial**

**Park**

Burntroot Lake

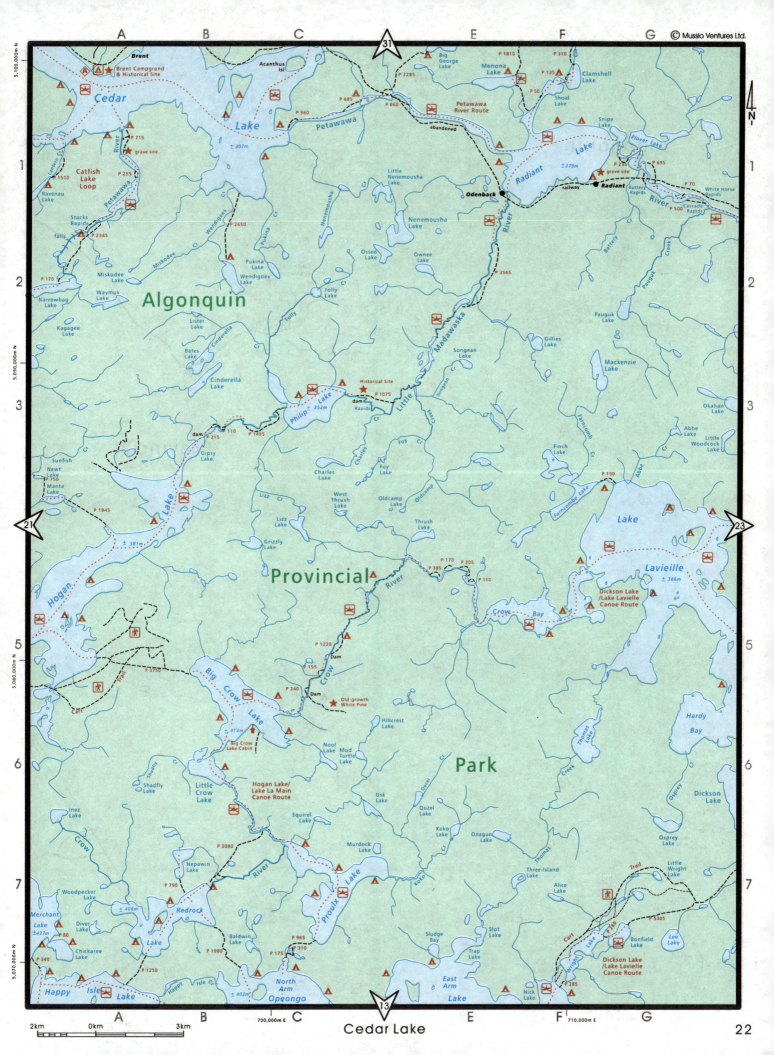

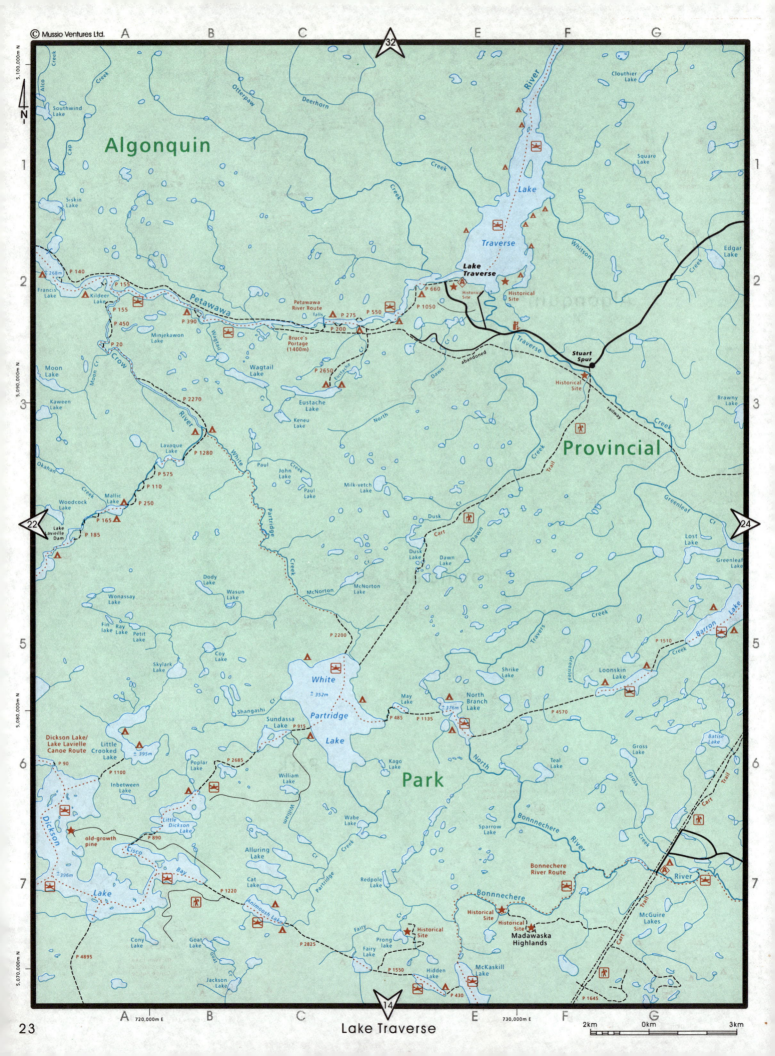

A B C D E F G

N

**Algonquin**

Southwind Lake

Siskin Lake

Otterpaw Creek

Deerhorn Creek

Clouthier Lake

Square Lake

Edgar Lake

Traverse Lake

Lake Traverse

Whitson

1

Francis Lake
P 268m
P 140
Kildeer Lake
P 155
P 155
P 450
P 390
Petawawa River Route
Minjekawon Lake
P 20
Crow River
Wagtail Creek
Wagtail Lake
Petawawa River Route
falls
P 275
P 550
P 200
P 660
Historical Site
P 1050
Historical Site
Traverse
Stuart Spur
Historical Site
railway
2

Moon Lake
Kaween Lake
Okahan Creek
P 2270
Lavaque Lake
P 1280
Bruce's Portage (1400m)
P 2650
Eustache Lake
Keneu Lake
Eustache
Paul Creek
John Lake
Paul Lake
Milk-vetch Lake
North
Dawn
Creek
Dusk
abandoned
Dawn
**Provincial**
Brawny Lake
3

Woodcock Creek
Mallic Lake
P 575
P 110
P 250
P 165
Lake Lavieille Dam
P 185
White River
Partridge
Greenleaf Cr
Greenleaf Lake
Lost Lake
22    24

Wonassay Lake
Dody Lake
Wasun Lake
McNorton
McNorton Lake
Dusk Lake
Dawn Lake
Cart
Dawn
Travers Creek
Greenleaf Creek
Barron Lake
Fin lake
Ray Lake
Petit Lake
Skylark Lake
Coy Lake
P 2200
White Lake
± 352m
Shrike Lake
P 1510
Loonskin Lake
5

Shangashi
Sundassa Lake
P 915
Partridge Lake
May Lake
± 376m
North Branch Lake
P 485
P 1135
P 4570
Dickson Lake/ Lake Lavieille Canoe Route
P 90
Little Crooked Lake
± 395m
Poplar Lake
P 2685
P 1100
William Lake
Kago Lake
**Park**
North
Teal Lake
Gross Lake
Batise
6

Inbetween Lake
Little Dickson Lake
old-growth pine
P 890
Cisco Bay
± 396m
Dickson Lake
Alluring Lake
Cat Lake
William Creek
Wabe Lake
Partridge
Redpole Lake
Sparrow Lake
Bonnechere River
Bonnechere River Route
Carr Trail
River
McGuire Lakes
7

Cony Lake
Goat Lake
Animoosh Lake
P 1220
Fairy Lake
Prong lake
Historical Site
Bonnechere
Historical Site
Historical Site
Madawaska Highlands
Carr
P 4895
Jackson Lake
P 2825
Fairy Lake
Hidden Lake
McKaskill Lake
P 1550
P 430
P 1645
14

A    720,000m E    B    C    14    E    730,000m E    F    G

**Lake Traverse**

2km    0km    3km

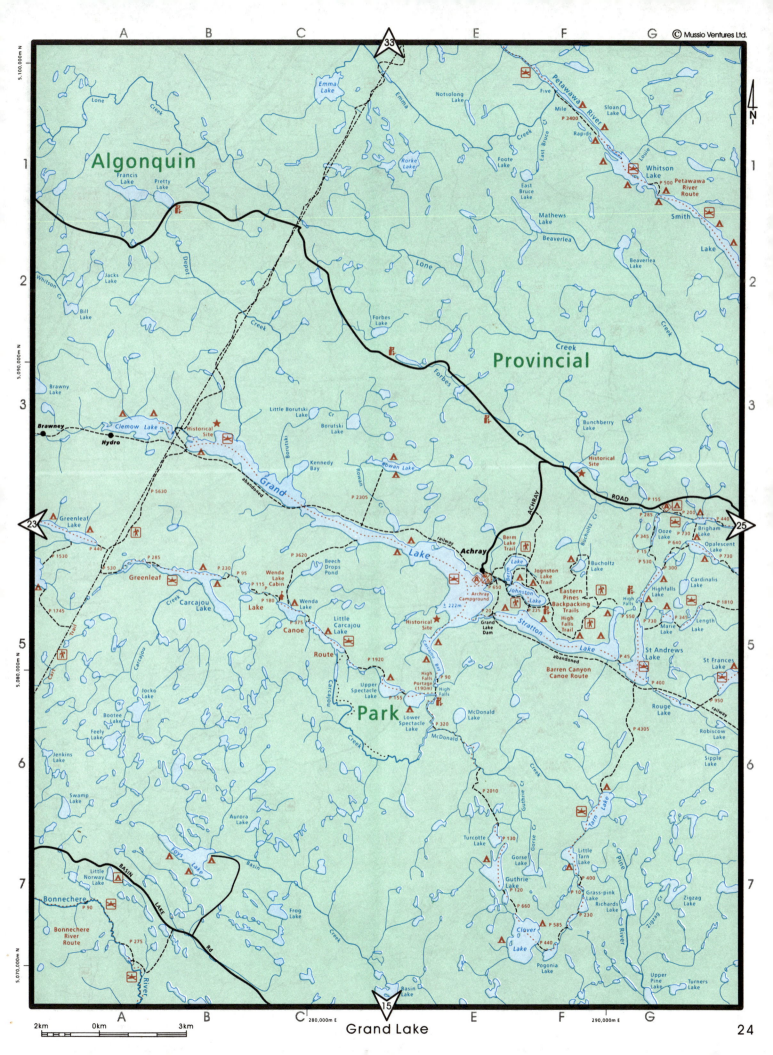

© Mussio Ventures Ltd.

Algonquin

Provincial

Park

Grand Lake

24

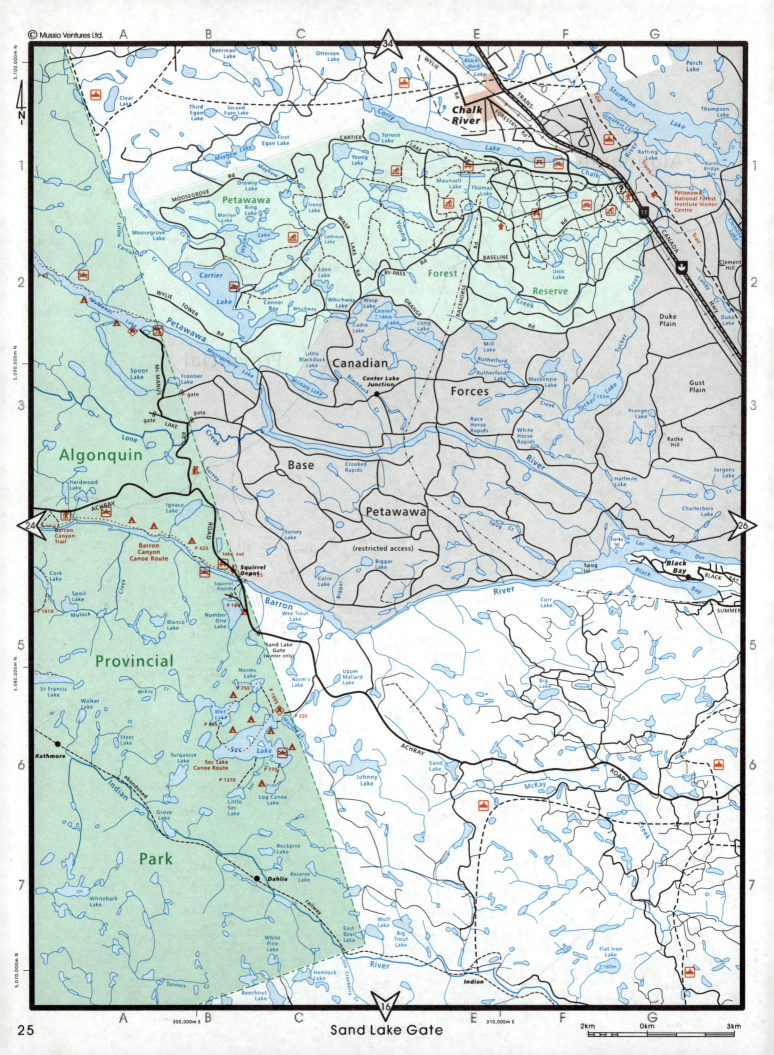

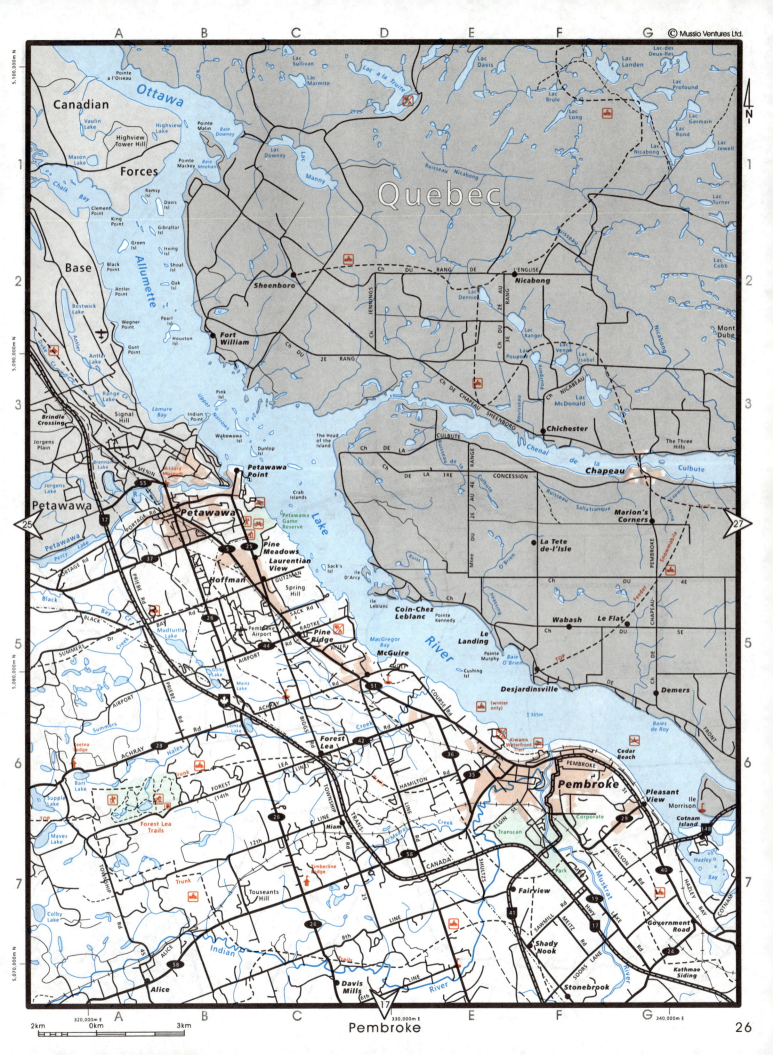

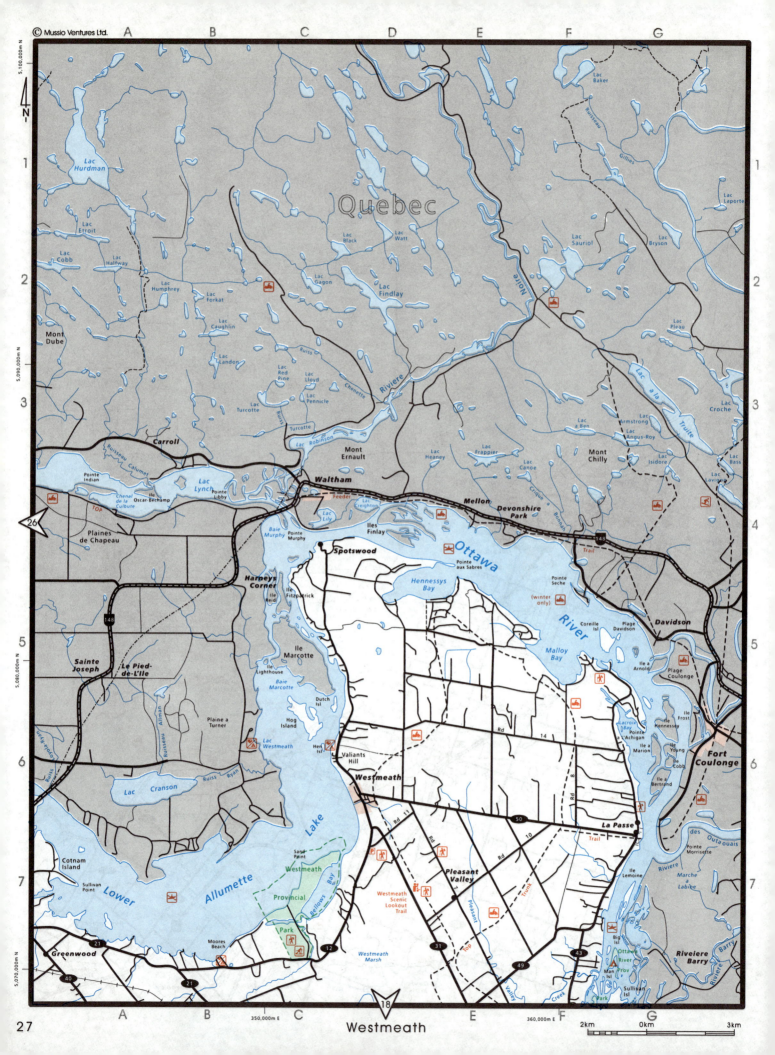

© Mussio Ventures Ltd.

Quebec

Lac Hurdman
Lac Etroit
Lac Cobb
Lac Halfway
Mont Dube
Lac Humphrey
Lac Forkat
Lac Caughlin
Lac Landon
Lac Turcotte
Lac Red Pine
Lac Lloyd
Lac Pennicle
Ruiss
Turcotte
Lac Robinson
Carroll
Pointe Indian
Ruisseau Calumet
Lac Lynch
Pointe Libby
Ile Oscar-Bechamp
Chenal de la Culbute
TOP
Plaines de Chapeau
26
148
Sainte Joseph
Le Pied-de-L'Ile
Ruisseau Allman
Plaine a Turner
Ruiss Ryan
Lac Cranson
Lac Westmeath
Cotnam Island
Sullivan Point
Lower
Allumette
Lake
Greenwood
21
40
21

Lac Black
Lac Watt
Lac Gagon
Lac Findlay
Riviere
Chenette
Ruiss
Mont Ernault
Waltham
Feeder
Lac Creighton
Lac Lily
Baie Murphy
Pointe Murphy
Spotswood
Harneys Corner
Ile Fitzpatrick
Ile Reid
Ile Marcotte
Ile Lighthouse
Baie Marcotte
Dutch Isl
Hog Island
Hen Isl
Valiants Hill
Westmeath
Iles Finlay
Sand Point
Westmeath
Provincial
Park
Bellows
Bay
Moores Beach
12
Westmeath Marsh
31
18
Westmeath

Lac Heaney
Lac Frappier
Lac Canoe
Mont Chilly
Crique a Branch
Mellon
Devonshire Park
148
Trail
Ottawa
Pointe aux Sabres
Hennessys Bay
Pointe Seche
(winter only)
River
Coreille Isl
Plage Davidson
Davidson
Malloy Bay
Rd
14
Rd
8
Rd 11
Rd
50
10
La Passe
Trail
Pleasant Valley
Westmeath Scenic Lookout Trail
Pleasant Valley
Top
49
43
Ottawa River Prov
Sullivan Isl
Man Isl
Big Isl

Lac Baker
Russeau Gillies
Lac Sauriol
Lac Bryson
Lac Pleau
Lac Laporte
Noire
Lac Croche
Lac Ben
Lac Armstrong
Lac Angus-Roy
Lac Isidore
Lac Bass
Lac Lavigne
Truite
Lacroix Bay
Pointe a l'Achigan
Ile a Arnold
Plage Coulonge
Ile a Marion
Ile Hennessy
Ile Young
Ile Cobb
Ile Frost
Fort Coulonge
Ile a Bertrand
des Outaouais
Pointe Morrisette
Riviere
Marche a Labine
Ile Lemoine
Riviere Barry
Riviere Barry

27

2km    0km    3km

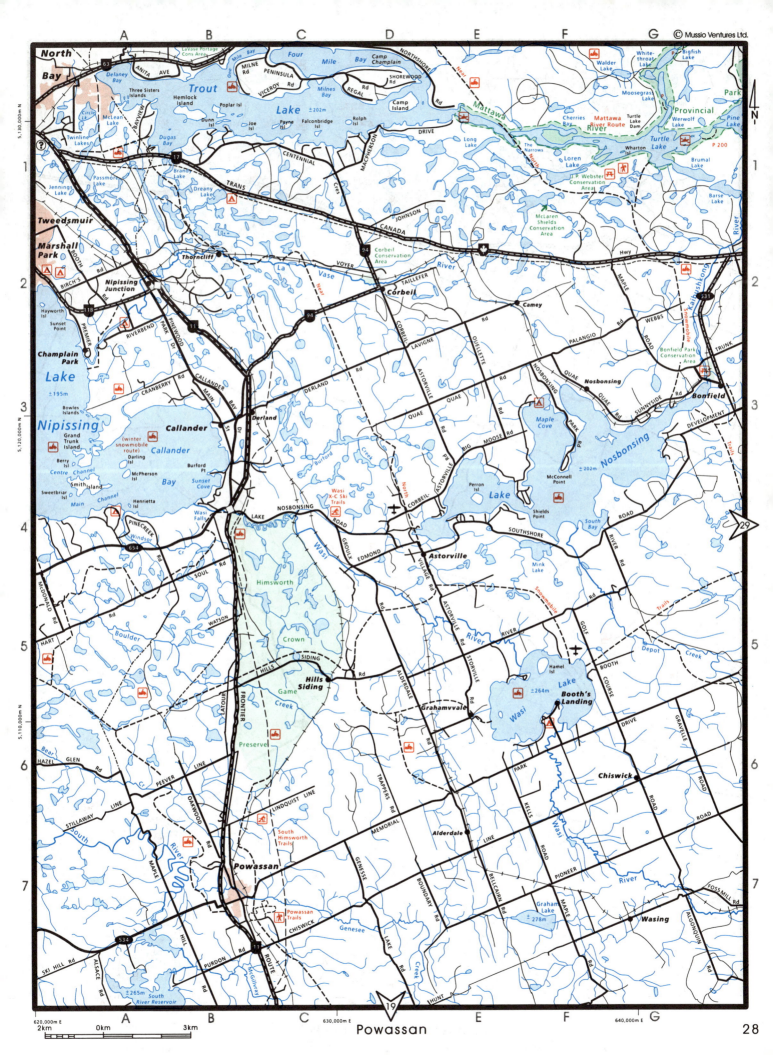

Powassan

28

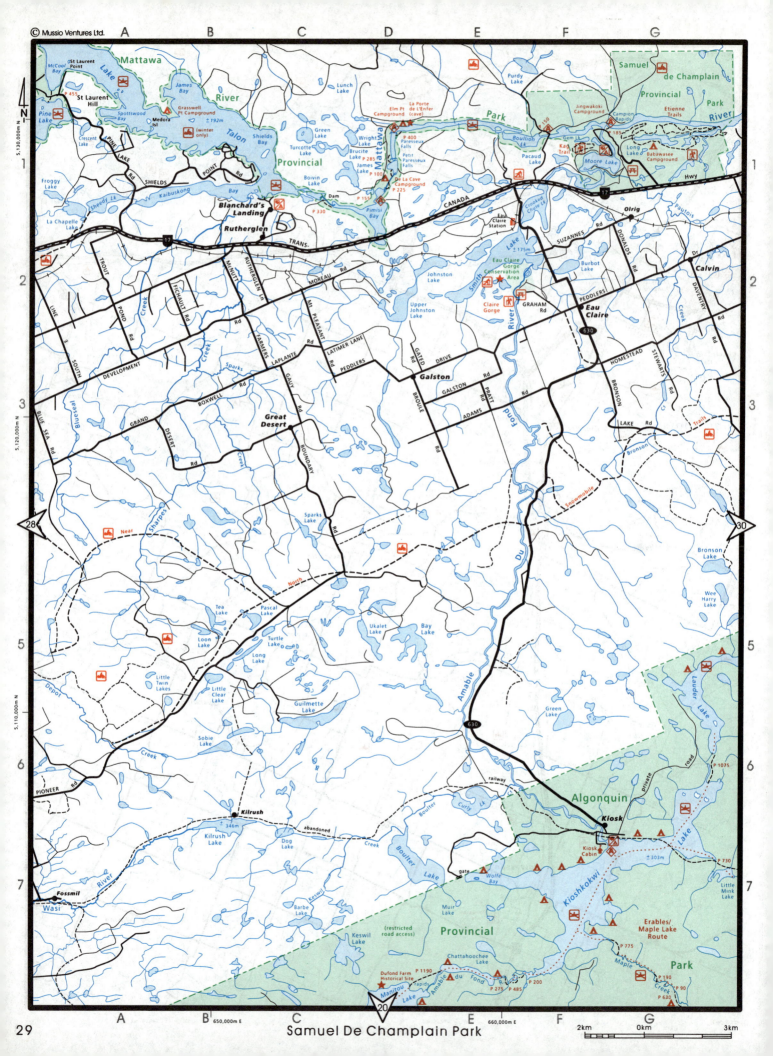

Samuel De Champlain Park

29

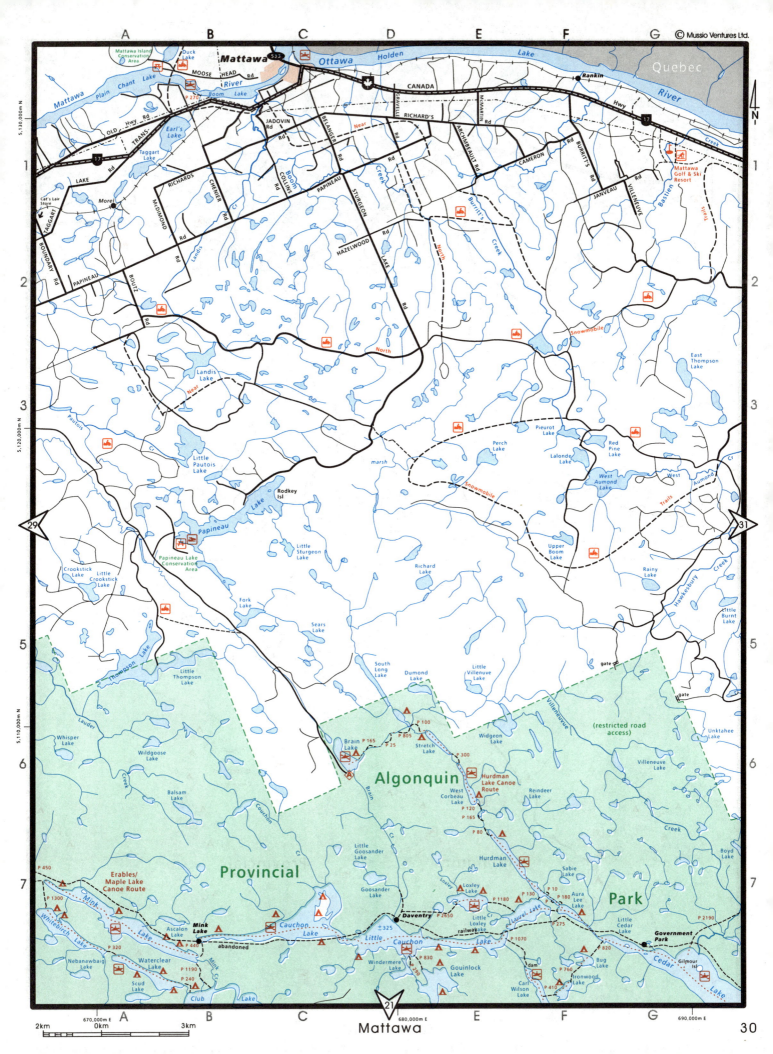

© Mussio Ventures Ltd.

Quebec

Mattawa

Rankin

**Algonquin**

**Provincial**

**Park**

Daventry

Government Park

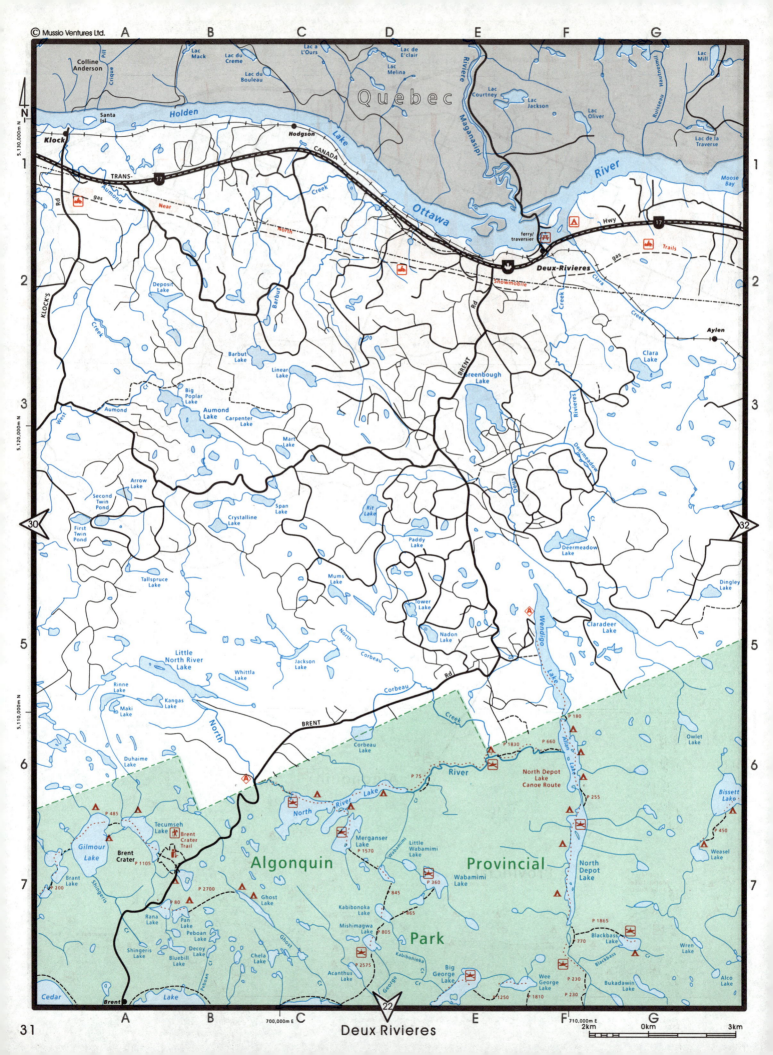

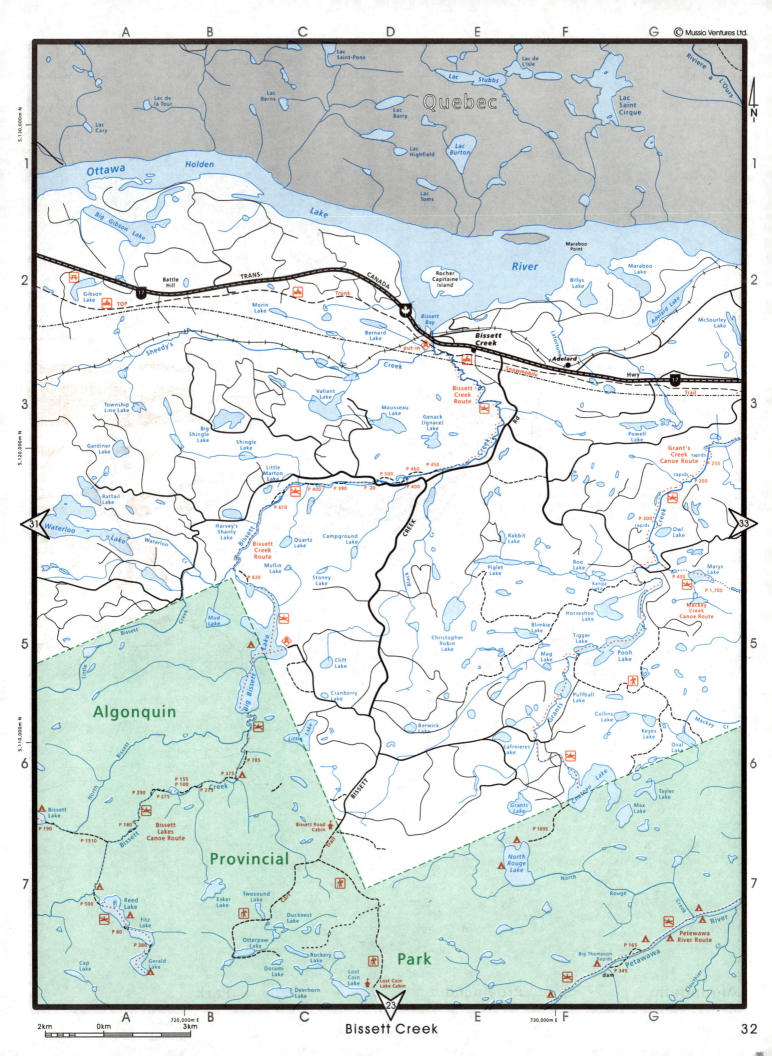

Quebec

Lac de L'Isle
Lac Stubbs

Lac Saint-Pons
Lac Cirque
Lac Saint

Lac Berns

Lac de la Tour

Lac Cary
Lac Barry
Lac Highfield
Lac Burton

Ottawa Holden Lake
Lac Toms

Riviere a L'Ours

1

Big Gibson Lake

Maraboo Point

River

Maraboo Lake

Billys Lake

Adelard Lake

McSourley Lake

TRANS-
CANADA

Battle Hill

17
TOP
Gibson Lake

Trunk
Rocher Capitaine Island

Bissett Bay

2

Bissett Creek

Adelard

Snowmobile

Hwy
17
Trail

Morin Lake

Bernard Lake
put-in
Creek
Bissett Creek Route

Powell Lake

Grant's Creek Canoe Route
rapids
P 250

Valiant Lake
Mousseau Lake
Genack (Ignace) Lake

Creek Rd

3

Township Line Lake
Big Shingle Lake
Shingle Lake
Little Marton Lake
P 500 P 460 P 450
P 400

rapids P 200

Gardiner Lake
P 400 P 390 P 20
P 610

Owl Lake

P 300 rapids

Rattail Lake
Harvey's Shanty Lake
Quartz Lake
Campground Lake

Rabbit Lake

Marys Lake
P 400 P 1,700
Mackey Creek Canoe Route

31
Waterloo Lake
Waterloo
Bissett Creek Route
Mullin Lake
P 630
Stoney Lake

BLACK CREEK

Piglet Lake
Roo Lake
Kanga

33

Mud Lake
Cliff Lake
Christopher Robin Lake
Blimkie Lake
Horseshoe Lake
Tigger Lake

5

Cranberry Lake
Mag Lake
Pooh Lake

Algonquin

Big Bissett Lake
Berwick Lake
Puffball Lake

Little
Little Lake
Lafrnieres Lake
Collins Lake
Keyes Lake
Oval Lake
Mackey Cr

P 785

Grants
Grants Lake
Chateau Lake
Max Lake
Tayler Lake

Little
North Bissett
P 155 P 375
P 100
P 290 P 275 P 275

Provincial
Trail
Bissett Road Cabin

North Rouge Lake
P 1895

6

Bissett Lake
P 180
P 190
P 1510
Bissett Lakes Canoe Route

BISSETT

North
Rouge

7

P 500
Reed Lake
Fitz Lake
P 60
Esker Lake
Twosound Lake
Ducknest Lake
Trail

Park

Big Thompson Rapids
P 165
Petewawa River Route
P 345
dam

River

Petewawa River Route

Cap Lake
Gerald Lake
P 380
Otterpaw Lake
Rockery Lake
Dorami Lake
Deerhorn Lake
Lost Coin Lake
Lost Coin Lake Cabin

Bissett Creek
23

32

5,130,000m N
5,120,000m N
5,110,000m N

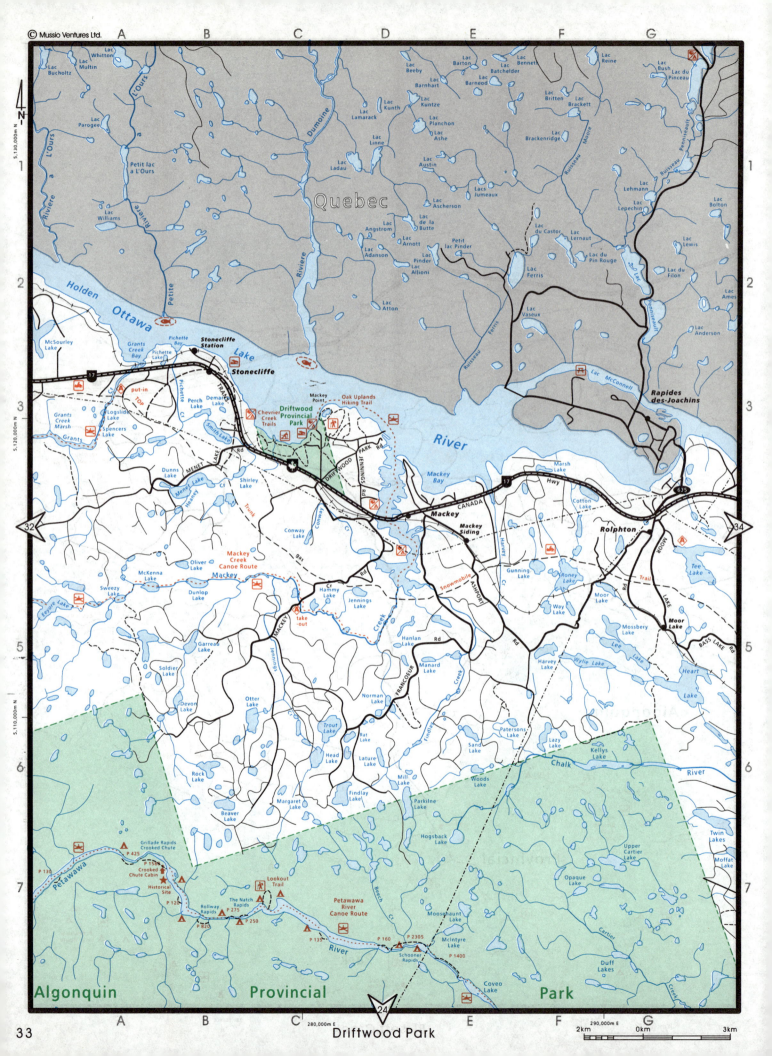

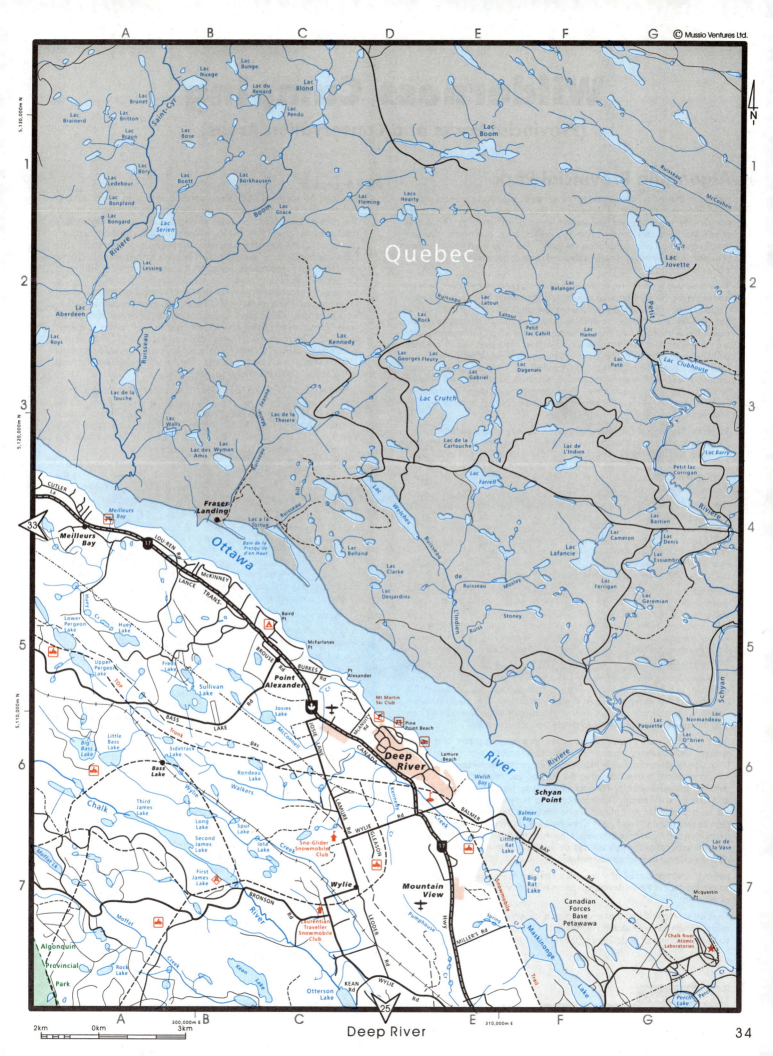

© Mussio Ventures Ltd.

**A**    **B**    **C**    **D**    **E**    **F**    **G**

## Quebec

Lac Brainerd
Lac Brunet
Lac Britton
Lac Nuage
Lac Bunge
Lac du Renard
Lac Blond
Lac Boom

Saint-Cyr
Lac Bose
Lac Braun
Lac Pendu
Lac Bory
Lac Ledebour
Lac Boott
Lac Borkhausen
Ruisseau
McCoshen

Lac Bonpland
Lac Grace
Lacs Hearty
Lac Fleming

Lac Bongard
Lac Serien
Boom
Lac Jovette

Riviere
Lac Lessing
Lac Belanger
Lac Latour
Ruisseau
Petit
Lac Aberdeen
Lac Rock
Lac Latour
Latour
Lac Hamel
Lac Roys
Lac Kennedy
Lac Georges Fleury
Petit lac Cahill
Lac Pato
Lac Clubhouse
Lac de la Touche
Lac Gabriel
Lac Dagenais
Ruisseau
Lac Walls
Lac de la Theiere
Lac de la Cartouche
Lac de L'Indien
Lac Barry
Lac des Amis
Lac Wyman
Lac Farrell
Petit lac Corrigan
Marie Jeanne

Riviere
Lac Welches
Lac Bastien
CUTLER La
Meilleurs Bay
Fraser Landing
Lac a la Tortue
Lac Cameron
Lac Denis
33
Baie de la Presqu'ile d'en Haut
Lac Essiambre
Meilleurs Bay
Ottawa
Lac Belland
Ruisseau
Lac Lafancie
LOU-REN Rd
Lac Clarke
de
Lac Ferrigan
Lac Geremian
17
McKINNEY
Lac Desjardins
Ruisseau Mosley
Stoney
LANCE TRANS.
Baird Pt
L'Indien
Ruiss

Huey Cr
Lower Pergeon Lake
Huey Lake
McFarlanes Pt
BROUSE Rd
BURKES Rd
Pt Alexander
Lac Normandeau
Fred Lake
Mt Martin Ski Club
Riviere
Upper Pergeon Lake
Sullivan Lake
Point Alexander
Pine Point Beach
Lac Paquette
Lac O'brien
TOP
Josies Lake
Deep River
Schyan
BASS
LAKE Rd
McConnell
gas
Lamure Beach
River
Big Bass Lake
Little Bass Lake
Sidetrack Lake
Rondeau Lake
JOSIE LANE
CANADA
Welsh Bay
Schyan Point
Bass Lake
Walkers
BALMER
Balmer Bay
Chalk
Third James Lake
Wylie
Spur Lake
Iota Lake
Lamure Rd
WYLIE
Kennedy Cr
Little Rat Lake
Lac de la Vase
Long Lake
Sno-Glider Snowmobile Club
GLEASON
17
Big Rat Lake
Second James Lake
Creek
Mountain View
Snowmobile
Mcquestin Pt
First James Lake
Wylie
Pumphouse
BRONSON Rd
River
Laurentian Traveller Snowmobile Club
LEODER Rd
Hwy
Spring Cr
Canadian Forces Base Petawawa
Moffat Lk
Moffat
MILLER'S Rd
Maskinonge
Chalk River Atomic Laboratories
Algonquin Provincial Park
Rock Lake
Kean Lake
KEAN Rd
WYLIE Rd
Trail
Otterson Lake
Perch Lake
Perch Cr

2km   0km   300,000m E   310,000m E

**A**    **B**    **C**    **D**    **E**    **F**    **G**

25

## Deep River

# Wilderness Camping
## (Provincial Parks and Conservation Areas)

## Algonquin Provincial Park

Algonquin Provincial Park is world renowned for its spectacular scenery and its rustic wilderness camping. The interior of the park has long been the main attraction for adventure and soul seekers from around the world. Thousands of primitive campsites dot the seemingly endless lakes and rivers. You can literally spend a lifetime exploring the park. The Algonquin interior offers seclusion from our busy urban lifestyles and helps us get a little more in touch with nature.

Wildlife viewing is a favourite pastime of interior trippers. Moose, deer, beavers and bears are the more popular four legged attractions of the park. You have a good chance of seeing at least one of these creatures on an interior canoe trip. Fishing opportunities are endless. The predominant species being the elusive brook trout and lake trout. In spring, just after ice off, fishing enthusiasts are the first to brave the interior in search of trout. The blackflies of late May and June soon keep the bulk of canoe trippers away. It would be a wise choice to avoid the peak of blackfly season in Algonquin (or Central Ontario, for that matter). After blackfly season, mosquitoes take their place. They are never as bothersome as blackflies but they keep some campers away nonetheless. Seclusion seekers will find this period (June and early July) some of the best times to be in the park.

As the heat of August comes on, camping on a lazy lake of the interior is a great way to enjoy summer. The heat can be easily forgotten after a refreshing swim in a cool Algonquin lake. One of the best times to travel in the park, however, is during September and into early October. The park is a lot quieter and if you time it right, you can travel through the park during its annual autumn display. The fall colours are truly magnificent.

There are 29 interior access points to Algonquin Provincial Park and 1,946 interior campsites. The interior experience is the essence of Algonquin. There is no better feeling than pulling up in your loaded canoe to a rustic campsite. Unlike busy campgrounds, the interior offers campers the chance to get away from it all. The majority of interior sites have beautiful lakeshore settings. Other sites lie on the banks of meandering rivers and streams. Prized island campsites are also scattered throughout the interior on a number of different lakes.

Although the park may intimidate many would be canoe trippers, campsites and portages are easy to locate. Portage points are marked with yellow signs and campsites are marked with orange signs. This helps make your trip go a little smoother. In maintaining the rustic experience there are no facilities at interior campsites other than, at the most, simple privies. If you're looking to brave the elements of a rustic canoe trip, an Algonquin Park interior trip is the best way to experience it.

Although Algonquin is often referred to as a wilderness park, it is far from wilderness in the true sense of the word. Ironically, we love and depend on the park so much that we have changed its wilderness forever. With over one million visitors to the park annually, we cannot classify it as wilderness, but we can help manage the flow of people to create that 'wilderness feel'.

As of 1998, all park interior access points have become a part of a quota system. Only so many trippers are permitted to access certain areas. This helps control use and maintain that outdoor experience that we are all looking for. In addition, before accessing the interior, you must have an itinerary detailing your planned trip. For each night of your trip, you must designate a lake where you will camp. This is important so that you will know if campsites will be available for your trip. It is also important that you stick to your trip plan so that you don't end up in a reserved site. If everyone uses the system properly, it can help make everyone's trip more rewarding. To help maintain the park experience for yourself and others, be sure to leave your campsite clean or cleaner than when you arrived.

Parking is permitted at all access areas for as long as you are in the park. We have listed each of the interior access points below along with a brief description of the area.

The best way to find the most information about your planned trip is to cross reference with the other sections of the book. Other sections describe the lakes you will be fishing or paddling and the routes or trails you will be travelling.

## East Access

**Grand Lake-Achray (Map 24/E4)** is a popular access point on weekends in summer, due to its close proximity to the magnificent Barron Canyon. The cliffs of the canyon are awe-inspiring and are one of Algonquin's most amazing natural sites. The launching point of day trips to the canyon is Stratton Lake, which offers several campsites on its eastern shore. The lakes and portages are generally small en route to the canyon and most lakes have interior campsites available. If you wish to travel to the Barron Canyon but would like to avoid the people, weekday trips will always be less busy. The best time of year, however, is in the fall after the first weekend in September. There are few biting insects and most people are back to work or school. Other great routes can also be accessed from Grand Lake-Achray. A trip down into Clover Lake or even further is always secluded. The route to Carcajou Lake past the Wenda Lake Cabin is quite scenic, although a little more busy. To find the access point travel 19.2km west of the Sand Lake Gate. On the left, you will see the road to the access point and Grand Lake.

**Lake Travers (Map 23/E2)** is a popular put-in for whitewater canoeists. From Lake Travers, the lower stretch of the mighty Petawawa River can be accessed. The Petawawa is Algonquin's and perhaps Ontario's, most revered whitewater river. The Lake Travers access is found about 55km past the Sand Lake Gate. The put-in is located at the mouth of the Petawawa River on scenic Lake Travers.

**McManus Lake (Map 25/A2)** can be accessed by the road found 6.4km past the Sand Lake Gate. At this point you turn right and travel to the end of the road. There are some campsites on McManus Lake but the area is mainly the pick-up site for Petawawa River trippers.

**Sec Lake (Map 25/C6)** is one of the hidden gems of Algonquin Park. The road to the Sec Lake access can be found off Achray Road 2.5km before it reaches the park boundary. 16 interior campsites are available on Sec Lake. The lake can be marginally busy on summer weekends, especially long weekends, although the access is rarely full to capacity. During the week Sec Lake can be deserted. The lake is a good spot to set up base camp for further exploration of the surrounding lakes. There are 5 other lakes that can be accessed by canoe from Sec Lake.

### Highway 60 Corridor Access

All kilometer markings on Hwy 60 are from west to east across the corridor. Kilometer zero is the West Gate.

**Cache Lake (Map 12/G5)** can be accessed off the south side of Hwy 60 at kilometre 23.5. This is a popular access point to the southern Algonquin Park interior. Adding to the activity on the lake is the numerous cottages and camps on Cache Lake. During summer, the lake is a buzz with activity. It is likely that you will see a number of trippers on the chain of lakes that lie to the south of Cache Lake. In late September, however, these lakes can be deserted, making it an ideal trip location. Permits can be picked up at the Canoe Lake Access Point Office.

**Canoe Lake (Map 12/D6)** access point is perhaps the busiest in Algonquin Park. The popularity of this area is due to the few short portages that provide a direct route to northern interior lakes. The access point is so busy that the route from Canoe Lake to Big Trout Lake has earned the nickname of 'Yonge Street' (after the busy street in Toronto) from park regulars. However, the lakes north of Canoe Lake are indeed beautiful. The fishing is good, the scenery is great and the route is historic.

Tom Thompson Lake is one of the historic lakes that can be accessed from the Canoe Lake put-in. It is unknown whether or not the lake was a favourite of Thompson's, although it is sure that he must have spent some time there. In remembrance of one of Canada's most heralded painters, the name of the lake was changed from Black Bear Lake to Tom Thompson Lake in 1946.

To limit your exposure to the Canoe Lake rush, it is recommended to travel during the week or in the fall. The short road to the access can be found off the north side of Hwy 60, at kilometre 14.1 of the corridor. Interior camping permits are available at the Access Point Office on the lake.

Galeairy Lake-Whitney (Map 13/G7) can be accessed from Ottawa Street in the town of Whitney. To find Ottawa Street take Post Street off Hwy 60 about 5.6km past the East Gate. The access is located on the large Galeairy Lake. The western portion of the lake lies within the park and interior camping permits can be purchased at the East Gate. The access sees a steady flow of trippers throughout the year, although is never overly busy. From Galeairy Lake, a number of different route options are available.

Lake Opeongo (Map 13/D3) is the largest lake in Algonquin Provincial Park. The size of the lake is often a deterrent for canoeists. At times, the wind on the big lake can slow your rate of progress to a crawl. On light wind days, it still takes a full day's paddle to get to the north end of the lake. For this reason, many trippers take the Opeongo Water Taxi to their desired destination.

In spring, many trippers head towards the lakes north of Opeongo. Lakes such as Happy Isle, Big Crow, Hogan, Laveille and Dickson see their share of fishermen, although are not overcrowded. The flow of trippers starts at ice out and slows considerably during blackfly season. From mid-July to Labour Day weekend (1st weekend in September) the flow of trippers is consistent.

The Opeongo access is found off Hwy 60 at the end of Opeongo Road. Permits are available at the Access Point Office. The Opeongo Water Taxi is run by Opeongo Algonquin (613) 637-2075 and Opeongo Outfitters (613) 637-5470.

Pinetree Lake (Map 13/F5) access point was developed to help reduce the pressure on the more popular Hwy 60 corridor access points. The Pinetree Lake access point is found off Hwy 60 at the 49.9km mark. From the parking area, a 1,885m portage leads to Pinetree Lake. From Pinetree Lake you can choose to travel north towards the highway or south towards Galeairy Lake. This area receives a lot less use than the other corridor access points, making it a good choice. Some of the portages can be a little more difficult to travel due to deadfall, especially in spring. Permits are available at the East Gate.

Rock Lake (Map 13/C6) can be accessed off Hwy 60 at kilometer 40.3. Turning south at this point leads to the Coon Lake and Rock Lake Campgrounds. Permits for interior camping are available at the Rock Lake Campground office. After passing the road to the Coon Lake Campground, stay right towards the Madawaska River. The put-in is located on the river shore where you make your way to Rock Lake.

The north end of Rock Lake is often busy with traffic from the campground and the numerous cottages that dot the northern portion of the lake. Rock Lake leads to the popular Lake Louisa and Pen Lake.

Rock Lake is a popular access point in spring and throughout the summer months. The only time of year you can expect to find some isolation is in June or in the fall. However, during weekdays the routes are a little less busy.

Smoke Lake (Map 12/D6) is one of the busiest lakes in the park. There are numerous cottages and camps on the shore of the lake and the access point is extremely popular. In spring, fishing enthusiasts often head towards Ragged and Big Porcupine Lakes in search of trout. During summer, the convenient access and short portages of the area make two-day canoe trips attractive. However, similar to most areas in the park's interior, the more distance you put between you and civilization the more secluded you will be. The access point can be found south off Hwy 60 at kilometre 14.1. Permits are available at the Canoe Lake Access Point Office.

Source Lake (Map 12/F5) access point is the ideal alternative to avoid some of the clutter of the Canoe Lake Access. Although there are longer portages to get to Burnt Island Lake, the route is usually less busy. The access can be found off the north side of Hwy 60 at kilometre 20.1. There is a short road from the highway that leads to the lake. Permits can be purchased at the Canoe Lake Access Point Office.

Sunday Creek (Map 13/D4) access point can be found off the south side of Hwy 60 at kilometre 42.5. Parking is available at the Spruce Bog Boardwalk trailhead. This access is one of the least busy along the park corridor and is a great area for a quiet getaway. Interior camping permits can be picked up at the East Gate of the park.

## North Access

Big Bissett Lake (Map 32/C5) interior access point is found at the north side of the park off Hwy 17. Take Bissett Creek Road for about 13.5km from the highway and turn right. It is about 4km to Big Bissett Lake along a rough and somewhat overgrown road. To get to the interior lakes you must first travel up the Bissett Creek. There are numerous portages along the creek that are not regularly used. Deadfall can be a problem. Permits can be picked up at the Yates Store in Stonecliffe, off Hwy 17.

Brain Lake (Map 30/D6) is a seldom used access point of the park. The campsites at the lake itself are used periodically throughout the summer, however, the lakes below Brain Lake see little use compared to the rest of the park. It is not too hard to find privacy from this access point. Interior camping permits can be found at the Cats Lair Store on Boundary Road, south of Hwy 17. The road leading to the access point can be reached at the end of Daventry Road.

Cedar Lake-Brent (Map 22/A1) interior access point is a hidden treasure in the park. From Cedar Lake, you can choose from numerous canoe route options, which helps to spread out trippers making it easy to find seclusion. The mighty Petawawa River also flows in and out of Cedar Lake and offers whitewater thrills.

Just after ice off, fishing enthusiasts head out on the big lake in search of their favourite fishing spots. By June, blackflies keep most visitors away from Brent but by mid-July traffic begins to pick up. Weekdays are generally slow at the access point but on weekends, the traffic increases, although is never close to what the corridor access points experience. The rough Brent Road can be found off Hwy 17 about 2km west of Deux-Rivieres. About 16km from the highway, the Access Point Office can be found. Interior camping permits can be picked up here.

Kioshkokwi Lake-Kiosk (Map 29/G7) access point is found at the end of Hwy 630 from Eau Claire. Interior camping permits can be picked up at the Kiosk park office. From Kioshkokwi Lake there are a number of different canoe routes to choose from. The access point can be busy on weekends during the summer, although rarely as busy as the corridor access points. It is generally easy to find some seclusion in this part of the park. Fishing is a major attraction in the spring with trout seekers being primary visitors. In fall, the area is quite vacant.

North River (Map 31/B6) is an attractive access point due to the canoe route to North River Lake. The fishing possibilities of the lake and the surrounding smaller lakes keep this access busy in spring. Although you will usually find someone on North River Lake in spring, it is far from crowded. During weekdays in summer, the area is quite isolated. To find this access point follow the same directions as the Cedar Lake-Brent access point. En route to Brent you will pass the North River access point.

Wendigo Lake (Map 22/B2) access point can be found about 2km from the Access Point Office on Brent Road. From Wendigo Lake, you can travel south towards Radiant Lake. The area is quite busy compared to the remoteness of the access. During the long weekend in May, Allen and North Depot Lakes are usually close to camping capacity. Of course, the fishing is the main draw. As the bugs of June chase campers out and the trout move to deeper waters, the traffic begins to subside. The flow is steady during weekends in summer but not crowded. During weekdays and in fall, the access and the lakes can be deserted. Interior permits can be picked up at the Access Point Office.

## West Access

Kawawaymog (Round) Lake (Map 19/G4) access point can be busy throughout the year because of its close proximity to the Toronto area. In spring, trout seekers travel to North Tea Lake and the surrounding lakes in search of the elusive fish. During this time, flow at the access point is consistent, especially on weekends. North Tea is quite big and has a good supply of interior campsites. Finding room on North Tea or other lakes is usually not a problem.

In summer, North Tea Lake experiences a steady flow of visitors since there are many canoe route options. Weekends are usually the busiest periods. Fall can also be a great time of year to explore this area. To find the Kawawaymog access point, take Hwy 11 to South River and head east on Chemical Road. The road leads right to the lake and the access point.

Magnetawan Lake (Map 11/D3) interior access point is quite busy with fishermen after spring ice off. Another bonus of this access point is that there is an endless array of canoe route possibilities, with generally short portages and easy paddling.

Butt Lake is often close to capacity during the May long weekend and on summer long weekends. During other times of year, the area sees a little less use. Weekdays in summer and fall seem to be a good time to visit the area. An additional feature of a fall interior trip in this area is the superb array of autumn colours. It would definitely be a trip to remember. The access point is located at the end of Forestry Tower Road, which can be found off Hwy 518. Park permits can be picked up at the Park Office in the Kearney Community Centre.

**Rain Lake (Map 11/E4)** interior access point can be found by following Rain Lake Road to Rain Lake and the canoe access point. Park permits are available at the Park Office in the Kearney Community Centre. This access point doubles as the western access point to the Western Uplands Backpacking Trail and there is a small campground in the area.

The Western Uplands Trail, the campground and the canoe routes off Rain Lake keep this access area occupied throughout the year. Regardless, the area is still a great place to visit. The old Ottawa, Arnprior and Parry Sound Railway once passed right through here. All that remains now, however, is the old railbed. Ironically, one of Canada's busiest commercial railways is now part of one of Canada's greatest recreation trails.

**Tim River (Map 11/B1)** is a slow meandering river that is a peaceful route to travel on canoe. From the Tim River interior access point, you travel the Tim River to Tim Lake. From Tim Lake, there are a number of different route directions to choose from. The main route traveled by trippers is from Tim Lake to Rosebary Lake. Portages on this stretch are well used. However, most of the other portages in this area are low use and deadfall could pose problems. The access point is most busy during the spring. The fishing in the smaller interior lakes draws people to the area, although this subsides by early June. By mid-July use begins to increase again but mainly on weekends.

To find the access point, take the Forestry Tower Road from the village of Kearney and follow the signs to the access area. If you cross over the Magnetawan River, you've gone too far. Park permits can be picked up at the Park Office in the Kearney Community Centre.

## South Access

**Aylen Lake (Map 15/B4)** interior access point is located on the southwestern shore of Aylen Lake. To find the access point, take Aylen Lake Road off the north side of Hwy 60. The 1,425m portage to O'Neill Lake and the park boundary is located at the northern tip of Aylen Lake. From O'Neill Lake, it's a 1,235m portage to Robitaille Lake in the interior of the park. Due to the length of these portages, this is one of the lesser used park access points. The flow of trippers is slow but steady throughout the year. If you are willing to work a little harder, this access is a great way to find a more secluded section of the interior. Permits are available at the Aylen Lake Marina at the put-in.

**Basin Lake (Map 16/A2)** access point offers more variety than the majority of other interior access areas. There are really three separate areas that can be traveled from the Basin Lake access point. Permits for this access can be picked up at Turner's Camp, east off Hwy 62. From Turner's Camp, Basin Lake Road leads to Basin Lake where interior campsites are available. Basin Lake was once the site of a bustling supply depot for Algonquin logging companies. The depot was used until about 1913, at which time up to ten buildings and a post office stood there.

Further up the road, you can also access Foys Lake. Interior sites are also offered at Foys Lake. If you continue up the road, you will come to a power line crossing. Here the road travels south and to the Bonnechere River access. From here, you can travel the river all the way to Turner's Camp or Round Lake. The river flows through a number of lakes but the route involves primarily river travel. The main deterrent to the trip, however, is a grueling 6,400m portage along the last stretch of the route. This is a secluded canoe route through the heart of the east side of the park. Surprisingly, the campsites at both Foys and Basin Lakes are rarely full to capacity.

**Hay Lake (Map 5/B2)** can be reached by taking McRae-Hay Lake Road off Hwy 127. The boundary of the park is about 4km from the canoe put-in. This access is a great way to enter the under used panhandle of the park. There are numerous route options and plenty of opportunities to explore. Deadfall on the trails can slow you down, although is never a big problem. The fishing is good, the scenery is wonderful and the routes are secluded near this access. Permits for the Hay Lake interior access point can be picked up at the East Gate of the park.

**Hollow River-Dividing Lake (Map 3/C3)** access has really one purpose, to lead trippers to Dividing Lake Provincial Nature Reserve Park. The reserve helps protect one of the last remaining stands of old growth white pine in southern Ontario. These magnificent trees are the main attraction of the area. Most of the park and southern Ontario used to be dominated by these great trees. The access point, which is generally slow throughout the year, is located at Livingstone Lodge on Livingstone Lake. Interior camping permits can be purchased at Tower Hill Marine on Hwy 35. Further access into Algonquin Park is available from the Dividing Lake Provincial Nature Reserve.

**Kingscote Lake (Map 5/A7)** access point is perhaps one of the most under used access areas of the park. This is baffling since there are easy portages to a number of fishing lakes and the York River. If you drop a second vehicle off at the Hay Lake access, you can probably travel right through the interior of the panhandle. You would be hard pressed to find another canoe on this route. Permits can be purchased at the Pine Grove Point Lodge on Benoir Lake. The access point is at the end of the Kingscote Lake Road.

**Shall Lake (Map 14/D3)** access point is actually located on the Opeongo River between Farm and Crotch Lakes. However, it does provide access to Shall Lake. The main lake that trippers stay on is Booth Lake. In spring, most of the sites will be taken as visitors try their luck for trout. In summer, the flow of paddlers is steady but never overbearing. Booth, Crotch and Farm Lakes are the busiest at the access. Once you travel a little further into the interior, seclusion is easier to find. To get to the access point follow Major Lake Road from the village of Madawaska. The road leads right to the lake and the Access Point Office where permits can be picked up.

## Paddle-In Campsites

Along the Hwy 60 corridor, there are a few areas where paddle-in campsites are available. These sites are for those individuals that wish to have a canoe-in feel to their camping but do not wish to travel into the interior of the park. From these sites you are only a few minutes away from your vehicle and can access the modern facilities of the park. For more information on paddle-in camping, call (705) 633-5572. For reservations call (888) ONT-PARK.

**Canisbay Lake (Map 12/G5)** has 16 paddle-in sites available. These sites are only a short paddle away and offer a little more privacy than vehicle access campground sites. These beautiful lakeside sites can be quite busy during summer months. For a day trip, you can travel from your site on Canisbay by canoe and portage to Polly Lake or Linda Lake. All three lakes offer fishing and swimming opportunities. It is always recommended to make reservations in advance of your trip.

**Crotch Lake (Map 14/D3)** has six paddle-in campsites that can be accessed by the Shall Lake interior access point. The sites lie on the eastern shore of Crotch Lake and are usually less busy than the Canisbay Lake paddle-in sites. Several other lakes are within a portage or two from Crotch Lake making these sites a good choice if you enjoy day tripping. Fishing and swimming can be enjoyed in Crotch Lake. All sites are a short paddle from the access point. Although Crotch Lake may not be as busy as Canisbay Lake, there are only six sites available. It is recommended to make reservations before your trip.

## Old Ranger Cabins

Over the history of Algonquin Park, there have been many different management perspectives in place. In the early 1900's park rangers traveled on foot and by canoe through the park in search of poachers. Cabins were built throughout the park to house equipment and provide a more comfortable place to stay while the rangers were on duty. Rangers would travel from cabin to cabin, covering and managing large tracts of land on the way. As the management practices of the park changed, the cabins saw less and less use. Over the past few years Algonquin Park has repaired a number of the cabins and began the cabin rental program.

People can now rent cabins for a night or even a week at a time. The program will help the park preserve the historical cabins and provide visitors with a unique park experience. A few cabins have drive-in access, although most involve canoe tripping or a hike to access them. Most cabins are equipped with a wood stove, table, chairs and bed frames. Users must supply bedding and sleep cushions. Most cabins accommodate four people unless otherwise noted. Call Algonquin Park Information at (705) 633-5572 for reservations and prices.

**Big Crow Cabin (Map 22/C6)** is found on Big Crow Lake north of Opeongo Lake. Access is by canoe only and begins at the Opeongo Lake access point. You can either canoe directly to Big Crow Lake or you can take a water taxi on Opeongo Lake to the Proulx Lake portages. After three portages to Proulx Lake it is an easy paddle to the cabin. With the water taxi the trip can be done in one day, without it the trip would take two days. The cabin is an old fire ranger cabin that was built in 1956. The frame construction cabin is equipped with a kitchen, living area and two bedrooms. Fishing is available on Big Crow Lake as well as many other nearby lakes.

**Birchcliffe Cabin (Map 20/G3)** is a two bedroom log cabin that was constructed in 1962 to house employees of the Osler Township Fire Lookout Tower. The tower was on a hill not far from the cabin and remained active until the early 1970's. Since then, the cabin has been used by a mix of park employees and the public. The cabin offers a splendid waterfront view of Birchcliffe Lake. Fishing is available in Birchcliffe Lake and Calm Lake, which is a 1395m portage away from the cabin. A 2km walk from the cabin leads to the old fire tower site. Along with the two bedrooms, the Birchcliffe Cabin also has a kitchen and dining area. The cabin can be accessed from either the Kawawaymog or Kiosk access points. It is recommended to begin at the Kawawaymog access point since it is an easier one day trip. From the Kiosk access point, the trip would take at least two days and involves more portages.

**Bissett Road (Twelve Mile) Cabin (Map 32/D7)** is an easily accessed cabin found not far off Bissett Creek Road. The road leads to the park boundary, from here it is less than a 1km walk to the cabin. The cabin is situated in a beaver meadow and is a great base camp location for wildlife viewing or fishing. Fishing opportunities are available in nearby Big Bissett and North Rouge Lakes. The cabin was constructed in 1922 as a hunting camp and was later used by park rangers as a patrol outpost until the late 1950's. The cabin is locally known as the Twelve Mile Cabin due to its distance from Bissett Creek. It is a one room log construction cabin set amid a beautiful mature stand of White Pine.

**Crooked Chute Cabin (Map 33/B3)** was erected in 1929 for a total cost of $33.97. The cabin was built to provide shelter for park rangers who monitored the area during the Petawawa River log drives. The cabin remained in use for several years, although by the 1990's the cabin was in considerably poor shape. In 1997, the original structure was salvaged and a replica of the old building was built in its place. The cabin lies on the mighty Petawawa River south of the treacherous Crooked Chute. To access the cabin, take the Lake Travers access point to the Petawawa River. Although the cabin can be reached in a day's travel, two days is a more relaxed journey. Be aware of rapids and portages on the Petawawa River. This is one of two cabins in the park that can accommodate up to eight people per night.

**Highview Cabin (Map 20/F5)** is located near the serene Nipissing River on the west side of the park. The cabin was built in 1928 after the original cabin was set ablaze by a lightning strike. It was used as a fire ranger headquarters for this corner of the park. Fishing is offered in the Nipissing River and Gibson Lake, only a 2.5km walk away. The one room cabin can be accessed from a number of different points, although the recommended route is from the Tim River access point. A two day trip should be expected to reach the cabin.

**Kiosk Cabin (Map 29/F7)** is found at the Kiosk access point and is one of the few cabins in the park that has vehicle accessability. This log cabin is also one of the more modern cabins. It was built in 1936 on Kioshkokwi Lake and offers electricity along with all the comforts of home including a refrigerator, stove, electric heat, couch and a table with chairs and running water. Fishing is offered in Kioshkokwi Lake for lake trout and there is a nearby boat launch and lovely beach area.

**Kitty Lake Cabin (Map 14/C2)** is a one room cabin that can be reached by a short paddle from the Shall Lake access point. It was constructed in 1935 and is one of the largest cabins available in the park. The cabin sits on the quiet Kitty Lake and offers plenty of fishing opportunities in one of the many nearby lakes. Up to eight people can be accommodated year round.

**Lost Coin Lake Cabin (Map 32/D7)** is a one room log cabin that was built in 1936 by the Ontario Forestry Branch. The access point closest to the cabin is the Big Bissett Lake access point. Bissett Creek Road leads to the park boundary and a cart trail leads to the cabin. It is a 7km hike to the cabin from the park boundary. Although the trip is long and labourious, you will be rewarded with the serenity and isolation of Lost Coin Lake. Fishing is also available in the lake.

**McKaskill Lake Cabin (Map 14/E1)** has two access points. The first option is to travel from the Shall Lake access point by canoe. You have to cross five lakes with challenging portages. It would take a full day to access the cabin. An alternative route is to travel the Basin Lake Access Road to the hydro line. At the hydro line, a cart trail travels 8km to the lake. Both options involve some effort, although the canoe route would be more scenic. The one room log cabin was built in 1932 and sits on the majestic McKaskill Lake. Fishing is offered in the lake or for the more adventurous there are several other fishing lakes within a portage or two from McKaskill Lake. The cabin is also available for winter use.

**Rain Lake Cabin (Map 11/E4)** is one of the more modern cabins in the park and has vehicle access from the village of Kearney along Rain Lake Road. It was originally built on Cache Lake and was a private cottage for several years. In the late 1970's, the cabin was moved to its current location on Rain Lake. The cabin is equipped with a propane stove, fridge, lights and heat. Rain Lake is the perfect base for exploring the interior of the park. There are a number of different canoe route options and the Western Uplands Backpacking Trail is also accessed from this area.

**Tattler Lake Cabin (Map 13/G3)** was originally constructed as a shelter for the person who manned a nearby fire tower. It is estimated that the cabin was built around the time the tower was erected in 1932. Since those days, the cabin has been significantly repaired. Today it is a great location to enjoy Tattler Lake. The cabin can be reached by an easy one day canoe trip from the Shall Lake access point.

**Wenda Lake Cabin (Map 24/C5)** is a one room log cabin that was built in the early 1920's. It sits on picturesque Wenda Lake amid a mature stand of Red Pine trees. There are two routes to the cabin. The most direct route is to travel from the Achray access point to the 3.6km portage off Grand Lake. Although this route is direct, it is an arduous 2 day journey due to the hilly terrain of the portage. Alternatively, you can travel from the Achray access across Carcajou Bay and the Spectacle Lakes to Wenda Lake. This is a more scenic and less strenuous route. Fishing opportunities exist at Wenda Lake and at a number of other lakes close by.

## Vehicle Campgrounds

There are a number of vehicle access campgrounds in Algonquin Park. These campgrounds offer some modern conveniences like showers and running water. They are scattered along the park's more popular access points, although the bulk of the campgrounds are found along the Hwy 60 corridor. Overnight fees vary depending on the amenities available and time of year. The park can be busy during summer months and it is recommended to call ahead for reservations. For reservations call (888) ONT-PARK. For more information call (705) 633-5572.

**Achray Campground (Map 24/E4)** is located on the eastern side of the park. Turn left at about the 19.2km mark from the Sand Lake Gate. There are 39 sites at the campground along with comfort stations that provide running water and flush toilets. The Eastern Pines Backpacking Trail and the Berm Lake Trail can both be accessed from the campground. There is a canoe access point onto Grand Lake, which leads to a number of possible canoe routes and good fishing.

**Brent Campground (Map 22/A1)** is found at the Kioshkokwi Lake-Kiosk access area. The campground offers 28 campsites with a store nearby. There is canoe access onto the large Cedar Lake where a number of canoe routes can be explored, including a trip down the mighty Petawawa River. Fishing is offered on Cedar Lake.

**Canisbay Lake Campground (Map 12/G5)** offers visitors several of the amenities of home including full comfort stations equipped with showers, running water and laundry facilities. Canisbay Lake is one of the larger campgrounds in the park and is located off the north side of Hwy 60 on the charming Canisbay Lake. There are 248 regular and 66 electrical campsites at the campground. A sandy beach, fishing and a number of hiking and biking trails are all close by.

**Coon Lake Campground (Map 13/D6)** is in a central location to a number of different hiking and biking trails. The campground is not far off the south side of Hwy 60. There are 49 campsites and a small beach area, although there are no comfort stations. There is also fishing at nearby Loon Lake.

**Kearney Lake Campground (Map 13/C5)** is another Hwy 60 corridor camping area with 103 sites set amid splendid stands of pine trees. Comfort stations at the campground include showers and flush toilets. Kearney Lake also has a beach area and fishing A number of recreation trails are within a short walk from the campground.

**Kiosk Campground (Map 29/G7)** has 17 sites along with flush toilets. Found at the north end of the park, this campground is used as a staging ground for the Kioshkokwi Lake-Kiosk. From Kioshkokwi Lake, a number of different canoe routes can be followed. Fishing and swimming are also available on the lake.

**Lake of Two Rivers Campground (Map 13/A5)** is located off the south side of Hwy 60. It is one of the larger campgrounds in the park with 241 regular campsites and another 160 electrical sites for overnight use. Full comfort stations are available providing showers, flush toilets and laundry facilities. The Two Rivers Store at the campground is open throughout the summer months and provides basic supplies and snacks. The Madawaska River flows to the south side of the campground and a beautiful sandy beach lies at the water's edge of Lake Of Two Rivers. Hiking and biking trails, fishing opportunities and swimming are all possible activities to enjoy.

**Mew Lake Campground (Map 13/A5)** is a year round campground, although it is only staffed during the spring to fall camping period. It can be found off the south side of Hwy 60 and offers 131 regular campsites and 66 electrical sites for overnight use. Comfort stations are equipped with flush toilets, showers and laundry facilities but they are closed during the winter season. During this time, vault toilets are the only facilities available.

Hiking, biking, cross-country skiing and snowshoeing trails are all found close to the campground. The beach area on Mew Lake is a popular spot during the summer. Roofed accommodation called yurts, are also available throughout the year. They are tent accommodations that are equipped with electric heat, table, chairs and a bed frame. It is recommended to call ahead for reservations at (888) ONT-PARK or in the off season at (613) 637-2780.

**Pog Lake (Map 13/B5)** campground is one of the largest campgrounds in the park. It is located off the south side of Hwy 60, just past Lake of Two Rivers. There are 286 regular campsites and another 83 sites with electrical service. Comfort stations include flush toilets, showers and laundry facilities. A number of recreation trails are within close proximity of the campground including the Old Railway Bike Trail and the Highland Backpacking Trail. Canoeing and swimming at the sandy beach areas are also popular pastimes on the quiet Pog Lake.

**Rain Lake (Map 11/E4)** campground is the smallest campground in the park with only 9 regular campsites. The campground is found at the Rain Lake interior access point at the end of Rain Lake Road, from the village of Kearney. The campground lies on the shore of Rain Lake and is a great base for further exploration of the interior of the park. The Western Uplands Backpacking Trail can be accessed from the area as well as a number of different canoe routes from Rain Lake. Fishing is available in Rain Lake and many other lakes are within one or two portages.

**Rock Lake (Map 13/D6)** campground lies on the picturesque Rock Lake. The road to the campground is found on the south side of Hwy 60 near the 40km mark of the corridor. There are 124 regular campsites and 72 electrical sites along with full comfort stations. Comfort stations are equipped with flush toilets, showers and laundry facilities. The Booth's Rock Trail, Old Railway Bike Trail and the Centennial Trail are all within a few minutes walk of the campground. Fishing and paddling opportunities are available on Rock Lake and at a number of the surrounding lakes in the area. There are also two beach areas near the campground for swimming.

**Tea Lake (Map 12/C7)** campground is found off the north side of Hwy 60. This campground offers 43 regular campsites, although the only amenities at the campground are vault toilets and running water. Fishing can be enjoyed on the lake and a number of recreation trails are within close proximity of the campground. There is a small beach area for swimming.

**Whitefish Lake Group Campground (Map 13/C5)** is located off Hwy 60 on Whitefish Lake. There are 18 sites for groups ranging in size from 10-40 people. Facilities include vault toilets and running water. The area was designed specifically to accommodate youth and special groups, although certain adult groups are permitted (i.e. family reunions). The Madawaska River flows behind several of the group sites and Whitefish Lake provides swimming and fishing opportunities. The Old Railway Bike Trail and a number of other recreation trails are close by.

# Other Parks and Conservation Areas

## Arrowhead Provincial Park (1/G2)

This is a 1,237 ha park is set amid the beautiful Muskoka region and can be accessed off Hwy 11, north of Huntsville. The park encompasses Arrowhead and Mayflower Lakes, which offer fishing and canoeing or you can swim and relax at one of the sandy beaches. A peaceful stretch of the Big East River meanders through the south side of the park and is a great spot for an easy canoe ride. There are also over 12km of easy hiking trails throughout the park that give you a chance to explore the area even further.

The Park has 388 campsites, with electricity at 115 of these sites. Other amenities at the park include a small store and full bathroom facilities, with toilets and showers. In winter, the park activities continue with cross-country ski trails, tobogganing and skating on Arrowhead Lake. Cross-country skis can be rented from the park concession. In summer, the park can be quite busy at times and it is recommended to call ahead to make reservations. Call (705) 789-5105 for more information.

## Bell Bay Provincial Park (15/A7)

This is a non-operating provincial park found off Hwy 60 east of the village of Madawaska. The main portion of the park protects a large section of Bark Lake's northern shoreline. There are also a few other separated parts of the park just west of the main portion. These other sections protect a stretch of Parissien Lake and Pergeon Lake's shorelines. In total, the park covers 404 hectares of land and is home to the very rare Encrusted Saxifrage. This plant grows mainly on the park's large cliff overlooking Bark Lake. The plant is a remnant of the glacial retreat over 10,000 thousand years ago.

Bell Bay Provincial Park has no facilities, although hiking along the old roadway through the park can be enjoyable along with nature viewing. The road makes an ideal bike ride or hike through the interior of the park. A few older unmaintained trails also exist in the park, although they can be difficult to locate. Other activities include canoeing or fishing on Bark Lake. To access the main portion of the park, follow the rough 4wd road that travels from Hwy 60.

## Bonfield Park Conservation Area (Map 28/G3)

The Bonfield Park Conservation Area is part of the North Bay-Mattawa Conservation Authority. The day-use park is 8ha in size and lies off Hwy 531 on the Kaibushkong River, north of the village of Bonfield. There is a parking and picnic area, a small beach on the river for swimming and sunbathing as well as a kid's playground.

## Bonnechere Caves (Map 18/A7)

The Bonnechere Caves are a series of underground caves that were carved into the limestone thousands of years ago by ancient water passages. They were first discovered in 1853 by European settlers, although they were never publicized and were soon forgotten. The caves were somewhat rediscovered in the early 1950's and were finally opened to the public in 1955.

In the caves, there are a number of interesting things to see including stalactites. Stalactites are rock icicles that hang from the cave ceilings and have been formed by the buildup of minerals over thousands of years. The caves are also the site of coral and sea fossils that were remnants of predinosaur life forms. These fossils have led to the theory that the caves were once the bottom of a tropical sea over 500 million of years ago. A present day example of how the caves were formed can be found at the Fourth Chute.

The Fourth Chute is a windy stretch of the Bonnechere River that has been carved through limestone much like the caves were formed thousands of years ago. The caves are located outside of the village of Douglas, not far of Hwy 60. Guided tours are required to explore the caves for a nominal fee. Tours are frequent throughout the day and run from the beginning of May to the 2nd Monday in October.

## Bonnechere Provincial Park (Map 26/B2)

Bonnechere Provincial Park is located off Hwy 62 on the picturesque Round Lake. The historic Bonnechere River flows through the park and into the 3,075 hectare Round Lake. The river was once one of the major transportation veins for moving Algonquin timber out of the vast park. Logging sustained the first settlers of the area and the Bonnechere River played a vital role during the annual log drives.

Today, the park protects a portion of the river and offers a variety of recreation opportunities including hiking, fishing, boating and water sports. Three hiking trails totaling over 5km take you throughout the park and along the Bonnechere River. Guided nature tours along the trails are also offered throughout the camping season. There are fishing opportunities on both the Bonnechere River and Round Lake, which is also the ideal place for a beach picnic or a swim.

Canoeing the river is a popular pastime at the park and you can take an overnight trip up the river to more remote lakes or even into Algonquin Park. Kayaking is becoming increasingly popular and opportunities are available on both the Bonnechere River and Round Lake. Canoes and kayaks can be rented at the park for a nominal fee.

At the park, there are 128 camping sites and another 24 sites that provide electricity. Most sites at the park are suitable for both tents and trailers. The park offers full modern facilities including showers and a laundry area. Bonnechere Provincial Park can be busy during summer months and it is recommended to call ahead for reservations. For more information call (613) 757-2103. For reservations call (888) ONT-PARK.

### Bonnechere River Provincial Park (Map 15/G2)
This is a waterway provincial park created to protect the historic Bonnechere River and its shoreline. The park stretches from the Algonquin Park boundary to Bonnechere Provincial Park on Round Lake. The park encompasses 1,198 hectares of Bonnechere River shoreline. The park is a non-operating park, although you can camp and canoe on the waterway.

The river travels through a maple and pine dominated forest and you may catch a glimpse of wildlife such as moose, bear and waterfowl. Between Round Lake and Algonquin Park, there are six recognized park campsites available for use. These wilderness sites are mainly canoe access only. The river is quite meandering and there are not many areas of difficulty. The stretch towards Algonquin Park is more rustic and the opportunity to find seclusion is better than closer to Round Lake.

### Carson Lake Provincial Park (Map 15/E7)
This is a small recreation park found off Hwy 60, about 6km west of Barry's Bay. The park sits on the shore of Carson Lake and across the highway from Trout Lake. There are 34 camping sites at the park and a picnic area. Swimming is a major attraction of the park as well as boating on Carson Lake or nearby Trout Lake. Both lakes provide opportunities for fishing and are good locations for canoeing day trips. The park lies amid the Algonquin Highlands and is just minutes away from Algonquin Park. It is recommended to call ahead for reservations, as the park can be busy during the summer. For more information call (613) 756-3061. For reservations call (888) ONT-PARK.

### Centennial Lake Provincial Nature Reserve Park (Map 8/G6, 9/A6)
This is a 530 hectare, non-operating nature reserve park that was established to protect rare, indigenous plant species, such as the Purple Cliffbrake. The park encompasses a few small water bodies including Oakhill Lake and a portion of Big Limestone Lake. The area is characterized by rolling highlands similar to Algonquin Park. There are no facilities at this park and access is limited to maintain the natural state of the area. The park is found west of the town of Calabogie and spans the area. The reserve is comprised of a number of islands on Black Donald Lake, although the main portion lies about 3km northwest of the lake.

### Conroy Marsh Game Preserve (Map 6/G5, 7/A5)
Conroy Marsh is located east of the town of Mynooth and is part of the York River system. The marsh has played a historical role in the development of the area since the arrival of the first settlers over 300 years ago. It was once an abundant wildlife and fishing area. It provided furs and fish to the first settlers and to natives for hundreds of years before them. In its entirety, the marsh is approximately 2,400 hectares and the game preserve is about 2,100 hectares.

The game preserve was established in 1962 to protect the over exploited wildlife in the marsh. Today it acts as a refuge to many fur bearing animals including fox, beaver and marten. The marsh is a unique and serene place that is the ideal location for nature seekers. A canoe trip through the marsh is a relaxing experience as you travel through the peaceful marsh. There are no established road access points to the marsh and for good intention. The main access to the marsh is Mayhews Landing up river. A canoe can be placed in the York River off the road near here and it is about a 4km paddle to the marsh.

### Corbeil Conservation Area (Map 28/D2)
This 38ha conservation area was established to protect the headwaters of the La Vasse River. The area is an important floodplain of the river helping to maintain proper water levels during spring thaws. The area can be accessed from Hwy 94, southeast of the city of North Bay. There is a small parking area off the highway where an interpretive trail can be found. The trail takes you on a 1.8km loop through the conservation area. An informative interpretive brochure can be picked up at the trailhead.

### Dividing Lake Provincial Nature Reserve Park (3/F2)
Divide Lake can only be reached by canoe from Rockaway Lake and involves a grueling 2745m portage from Kimball Lake. The trip is difficult, although the reward is well worth the effort. Dividing Lake Provincial Park was established to protect one of the last stands of old growth white pine in southern Ontario. The century old trees are found throughout the park and are best viewed along the portage from Rockaway Lake to Dividing Lake. There are a few rustic campsites at Rockaway and Dividing Lakes, allowing for a longer stay to enjoy the good fishing in the area. Algonquin Park permits must be acquired in order to camp.

### Driftwood Provincial Park (Map 33/C3)
This is a full recreation provincial park that is located on the shore of the Ottawa River off Hwy 17, west of the village of Rolphton. The park sits on a quiet bay of the Ottawa River that was formed in 1950 with the completion of the Des Joachims Hydro-electric Dam. The dam flooded the original Ottawa River shoreline and subsequently created the bay. The bay was a collection point for large amounts of driftwood from the flooding and hence the bay received its name, Driftwood Bay.

The park hosts a number of different recreation activities for the public to enjoy including fishing, hiking, water sports and boating. The Ottawa River has long been a good river for fishing. A boat launch is available at the park so you can get out, explore the river and find those prime fishing areas. There are a number of great hiking trails throughout the park. The trails traverse through a mixed forest and are available for cross-country skiing in winter. In summer, the trails are excellent for picking blueberries while in season (late July-early August).

The soft sandy beach that makes up much of the shoreline at the park is a great place to enjoy the sun and to take a dip in the bay. The park has 80 regular campsites and another 20 sites that equipped with electrical outlets, suitable for RV's. A comfort station provides running water, although there are no showers at the park. Boat and motor rentals are available at the park as well as canoe rentals. The park can be busy during summer months and it is recommended to call ahead for reservations. Call (613) 586-2553 for information. For reservations call (888) ONT-PARK.

### Eau Claire Gorge Conservation Area (Map 29/E2)
This 120ha conservation area was established in 1976 to help preserve the natural and historical features of the area. The area protects the magnificent Eau Claire Gorge and it's 18m (60ft) high rock walls. The Amable Du Fond River flows below the gorge and was an essential part of transporting logs to the Mattawa River. The gorge was a natural barrier to the transportation route and a log chute was built to bypass the gorge. Remnants of the chute and the logging camp can still be seen today. An interpretive trail takes through the conservation area and helps to explain more about the natural and historical features of the conservation area. To access the conservation area, follow Graham Road off Peddlers Drive. There is a parking area and picnic tables available.

### Foy Provincial Park (Map 16/C2)
This is a non-operating provincial park that was established to help protect a portion of Round Lake's shoreline. The park sits across the lake from Bonnechere Provincial Park and can be reached by a gravel road off Hwy 62. The park is 147 hectares in size and can be explored on foot if desired. The road through the park travels close to Round Lake's shore where canoes can be launched into the lake. The road can also be a good route for biking.

### Haliburton Forest and Wildlife Reserve (Map 3/F6, 4/A4)
This is a vast reserve with 50 lakes that covers over 20,243ha. The privately owned reserve offers guided and non-guided recreation opportunities and is reasonably priced and well organized . There is a restaurant on site and a store where you can pick up supplies before you head out on your adventure. You can also choose between staying in the lodge or spending your nights in a separate housekeeping unit. To enhance your visit, the reserve rents many types of equipment including mountain bikes, canoes, cross-country skis and even snowmobiles.

There are over 300km of trails that are utilized throughout the year for mountain biking, hiking, cross-country skiing, snowshoeing and snowmobiling. The magnificent Forest Canopy Trail is one of the outstanding trails and is a unique and invigorating experience. You can canoe and fish most of the lakes in the reserve and 17 of the 50 lakes have semi-wilderness camping sites. The Haliburton Forest Reserve also has outdoor educational programs to enhance your wilderness skills and knowledge. Accessed can be found on County Road 7 off Hwy 118. For more information call (705) 754-2198.

### J. Albert Bauer Provincial Park (Map 2/D2)

J. Albert Bauer Provincial Park borders on Solitaire and Estell Lakes, which offer canoeing and fishing opportunities. The park is 163ha in size and can be found off County Road 8 on Limberlost Road. It is a non-operating day-use area and there are no amenities for visitors. Solitaire Lake makes a good spot to go swimming on those hot and humid mid summer days.

### J.P. Webster Conservation Area (Map 28/F1)

This 132ha conservation area is located south of Turtle Lake. There is a rough access road to the area, where parking and picnic facilities are available. The picnic area has a small shelter and tables, offering protection from any unexpected rain. A 2km trail traverses in a loop through the conservation area, offering visitors a better chance to explore the area.

### Lake St. Peter Provincial Park (Map 5/E3)

This is a full recreation provincial park. Lying on the southern boundary of the great Canadian Shield, the park's landscape is characteristic of the Algonquin Highlands. The park forest is a mix of deciduous and coniferous trees, which are common to the transition zone of the area. The park is located on Lake St. Peter off Hwy 127, north of the town of Maynooth.

The park is 478 hectares in size and has 65 campsites for overnight use, with 46 of the sites able to accommodate trailers. The boundary of the park stretches from the shore of Lake St. Peter all the way north to McKenzie Lake. Lake St. Peter Provincial Park was established in 1956 in response to the increasing recreational demand on the area.

There are a number of recreational activities at the park such as swimming, hiking, boating and fishing. There is a sandy beach and picnic area on the west side of the park, which is an ideal location to get some sun or to cool off in the lake. There are two hiking trails totaling 4km that pass through the mixed forest of the park highlands. For fishing and boating enthusiasts, there is a boat launch onto Lake St. Peter.

Full modern facilities are offered at this park including showers and a laundry area. Lake St. Peter Provincial Park is close to Algonquin and Silent Lake Provincial Parks. For added adventure, day trips can be taken to both of these parks. Your park camping permit also allows you free entrance to several

interpretive programs of Algonquin Park. The park can be busy during summer months and it is recommended to call ahead for reservations. For reservations call (888) ONT-PARK. For more information call (613) 586-2553.

### La Vase Portage Conservation Area (Map 28/B1)

This 39ha conservation area was established in 1995 in order to protect a portion of the historic La Vase Portage. Natives and voyageurs of the early 19th century frequently used the portage. Currently, there are no established facilities at the area other than a rustic trail. The trail is great for hiking, snowshoeing or cross-country skiing. Further development is planned for the area in the near future.

### Leslie M. Frost Centre (Map 2/G7, 3/C7)

Leslie M. Frost Centre is a 24,000ha reserve of crown land in the Haliburton Highlands that has provided the base for a Ministry of Natural Resources training centre since 1971. The centre provides endless outdoor recreation opportunities for the public and is accessible from many areas along its border with the main access being from the Frost Centre itself, located on Hwy 35, south of Dorset. The complete Leslie M. Frost Centre is shown in the Cottage Country edition of the Backroad Mapbook Series.

There are a few cottages scattered along the shorelines of some of the larger lakes, although most of the smaller lakes are not developed. A variety of canoeing opportunities lie within the reserve including the Gun Lake and Red Pine Lake Canoe Routes. Along the shores of most of the lakes, there are user maintained camping spots, which are available free of charge. The portages between lakes are generally obstruction free.

There are many trails throughout the property that are used for hiking, biking, cross-country skiing, snowmobiling and snowshoeing. The two main trailheads are located behind the main buildings and from the parking area across the highway from the Frost Centre. Washrooms are available in the main building on Hwy 35 and a couple warmup shelters are found on the cross-country trails.

### Lower Madawaska River Provincial Park (Map 7/F6, 8/B6)

This is a waterway park that was established to protect a 21km stretch of the Madawaska River. The protected area totals 1,200 hectares and covers the shoreline of the river between the village of Griffith and just south of Hwy 515. This is a non-operating provincial park, although there are 36 canoe-in campsites on the river. These sites provide campers with a backcountry river experience.

Road access to the river park is limited, although there are a few areas that are vehicle accessible. The main access point is a 2wd gravel road that travels south from the village of Quadeville. The road leads to the river and a canoe put-in site. The same road travels all the way to the village of Griffith. Another access point is found off the road about 12km east of the first point.

Campsites are scattered along the river in various locations and are user maintained only. Be sure to leave your site as clean as when you arrived or even cleaner, so the next group of campers can enjoy their experience like you did. The river is an ideal canoeing destination with very few obstacles along the route. In a few locations, rustic and unmarked hiking trails can be found along the shoreline. They are unmarked but make a great day's outing for the adventurous camper. If you enjoy fishing, the river also offers some good angling opportunities.

### McLaren Shields Conservation Area (Map 28/F1)

The McLaren Family donated the McLaren-Shields Conservation Area to the North Bay-Mattawa Conservation Authority. Currently, there are no established facilities at the area. A picnic area and an interpretive trail are planned.

### Mattawa Island Conservation Area (Map 30/C1)

The Mattawa Island Conservation Area is a 3ha preserve that is available for day-use by visitors. There is a parking area available at the end of a 2wd dirt road, west of the town of Mattawa. Privies and a picnic area can be found near the parking area. The beach area and swimming in the Mattawa River are popular, especially in the heat of summer.

### Mattawa River Provincial Park (Map 28/F1, 29/D1)

Mattawa River Provincial Park was established in 1970 as Ontario's first waterway park. In 1988, the federal government designated the river as a Canadian Heritage River. The river was an essential native transportation and trading route for over 5,000 years. With the arrival of Europeans, the river not only moved people but also moved endless amounts of lumber to the mills of the St. Lawrence. The river continued to play a role until the early 20th Century. Today, the river is an important recreation and historical area.

The 3,257 hectare park protects the shoreline of the Mattawa River from Samuel de Champlain Provincial Park to Trout Lake. Rustic campsites can be found along the Mattawa River shoreline throughout the park. Alternatively, private campgrounds with full facilities are found along the river in a few locations.

Access points to the river are scattered mainly along the parks southern shoreline, although there are a few rougher access points on the northern shoreline. Canoe tripping is popular on the river. You can travel the river from Trout Lake to Samuel de Champlain Provincial Park, although canoe trippers should have some river travel experience. There are marked and well maintained portages along the route. The river can be difficult to read for a beginner.

A three day trip is the perfect way to travel the length of the Mattawa River Provincial Park. Wildlife can often be seen along the river and fishing is quite good for a variety of species. The river is also revered for its whitewater opportunities. In spring, experienced canoeists can run many of the rapids for an exhilarating experience. Whitewater rafting is also a popular outdoor pastime on the river.

### Opeongo River Provincial Park (Map 14/G3, 15/A5)
Opeongo River Provincial Park protects 955 hectares of river shoreline stretching from Algonquin Provincial Park to Hwy 60. Since this is a waterway park, there are no visitor facilities available. The park can be accessed from Hwy 60 or from the Shall Lake access point of Algonquin Park. There are no established camping sites along the river, although no-trace camping is permitted. Traveling the entire stretch of the river makes a great two or three day trip.

The most difficult section of the river is the section from Victoria Lake to where the Opeongo River meets the Aylen River. There are many rapids along this part of the river and portages are not marked making travel challenging. In spring, this is a popular whitewater area. It is recommended to have whitewater and rustic tripping experience to travel the river, especially at this time of year. Wildlife viewing is also a popular attraction of the river park.

### Ottawa River Provincial Park (Map 27/G7, 18/G1)
This is a collection of islands on the Ottawa River that can only be accessed by a whitewater capable boat. The water on this part of the river is quite challenging and involves a lot of whitewater travel. It is recommended that only experienced rafters attempt this area of the river. The park was established to preserve 125 hectares of the original river shoreline in its most natural form. The park is a non-operating park; therefore, there are no visitor facilities available. The park does offer bird watching opportunities from the shore.

### Oxtongue River/Ragged Falls Provincial Park (Map 2/G2)
Oxtongue River/Ragged Falls Provincial Park has been developed to protect a stretch of the Oxtongue River and offers limited facilities to the visitor. This day-use waterway park is found off Hwy 60 on the west side of Algonquin Provincial Park. The river can be accessed from both the west and east end of the park. A marked gravel road on the east side leads to the magnificent Ragged Falls. The river is a part of an rarely used canoe route that can begin in Algonquin Park. There are washrooms and a parking area at the park along with a small series of connecting trails that lead to a natural lookout over the falls. The lookout provides visitors with a scenic view of the rolling beauty of the Algonquin Highlands.

### Papineau Lake Conservation Area (Map 30/B4)
The Papineau Lake Conservation Area was developed to protect a portion of the Papineau Lake shoreline and surrounding area. A 2wd dirt road from the road to Brain Lake leads to a boat launch area. The area also hosts a parking area, picnic tables and basic privies. Swimming and fishing are the major attractions of this conservation area.

### Samuel de Champlain Provincial Park (Map 29/G1)
Samuel de Champlain Provincial Park can be found off Hwy 17, west of the town of Mattawa. The park is 2,550 hectares in size and helps protect a stretch of the Mattawa River and Amable du Fond River. The park lies in the Canadian Shield and its terrain is characteristic of much of this part of the province. The Mattawa River is a Canadian Heritage River and played an important role in Canada's early history. The river was the main trade route for natives for over 6,000 years and for the Europeans of the New World. The Mattawa River was the most grueling portion of the voyageurs trip from Montreal to Fort William on Lake Superior. At the Voyageur Heritage Centre, you can learn more about the voyageurs and the Mattawa River Valley.

The park is a full recreation park and offers visitors a variety of recreation opportunities. There is a great series of hiking trails offering over 30km of hiking possibilities. The trail systems are broken up into six different loops with scenic natural lookouts scattered along many of the routes. Four of the loops are coordinated with interpretive guides to help educate you on some history and geography of the area. Canoeing on the Mattawa River is also a popular attraction of the park. Whitewater canoeing and rafting is possible in spring when water levels create challenging whitewater stretches. In summer, the river is much more calm and easier to navigate. Along with the canoeing, the river also offers fairly good fishing. In the park, fishing enthusiasts can also test their luck in Moore Lake or Long Lake.

There are 215 regular camping sites at the park and another 73 sites with electricity. Full amenities are also offered including showers and laundry facilities. Canoe, bicycle and boat/motor rentals are available on a first come first serve basis. Nature hikes and other educational programs are organized on a frequent basis throughout the summer season. In winter, the outdoor fun continues with a series of cross-country trails that are maintained and groomed and can be used for a nominal fee. If you intend to camp at the park it is recommended to call ahead for reservations, as the park can be busy during summer months. For reservations call (888) ONT-PARK. For more information call (705) 744-2276.

### Upper Madawaska River Provincial Park (Map 14/E6)
This is a 1,085 hectare park that was established to protect an upper stretch of the Madawaska River. The park is little more than a band of shoreline spanning from Whitney to Madawaska. Since this is a waterway park, there are no facilities. Campsites along the river are not marked and are quite rustic. It is encouraged to practice no-trace camping to help preserve the area in its natural state.

This stretch of river is an ideal whitewater canoe or kayak destination and is quite popular in spring and early summer. The river can be accessed off a 2wd road off Hwy 60 that travels from Whitney to Madawaska. The road follows the river between the two towns and access can be found off the road in several locations. The main put-in is around Whitney and the take-out being Madawaska. For fishing enthusiasts, angling opportunities are available on the river.

### Westmeath Provincial Park (Map 27/C7)
Westmeath Provincial Park is a non-operating provincial park that protects 610 hectares of Ottawa River shoreline. The park is an important migrating birds and turtle nesting area. The park has an abundance of waterfowl and other shoreline species making it a popular area for bird watchers and nature lovers.

The park can be accessed by boat on the Ottawa River or by vehicle off County Road 12, south of the town of Westmeath. A short hiking trail is available that travels through the park and down to the park's shore. Sandy beaches along the park's shoreline make the area a perfect swimming location.

# Paddling Routes

## (Canoe and River Routes)

## Canoe Routes

The Algonquin Region has long been known as the canoeing centre of Canada and offers an endless array of rivers and lakes to travel. From leisurely one day outings to challenging week long trips, the area has plenty to offer. Algonquin Park is one of the most popular canoeing areas due in part to the maintained canoe routes and spectacular wilderness scenery. However, routes outside of the park should not be overlooked. You'll often find these routes experience low use, making it easy to find seclusion. Another advantage of travelling outside of the park is that you can save on park fees. For people who do plenty of tripping, this is a definite bonus.

In Algonquin Park, canoe routes that begin near the Hwy 60 corridor are normally busy throughout the year. Other popular areas are the west entrances to the park. In most cases, the easier it is to get to an access from metro-Toronto, the busier it will be. Summer is the most popular time of year, although spring can also be busy. If you are looking to find some seclusion, it is recommended to try a trip from one of the lesser used access points. Another suggestion is to plan trips during the week or in the fall. Otherwise, remember the golden rule - the more distance you put behind you, the less people you will see.

Trip equipment is very important to help reduce fatigue and increase enjoyment. For long tripping with numerous portages, a good lightweight kevlar canoe is recommended. This helps increase your endurance and reduce the physical stress of numerous portages. Good planning is essential to minimize your weight and maximize your comfort. If planning is not done properly, an enjoyable trip can easily become hard work. Experienced canoeists have a good idea of how far they can travel in a day, although in general during 4-6 hours travel time you should be able to cover 10-20km or about 8cm-15cm on our maps. Of course, a number of factors must be accounted for when estimating your rate of progress, such as the number and difficulty of portages, wind on large water bodies and of course your physical conditioning.

*Our difficulty rating of the lake routes is as follows:*

**Easy:** For novice canoeists, with short easy portages or none at all. Lakes along the route are smaller reducing wind problems.

**Moderate:** For intermediate canoeists, with a number of portages and a few that may be more rustic and/or longer.

**Difficult:** For advanced canoeists, with longer portages and/or portages that may be difficult to find or are grown over. Wilderness orientation skills may be required. Some challenging river travel may also be a part of the route.

*For Algonquin Provincial Park interior canoe trips, be sure to always reserve ahead of your planned trip. Have a detailed trip itinerary available with the lakes you plan to camp on. It is recommended to have a back up plan in case lakes are fully reserved. During your trip, be sure to stick to your itinerary, as everyone else's trips depend on the system also.*

### Barron Canyon Route (Map 24/G4)
**Access/Parking:** The put-in and parking area for this route is found at Algonquin Park's Grand Lake-Achray interior access point. Park permits can be purchased at the Sand Lake Gate.

The Barron Canyon is one of the most spectacular natural wonders of Algonquin Park. This easy route takes you along the Barron River, where it travels through the immense gorge that is truly an amazing sight. In areas, the canyon walls measure over 100m (330ft) above the river.

There are campsites available on almost all of the smaller lakes along the route but the most popular base camp area is Stratton Lake. There are 19 rustic canoe sites and another eight trail access sites on the lake. Most of the canoe sites are located on the south portion of the lake, which can be a little crowded during summer long weekends.

To begin your route, from the put-in at Grand Lake travel south to the Grand Lake Dam. There is a short portage around the dam into Stratton Lake. From Stratton Lake, there is a quick portage into St. Andrews Lake. From St. Andrews Lake, you travel across High Falls and Opalescent Lakes before entering Bringham Lake. Two portages from Bringham Lake lies the marvelous Barron Canyon. The river is quite slow through the canyon, allowing you time to relax and enjoy the scenery.

You can return to your base camp by the same route you came or alternatively, from Opalescent Lake you can head in a loop east. The loop travels over Cork, Length and Marie Lakes before meeting back up with St. Andrews Lake. Fishing opportunities are available on Opalescent, Cork and Length Lakes. Allow at least two days for the trip.

### Big Porcupine Lake Loop (Map 12/E7, 3/F1)
**Access/Parking:** The access point to this Algonquin Park interior route is the popular Smoke Lake. Parking and permits area available at the Access Point Office at Canoe Lake.

Beginning at the north end of Smoke Lake, paddle south to the dam and portage to Ragged Lake. During summer, Smoke Lake can be busy with canoeists and motorboats. At the south shore of Ragged Lake, there is a 590m portage into Big Porcupine Lake. Your endurance will definitely be tested on this portage, as the portage climb is quite steep. Big Porcupine Lake makes a great first day camping area. The 16 interior campsites are well spaced and secluded.

The next day will take you on a short loop from Big Porcupine Lake to neighbouring Bonnechere Lake. The loop is a great day trip and travels from Big Porcupine over Little Coon Lake, Whatnot Lakes and McGarvey Lake before reaching Bonnechere Lake. If you wish to spend your second night at McGarvey or Little Coon Lakes, there are some lovely wilderness camping sites available.

To limit the route to three days, you can return from Bonnechere Lake through to Big Porcupine Lake and retrace back to Smoke Lake. If time permits, this part of the park offers a variety of route options. Trout fishing is a popular attraction, especially in spring.

### Big Trout Lake Route (Map 12/F3, 21/F7)
**Access/Parking:** There are two main access points for the Big Trout Lake Route. The first access is the Canoe Lake put-in. This is the most popular access in Algonquin Provincial Park. The other alternative is the Source Lake interior access point. This put-in is not as busy, which can make your trip a little more enjoyable. However, the portages from the Source Lake are a little longer but well worth the effort. For our Big Trout Lake Route, we have chosen to describe it from the Source Lake interior access point. Permits can be found at the Canoe Lake Access Point Office.

This moderately difficult route takes five nights and six days to complete and offers fishing on most of the lakes. The first day of the trip crosses a number of small lakes beginning with Bruce Lake. From Bruce Lake, you will travel over Raven Lake en route to Owl Lake. Linda Lake is a 1,315m portage from Owl Lake. Both Lakes make an ideal first night camping lake. There are three nice sites on Owl and four on Linda Lake, including one great island site. If you like, you can plan to stay on Iris Lake, which is an 875m portage from Linda Lake. There is only one campsite on the lake allowing you to have the whole lake to yourself.

The portage from Iris Lake north to Alder Lake is a brutal 2,105m. Once at Alder Lake there is a short portage into Birdie Lake where access to the large Burnt Island Lake can be found. Burnt Island is a popular lake due to its proximity to the Canoe Lake access point. At the northeast part of the lake there is a portage into Little Otterslide Lake. If you paddle to the north side of Little Otterslide, you'll find a small creek leading to the larger Otterslide Lake. Both Lakes make a great place to camp.

The stretch down Otterslide Creek to Big Trout Lake travels through wetland habitat that is ideal for spotting small mammals such as otters and beaver. The Algonquin moose is also often spotted down this route. The portages are generally easy with the last one leading into a small inlet of Big Trout Lake.

The size of the big lake and the well spaced campsites help spread out the trippers evenly on the lake. You can also camp on White Trout Lake to the south and get a head start on the next day.

The southern portion of White Trout Lake empties into a seemingly endless marsh area. You will follow the marsh for over 3km before reaching the portage to Hawkins Lake. It is sometimes difficult to keep track of the route, pay attention to route markers. From Hawkins Lake, travel south over Canada Jay Lake and into Sunbeam Lake. Camp can be made on Sunbeam Lake or if you are ambitious, you can continue on to Burnt Island Lake. There are eight interior sites on Sunbeam Lake, including 3 nice island sites. There are 52 campsites on the popular Burnt Island Lake. From Burnt Island Lake, retrace your original route back to Source Lake. The fifth night can be spent at one of the lakes between Burnt Island and Source Lakes.

### Bissett Creek Route (Map 32/D4)
**Access/Parking:** The put-in for this route is located off Hwy 17. Park on the other side of the highway, off the side of the road. Alternatively, you can drive down Bissett Creek Road to a point where the road comes close to the creek and put-in there. A second vehicle can be parked at the Algonquin Park interior access point at Bissett Lake.

The Bissett Creek Route can be done in a day, although you would really have to travel quickly. If you are interested in making this a leisurely trip, it is recommended to take two days. The route is moderate in difficulty due to the unmarked and occasionally overgrown portage points along the route.

Beginning at Hwy 17, you will travel through private property for almost 4km. Please mind the rights of property owners. The first portage of the route lies quite a distance from the highway and can be found shortly after Black Creek dumps into Bissett Creek. Three short portages later, you will reach a logging road crossing. A small bridge crosses the creek at this point. If you are doing the trip in two days, this area is usually a good place to set up camp. Although there are no designated campsites along the creek, camping is permitted. Please practice no-trace camping to help preserve the natural state of the creek.

Fishing for brook trout is good throughout the route. If you enjoy fishing, there are many pools along the river that will entice you to wet a line. From the road crossing, it is over 6km to Big Bissett Lake. There are 4 portages along this stretch with two of them over 600m (1,970ft) in length. Once at Big Bissett, it is an easy paddle to the access point on the eastern shore.

### Bissett Lakes Route (Map 31/G6, 32/A6)
**Access/Parking:** The put-in for this Algonquin Park route is the Big Bissett Lake interior access point. Park permits can be picked up at Yate's Store, off Hwy 17 near Stonecliffe. Follow Bissett Creek Road off Hwy 17 to the access point on Big Bissett Lake. The road is rough in some sections and low clearance vehicles should proceed with caution.

The Bissett Lake route travels through a low use area and portages could be obstructed with deadfall. The moderate route is most frequently used during spring by fishing enthusiasts. It takes a full day to travel from Big Bissett Lake to Bissett Lake; therefore, it is recommended to stay the first night at Big Bissett.

At the south end of Big Bissett lies the Bissett Creek. The creek meanders through a marshy area before meeting the first portage. Shortly after the portage, there is an interior campsite on the south side of the creek. It's a good spot to stay at in spring or fall, otherwise the bugs can be annoying.

There are a total of nine portages along the creek. They are all generally easy, except for the first portage which travels 785m (2,575 ft) up a steep hill. At times, you will be walking more of the creek than paddling it. The creek will begin to open into more and more wetland. At this point you will soon find the 1,510m (4,950ft) portage to the North Bissett Creek. After this tough

portage, there is one more short portage to reach Bissett Lake. The lake is quite isolated and offers 4 superb campsites, including one island site.

Once at the lake you can take a day trip south into Little Weasel Lake. There is one 450m (1,480ft) portage en route and in summer, travel can be difficult due to low water conditions.

To return to Big Bissett Lake, retrace your route. For an alternative trip, head south towards Reed, Fitz and Gerald Lakes along Bissett Creek.

### Black Lake Loop (Map 2/F7)
**Access/Parking:** West off of Hwy 35 just south of Dorset, the Shoe Lake Access Road takes you directly to Shoe Lake where parking for about five vehicles is available.

This moderate, semi-wilderness route in the Leslie M. Frost Centre travels across a total of nine beautiful lakes and over 11 portages. The route passes a few cottages on Shoe Lake but civilization becomes scarce after a couple of portages. The total distance of the loop is about 34km with the longest portage being the 1,463m (4,800ft) trip from Raven Lake back to the parking area. Overall, most of the portages are generally short, although there are three that are over 1000m in length.

The loop can be done in two days and there are campsites scattered along the route. A number of great campsites are found on Black Lake, although there is a spot on Lower Pairo Lake that is one of the more beautiful places to stay. For bird enthusiasts, be sure to bring binoculars, as there are plenty of bird watching opportunities, especially through the wetland area closer to Wren Lake. Most of the lakes also offer fishing, with the predominant species being smallmouth and largemouth bass.

### Bonnechere River Route (Map 15/D1, 23/G7, 24/A7)
**Access/Parking:** The access point for this Algonquin interior trip is the Basin Lake access. Follow Basin Lake Road into the park past Little Norway Lake to the hydro line. Once at the hydro line the road turns south towards the river. The parking area is not far off the road. Permits can be acquired at Turner's Camp off Bonnechere Road. A second vehicle can be left at Turner's Camp or at Basin Lake.

Near the river, there is a campsite just off the road. This site is perfect if you arrive late in the afternoon. From the put-in, river travel is quite smooth for the first 5-6km. The first portage is very short and two scenic campsites are found off the river not far from there. About 5km after the campsites, much of the route involves portaging until you reach Basin Lake Road over 8km away. From the road, you can proceed to your vehicle (if you left it at Basin Lake), otherwise, a second night can be spent at a campsite on Basin Lake.

From Basin Lake, portage down the road back to the river. The route opens up from here and there are only a few short portages required before the river flows outside of the park and into Couchain Lake. The route from Couchain Lake to Turner's Camp is a much easier journey as it crosses over Curriers and Beaverdam Lakes.

The route is difficult due to the underused portages and the amount of river travel involved. There are also long portages, including one measuring around 6,400m (21,000ft) long, which is very physically demanding.

### Booth Lake Route (Map 14/B2)
**Access/Parking:** The put-in for this route is located at Algonquin Park's Shall Lake interior access point. Take Major Lake Road from Hwy 60 directly to the access. There is an Access Point Office on the Opeongo River at the put-in. Permits can be picked up here.

The Booth Lake Route is an easy 2-3 day trip. From the Opeongo River put-in, paddle up the river to Farm Lake. If you arrive late the first day, there are 4 interior campsites available at the lake.

The trip continues west towards Kitty Lake and past the Kitty Lake Cabin, which can be rented. The cabin is an old ranger cabin that is one of the oldest standing cabins in the park. Across from the cabin, a short portage takes you into Kitty Lake. At the west end of Kitty Lake, there is a portage around a small dam before you enter Booth Lake. There are 18 campsites on Booth Lake along with an excellent beach area on the eastern shore of the lake.

If you plan to spend some time on Booth Lake, you can travel into one of the nearby lakes for a day's exploration. In the early morning and late evenings, a trip down McCarthy Creek will often be rewarded with a moose sighting. Fishing opportunities are also available on Booth Lake and many of the lakes along this route. Return to the put-in along the same route used to access Booth Lake.

## Catfish Lake Loop (Map 22/A2, 21/F2)

**Access/Parking:** The Catfish Lake Loop is an Algonquin Park interior trip. The access point for this loop is the Cedar Lake-Brent access area. Interior camping permits can be obtained at the Access Point Office, at the turnoff to Wendigo Lake, before entering the park. There is a small campground located at the village of Brent as well as the Brent Store, where last minute supplies can be purchased.

The put-in for this moderately difficult trip is on the north shore of Cedar Lake. The first portage is found on the south side of Cedar Lake directly across from the put-in where the Petawawa River flows into the lake. Along the portage, there is a short side trail that leads to the river and a view of some gorgeous falls.

The river section requires portaging around two more sets of falls, including a challenging 2,345m (7,690ft) portage, as well as a short whitewater run. There are scenic campsites located at the end of the portages. A quick paddle across a pond takes you to a short portage into Narrowbag Lake. At the west end of Narrowbag Lake, there is a short portage that takes you into Catfish Lake, which is a perfect place to spend a few days. There are 13 campsites at the lake, including three picturesque island sites. A few lakes near Catfish Lake are within ideal day tripping distance. You can also check out the remains of an old steam tug found on one of the northern islands of the lake. The tug is called an alligator and had the ability to pull log booms across large bodies of water. Its amphibious name was indicative of its dual ability to travel on land. The machines were widely used in the late 1800's and early 1900's during log drives.

Other camping areas are found at Lynx or Luckless Lakes, which are accessible from the western side of Catfish Lake. A full day is required to complete the loop from either lake. Once at Luckless Lake, the longest portage of the trip awaits at the north end of the lake. The portage is a grueling 2,875m (9,430ft) to the Nipissing River. From the portage point, the Nipissing River flows over 8km down into Cedar Lake. There are two portages on this stretch of the river, one at 230m (750ft) and one at 915m (3,000ft).

## Cache Lake Loop (Map 12/G6, 13/A7)

**Access/Parking:** This Algonquin Park route starts from the Cache Lake interior access point, found off the south side of Hwy 60. Park interior camping permits can be aquired at the Canoe Lake Access Point Office.

Cache Lake is one of the busiest lakes in the park due to the number of cottages that lie along its shoreline and its close proximity to Hwy 60. Once you begin to travel further into the park, you will begin to feel a little more isolated. In the fall, the route is spectacular. The autumn colours make this trip a real pleasure. The route is a moderate loop that travels over generally short portages and across mainly small lakes. The trip can be completed comfortably in three days.

The first day travels from Cache Lake to Bonnechere Lake. This is the most physically demanding stretch of the route. There are nine portages and eight lakes you must cross before reaching Bonnechere Lake. The longest portage in this stretch is the 965m (3,170ft) portage from Delano Lake to South Canisbay Lake. If you wish to add an extra day to the trip, your first night can be spent at Hilliard or Delano Lake. There is a single site on both lakes offering some privacy from the bustle of Cache Lake. Bonnechere Lake also offers a number of secluded interior campsites.

At the north east corner of Bonnechere Lake, you will paddle through a narrows into a small pond before reaching the short portage into a creek. The shallow weedy creek leads to Phipps Lake. At the east side of this lake, there is a small waterfall that must be carried around before reaching Kirkwood Lake. If you don't mind a little extra work to get back to Cache Lake the next day, Kirkwood Lake makes a good second night choice. There are two exquisite sites on the lake, including a small island site in the middle of the lake. On the east end of Kirkwood, there is a portage that splits near the end leading to Lawrence and Paradee Lakes. Both lakes are ideal locations to camp for the second night. There are three sites to choose from on Lawrence Lake and two on Paradee Lake.

From Paradee Lake, there is a short portage into Harness Lake, which has 11 campsites, including five hiking campsites reserved for users of the Highland Backpacking Trail. Two 1,000+m (3,280 ft) portages and the crossing of Head Lake are all that remains of the route before concluding at Cache Lake.

## Canoe Lake Route (Map 12/C4)

**Access/Parking:** The Canoe Lake Route begins at the Canoe Lake interior access point off Hwy 60. Permits for interior camping can be picked up at the Canoe Lake Access Point Office.

Canoe Lake has long been the most popular access into Algonquin Park's interior. The main reason is due to the many short portages that offer quick access to the interior. The lake's close proximity to Hwy 60 also increases the traffic flow. The canoe traffic on the stretch from Canoe Lake north through Joe and Tepee Lakes is so popular it has been nicknamed 'Yonge Street' (the main street of downtown Toronto). This easy route can be completed in three days, although allowing four days can help reduce your progress rate to a more leisurely pace.

Beginning at Canoe Lake, it is about a 4km paddle north to the first short portage around the Joe Lake Dam. Before you proceed to the portage. Be sure to check out the cairn to Tom Thompson on the north west point of the lake. Thompson was a member Canada's reveled 'group of seven' painters, one of the country's most celebrated artists. He is most famous for his Algonquin paintings and in 1877 his drowned body was found on Canoe Lake. To this day, it is unclear of the actual cause of his death.

From the Joe Lake Dam portage, a short paddle north under the old railway bridge leads into Joe Lake. Stay to the left of Joe Island and proceed to Tepee Lake. From Tepee Lake, there are no portages en route to Littledoe and Tom Thompson Lake, which both offer scenic campsites for your first night. If preferred, you can travel north to the smaller Bartlett Lake for the night. There are 13 interior campsites on Littledoe Lake, 18 on Tom Thompson Lake and another four sites on Bartlett Lake. Most of the sites are spacious, although remember that this is one of the busiest routes in the park.

The next day takes you from Bartlett Lake to Burnt Island Lake via Sunbeam Lake. From Bartlett to Sunbeam there are four easy portages, with the longest being 470m (1,540ft). If you plan on staying an extra day on the route, Sunbeam Lake has seven interior sites to choose from. The trip from Sunbeam Lake to Burnt Island Lake involves four more portages over some hilly terrain, with the last one being the longest at 680m (2,230ft).

Burnt Island Lake is a large lake and winds can sometimes play havoc with your paddling progress. Nonetheless, Burnt Island Lake makes a popular last night stop with 56 well spaced interior campsites. The lake can be full of campers some nights and the only telltale sign of life are the lanterns and cooking flames in the night. The portage out of Burnt Island Lake is found at the most southerly tip of the lake. There is a short portage around a dam and into Baby Joe Lake. From Baby Joe there are two easy portages to the east arm of Joe Lake before the return back to Canoe Lake.

## Conroy Marsh Route (Map6/G5, 7/A5)

**Access/Parking:** The access to this route is found at McKeek Lake on McPhees Bay. Off Hwy 515 there is an access road found about 4.5km north of the village of Jewellville. Parking is available at the access point.

The Conroy Marsh is a vast wetland that is truly a wonderful place. The marsh has played a number of roles in history, from a great provider to natives, to a transportation line for the early log drives. Today, the marsh is wetland habitat for waterfowl and other birds, including the great blue heron. Walleye used to abound in the marsh, although increased human pressure has reduced the fish species to a rarity.

From the access area on McKeek Lake, paddle into the York River past the mouth of the Madawaska River. From McKeek Lake, the York River is a meandering waterbody that slowly opens into the wetland. You can paddle for hours in the marsh, exploring the many bays and inlets. The route is quite easy and a relaxing day trip.

## Dickson Lake /Lake Lavieille Route (Map 13/E1, 22/A7, 23/A7)

**Access/Parking:** This Algonquin Park route begins at the Opeongo Lake interior access point. The access is found at the end of Opeongo Lake Road, off Hwy 60. Park permits can be acquired at the lake.

The Dickson Lake/Lake Lavieille Route is a difficult route due to a challenging portage and the large size of the lakes that are traveled. Beginning at the access point at the southern tip of Opeongo Lake, it is a full day's paddle to the first portage of the trip. Many visitors prefer to take an Opeongo Water Taxi, which is inexpensive and will get you to the portage point in about 25min. Be sure to reserve the taxi ahead of your trip date. If you choose to paddle, there are 17 campsites on Opeongo's East Arm where you can spend your first night. The first portage is a short one that takes you to Wright Lake. There is one pretty campsite found on the lake that makes a good overnight spot if you can work it into your itinerary.

A short portage from Wright Lake's east side takes you to Bonfield Lake. The next portage is a back breaking 5,305m (17,400ft) and never seems to end. However, you are rewarded with the beautiful Dickson Lake and Lake Lavieille. At the north end of Dickson, there is a short portage into Hardy Bay of Lake

Lavieille. You can literally spend days exploring the many bays and inlets along the lakes' shore. One particular site of interest is an old growth stand of Red Pine trees found on the north eastern shore of Dickson Lake. The giant red pines are over 340 years old and are quite impressive.

There are 12 interior campsites on Dickson Lake and 24 on Lake Lavieille. All sites are well secluded and there are a number of great island campsites on both lakes. Dickson Lake and Lake Lavieille are also popular destinations in spring for trout seekers. The large lakes hold good size lake and brook trout. To return to the access point, follow the same route back to Opeongo Lake. If you take the water taxi, be sure to return to Opeongo Lake in time for your pick up. The taxis do not wait for stragglers. For water taxi reservations call Opeongo Algonquin (613) 637-2075 or Opeongo Outfitters (613) 637-5470.

### Dividing Lake Provincial Park Route (Maps 3/F2)
**Access/Parking:** There are two access points to this route. For the first access, follow Kawagama Road to its end where a parking lot is available. The other access starts on Kawagama Road. At the second junction, turn right and follow it for about 23.5km to the road to Livingstone Lake Lodge. Parking is available off the road shortly after the lodge. Algonquin Park passes are required.

The Rockaway Lake route is a difficult trip due mainly to the extensive portage from Kimball Lake to Rockaway Lake. The portage is a grueling 2750m (4.3mi) that traverses through a soggy wetland area and then over some steep terrain. During high water levels Kimball Creek can sometimes be traveled a short distance to reduce the length of the portage, although even then the portage is still over 2250m.

Kawagama Lake can also offer problems to travel if winds are strong. The lake is quite large and can be unforgiving during periods of high wind. One of the rewards for this challenging trip are the campsites at the north end of Rockaway Lake. They are set amid a stand of ancient white pines, which are over two hundred years old and the last of their kind in Southern Ontario.

For the even more adventurous, you can continue onto Minkey Lake and then to Dividing Lake in the Algonquin interior. All the lakes in this route offer fishing, with fair to good brook trout fishing at both Rockaway Lake and Dividing Lake.

### Erables/Maple Lake Loop (Map 20/G1, 21/B1, 29/G7, 30/A7)
**Access/Parking:** The Algonquin Park Kioshkokwi Lake-Kiosk interior access point is the put-in for this canoe route. Permits for interior camping can be acquired at the Kiosk park office.

Kioshkokwi Lake is a large lake that can be challenging to paddle on windy days. Unlike most of the park's lakes, Kioshkokwi Lake continues to hold a native name. The lake's name is derived from native Algonkin meaning 'lake of many gulls'. This moderately difficult three day route begins at the put-in on Kioshkokwi Lake near the Kiosk campground.

From the put-in, paddle to the southeast corner of the lake. The lake narrows to a creek mouth where there is a 730m (2,390ft) portage from Kioshkokwi Lake to Little Mink Lake. After a short paddle across Little Mink, a 450m (1,480ft) portage takes you to Mink Lake, a long and narrow lake. The 1,190m (3,900ft) portage from this lake is found at the southeast corner of the lake, where it passes into a weedy narrows on Club Lake. Paddle through the narrows, to the southern half of the lake where two interior campsites can be found. Your first night can be spent on Club Lake or on Mouse Lake to the south. A 640m (2,100ft) portage separates the two lakes. There are six campsites available on Mouse Lake, all offering a scenic lakefront view.

The next day begins with a challenging 1,700m (5,580ft) portage over hilly terrain, which leads to Mink Creek. After a short paddle and portage you'll find Big Thunder Lake. The lake is small and only has one campsite, leaving the lake all to yourself. The 1,645m (5,400ft) portage out of Big Thunder Lake is also difficult due to the hilly terrain. At the end of the trek, you will be at the southern arm of Erables Lake.

The second night of the trip can be spent here or to the north on Maple Lake, the English cousin of Erables Lake. The lakes are referred to as cousins as the word 'erables' is French for Maple. Both Lakes are separated by a short 80m (260ft) portage and offer prime interior campsites as well as island campsites.

The last leg of the trip heads back to Kioshkokwi Lake via Maple Creek. From Maple Lake, the creek travels about 5.5km to Kioshkokwi Lake. There are six portages along the route averaging 437m (1,430ft) in length with the longest being 805m.

### Grants Creek Canoe Route (Map 32/G4, 33/A3)
**Access/Parking:** The access point to this route is found off Hwy 17, about 3km west of the village of Stonecliffe. Parking is available off the highway on one of the nearby bush roads. Be wary of private property and obey any land use signs.

This four day route is not maintained, although it is used throughout the year. The route is quite rustic due to overgrowth on the creek and portages may be hard to find or non-existent. Overall, the route is rated difficult.

From the put-in on Grants Creek, the route travels over Longslide and Spencers Lakes. Shortly after Spencers Lake, the creek widens into a marsh, providing a leisurely pace. However, the flow of the creek soon begins to pick up. It is necessary to portage or line your canoe along the creek in a number of locations. This lasts for about 5km or until you reach the first bridge, which must be portaged around.

About 3km upstream lies Pooh Lake. It is believed the lake was named after the famous Canadian cartoon bear, Winnie the Pooh. Your first night can be spent on Pooh Lake or on Tigger Lake, just to the west of Pooh Lake. There is a short carry over from Pooh to Tigger Lake (pronounced tig-ger after Winnie's favorite friend). There are no designated campsites on either lake so be sure to practice low impact camping.

Downstream from Tigger Lake lies Puffball Lake. From Puffball Lake, Grants creek travels about 2km before there is a tributary off the creek that leads to Chateau Lake. Along this 2km stretch there are a number of places where lining your canoe or a portage is necessary. An old logging road crosses Grants Creek just before the tributary to Chateau Lake. Watch for the bridge.

Chateau Lake's southern tip lies within the boundary of Algonquin Provincial Park, although no park permits are required to camp on the lake. Chateau Lake is a hidden gem. The lake is secluded and it offers a perfect outdoor setting to spend a few days.

You must retrace your route to return to the access point.

### Grants Creek/Mackey Creek Canoe Route (Map 32/G4, 33/D5)
**Access/Parking:** The access point is the same as Grants Creek Canoe Route. A second vehicle can be left at Driftwood Provincial Park or off one of the bush roads that crosses close to Mackey Creek.

This two day route travels in a loop from the put-in on Hwy 17 to Driftwood Provincial Park on Holden Lake. The rustic route is difficult due to overgrowth on the creek and on many of the portages, which may be hard to find or non-existent. The route used to be maintained by the Ministry of Natural Resources, although cutbacks stopped the program many years ago.

Beginning at the put-in, it is about a 2km upstream paddle through Longslide and Spencers Lake before entering Grants Creek Marsh. It is approximately 5km from the marsh to the creek that leads to Mary's Lake. If you come to a logging road bridge, you've gone too far. This creek is small, although you should be able to paddle upstream, especially during spring. The stream travels under a logging road about 0.5km from Grants Creek. Portage over the road and into the small pond on the other side. On the far shore, there is about a 400m rustic portage to Mary's Lake. The portage is not marked and can be difficult to find.

From the eastern corner of Mary's Lake there is another rustic portage that travels about 1,700m (5,580ft) to Eeyore Lake. Mackey Creek flows out of Eeyore Lake's eastern side. Follow the creek downstream to Sweezy Lake. You can camp on the shore or travel a little further downstream to McKenna Lake. Both lakes offer good brook trout fishing and superb scenery. Mackey Creek can be picked up again from McKenna Lake's eastern shore. It is about a 1km paddle to the next lake in the chain, Dunlop Lake. The stream travels about 3.75km from Dunlop Lake to a logging road crossing. Your second vehicle can be picked up here.

If you wish, the route can continue to Driftwood Provincial Park. It is about 5km to the open water of the Ottawa River system and from there approximately 9km to the Driftwood take-out on Holden Lake. Be sure to practice low impact camping to help preserve this natural area.

### Greenleaf Lake Route (Map 24/C5)
**Access/Parking:** The Greenleaf Lake Route lies within Algonquin Park. Park permits can be purchased at the Sand Lake Gate. The put-in and parking area is found at Algonquin Park's Grand Lake-Achray interior access point.

This moderate four day route travels across a number of small interior lakes en route to Greenleaf Lake. Beginning at Grand Lake, paddle south towards Carcajou Bay. Here you will find a little Canadian history. The beautiful Carcajou Bay was the backdrop of the famous 'Jack Pine' painting by the Group of Seven painter, Tom Thompson. The jack pine that Tom sketched in 1916 stood until the late 1970's. The fallen pine was later used as firewood by a group of campers.

If you wish to spend the night here, there are four wilderness campsites on the shore of the bay. From Carcajou Bay, you will travel over Lower Spectacle, Upper Spectacle and Little Carcajou Lakes before reaching Wenda Lake.

Secluded interior campsites are available on all four lakes or if you reserve ahead, the Wenda Lake ranger cabin makes a great place to spend the night.

The remainder of the trip involves numerous short portages and onelarge portage into Greenleaf Lake. Due to changing water levels between Wenda and Carcajou Lakes, the portage distances change throughout the year. Therefore, portage distances may vary from those marked on our maps. Three secluded campsites and impressive cliffs bank Greenleaf Lake, making the portages worth while. The rare Algonquin Wood Fern can befound on the cliffs.

The route returns the same way to Carcajou Bay. The word 'Carcajou' is a native derivation for wolverine. Despite the name, there are no records indicating the presence of the wolverine in Algonquin. Fishing opportunities are available on Carcajou and Greenleaf Lakes.

## Gun Lake Route (Map 3/A7)
**Access/Parking:** Take Kawagama Road off Hwy 35 and continue right at the first junction and take another right at the next fork in the road. Just past Minden Bay, turn right again to the Herb Lake access and parking area. A second vehicle can be left at the Raven Lake access point found off the road, just before the Herb Lake access road. Alternatively, you can walk the 2km back to the vehicle from Raven Lake.

Located in the beautiful Leslie M. Frost Centre this route is an easy 1-2 day trip. From Herb Lake you can travel to the more remote and often less busy, Gun Lake. Both lakes offer a great spot for weekend camping or a base for further exploration of the surrounding area.

From Gun Lake, it is a short portage to Raven Lake and on to the take-out point. Berry pickers will find an abundance of blueberries along the shorelines of all three lakes. To access Gun Lake there are only twoshort portages with the longest being a mere 170m. Fishing is offered on all the lakes along the route with the predominant species being smallmouth bass.

## Hogan Lake/Lake La Muir Route (Map 13/C1, 21/G5, 22/B6)
**Access/Parking:** The access to this Algonquin Park interior route is the Opeongo access point. The road to the access can be found off the north side of Hwy 60, just west of the Algonquin Visitor Centre Road. Permits for interior camping can be picked up at the Access Point Office on Opeongo Lake. An outfitting store is also located at the lake.

This moderate Algonquin interior trip takes 4-5 days to complete, although it is recommended to allow one or two extra days so you can explore some of the surrounding lakes. The route is not very busy during the year and can be traveled in three days if you choose to take the Opeongo Water Taxi to the Proulx Lake portage. Opeongo Lake is a big lake that demands a challenging paddle from even the most experienced canoeists.

Once at the Proulx Lake portage, it is about a 1,450m (4,760ft) carry to the lake. The portage can be shortened, somewhat, by paddling the small pond found shortly up the trail. However, this probably won't save you much time.

At the north end of Proulx Lake, there is a creek that leads north to Little Crow Lake. The 3.5km creek is quite marshy, making it a good area to spot moose. Big Crow Lake is found via a passage off Little Crow's east side. Both lakes offer prime interior campsites that are well spaced and maintained. There are 10 sites on Big Crow and three sites on Little Crow. There is also an old ranger cabin on Big Crow Lake's southeast shore. The cabin is available for rent. A trail behind the cabin leads to an old decommissioned firetower.

The Crow River flows out of Big Crow Lake from its eastern shore, where another trail can be explored. The trail is about 2.5km return and passes through a stand of virgin White Pine. The old growth trees are awe inspiring and stand over 35m (110ft) high.

At Big Crow's northern point lies a 3,750m (12,300ft) portage to Hogan Lake. Hogan Lake is the largest lake on the route and offers 10 wilderness campsites to choose from. Lake La Muir can be found via the Little Madawaska River that flows into Hogan Lake's southwest side. Moose often frequent the banks of the river. It is about 3.5km to the lake including a 685m (2,250ft) portage. Lake La Muir offers eight interior camping sites with two of them situated on a large island.

To return to Opeongo Lake, retrace your route back to the Proulx Lake portage. Be sure to be on time for your water taxi! For water taxi reservations call Opeongo Algonquin (613) 637-2075 or Opeongo Outfitters (613) 637-5470.

## Hurdman Lake Route (Map 30/E6)
**Access/Parking:** Brain Lake, in the northern end of Algonquin Park, is the starting point for this route. Park permits for interior camping can be picked up at the Cat's Lair Store, about 11km west of Mattawa. The road to Brain Lake is rough.

If you arrive late in the day, Brain Lake is an ideal spot for your first night. There are three campsites at the lake, with two of them on scenic islands.

The route is moderate in difficulty because of low use portages. Allow two days, although it is recommended to take at least three days so you can move at a more leisurely pace. The lake sees most of its visitors in spring shortly after trout season opens.

The route follows the Hurdman Creek all the way to Hurdman Lake. From Brain Lake to Stretch Lake, four portages cover over 1km of the 2.7km distance. From Stretch Lake there is a 300m (980ft) portage into West Corbeau Lake. You can plan to spend a night at Stretch or West Corbeau Lake. Each lake has a rustic campsite. Hurdman Lake can be found about 1.6km from West Corbeau Lake. There are three short portages along the Hurdman Creek before the lake. Hurdman Lake is a long, slim lake that measures nearly 3km in length and about 250m at its widest point. There are tworustic campsites on the lakes' northeastern shore. The return trip is via the same route.

## Madawaska Lake Route (Map 4/F3)
**Access/Parking:** From Hwy 127, north of the town of Bancroft take the McRae-Hay Lake Road to the public boat launch area where access and parking is available. Algonquin Park permits can be obtained from the East Gate.

This moderate route is a good trip for wilderness solitude since it does not see high use compared to some of the routes closer to the Hwy 60 corridor. From the Hay Lake access point, travel west to the Cauliflower Lake portage and on to Cauliflower Lake. From Cauliflower Lake the route travels down Cauliflower Creek. During spring, the creek is easier to travel compared to late summer, when water levels in some areas become quite low. There are a few portages along the creek, with the longest one being the 1440m (4,720ft) trip across the hydro line area to the South Madawaska River.

The South Madawaska River meanders through wetland areas all the way to Madawaska Lake, providing an excellent opportunity for bird watching and a chance to see an Algonquin Park moose. At Madawaska Lake, four beautiful camping sites are marked and easy to find. Once camp has been established, you can increase your chances of catching a glimpse of a moose by taking an early morning trip down the river. Fishing along this route is one of the main attractions for canoeists in the spring.

## Manitou Lake Loop (Map 20/2C)
**Access/Parking:** The access point to this Algonquin Park interior canoe loop is Kawawaymog Lake. The access and parking area can be found at the end of Chemical Road, from the town of South River.

The Manitou Lake Loop is a moderate 4-5 day trip that begins on the west shore of Kawawaymog Lake. The Amable du Fond River can be picked up at the east side of the lake and travels into North Tea Lake. North Tea Lake once went by the native name, 'Waskigomog Lake'. It is one of the biggest lakes in the park and is a popular access point into the west side of the park. There are over 70 rustic campsites found on the lake along with many island sites, which provide you with the privacy of your own island retreat. If you plan to arrive late the first day, North Tea Lake makes a good first night camping location.

The first portage of the trip is located on the north east shore of North Tea Lake just east of Lorne Creek. The portage is 1,920m (6,300ft) to Lorne Lake. There are six interior camping sites on Lorne Lake, including oneprivate island site available to the first lucky campers. From Lorne Lake it is a 1,535m (5,040ft) portage to Kakasamic Lake. 'Kakasamic' is the native Algonquin word for roast beaver or beaver jerky.

Two portages (455m and 200m) and a short paddle separate Kakasamic and Mattowacka Lakes. Both lakes make good second night camping spots, with three rustic campsites on each lake. If you think you can make it all the way to Fassett Lake on your second day, there are five secluded campsites available. The extra work into Fassett will save you from doing the 1,620m (5,310ft) portage the next morning. On Fassett Lake's northern shore there is a 1,025m (3,360ft) portage into the smaller Shada Lake. The Fassett Creek can be found from Shada Lake's eastern side, which travels down towards Manitou Lake.

En route to Manitou Lake there are three short portages and onechallenging portage measuring 1,325m (4,350ft). Manitou Lake is another large Algonquin Park lake and winds can play havoc with your rate of progress. There are about 50 interior campsites, including a number of great island sites. If you have time to do some exploring, paddle up to the north end of the lake to check out the clearing and remains of the old Dufond Farm. The Dufond family cleared the area in the early 1880's and lived there until 1916.

The last leg of the trip is the paddle down Manitou Lake and North Tea Lake. A short 410m (1,340ft) portage separates the two lakes. It is best to spend your last night at the south end of Manitou Lake or on North Tea Lake in order to limit your last day battle with potentially high winds. Another way to tackle the wind is to paddle in the early morning or at dusk.

## Misty Lake Route (Map 11/G3, 12/A1)

**Access/Parking:** The Misty Lake Route is an Algonquin Provincial Park interior canoe trip. The starting point for the route is located at the Rain Lake interior access point, at the end of Rain Lake Road. Park permits can be picked up at the park office in the Kearney Community Centre.

The Rain Lake access point is a popular area due to the easy access to numerous canoeing possibilities and the Western Uplands Backpacking Trail. There is a small campground at the access point along with 17 rustic canoe access sites on Rain Lake. From Rain Lake, the route travels to Misty Lake via several small interior lakes. Allow three days to enjoy this easy route.

The first portage is found at Rain Lake's north eastern side. The portage travels 310m (1,020ft) to Sawyer Lake. If you plan to arrive mid-day, Sawyer makes a good first night spot. There are six interior campsites found on this scenic lake. From Sawyer Lake it is a 550m (1,800ft) portage into Jubilee Lake and from there a 450m (1,480ft) portage takes you into the small, Juan Lake. After a short portage and paddle from Juan Lake you will find Moccasin Lake.

Moccasin Lake is shaped somewhat like a moccasin, the footwear common to North American Indians. A 440m (1,440ft) portage takes you to Bandit Lake. A 'bandit' was the nickname of rangers who cleared park portages.

From Bandit Lake it is a 540m (1,770ft) portage to Wenona Lake and then a 370m (1,210ft) portage to Muslim Lake. The portage between Muslim Lake and Misty Lake is the longest of the trip at only 1,030m (3,380ft). Misty Lake is a long picturesque lake with numerous inlets and bays to explore. If you plan to spend a few days on one of the 19 wilderness campsites, there are a number of lakes that can be visited in one or two portages from Misty Lake.

You can follow the same access route back to Rain Lake or alternatively, plan a longer loop trip. There are several loop trip possibilities from Misty Lake.

## Nipissing River Route
### (Map 19/G4, 20/G4, 21/E2, 22/A1, 29/F7, 30/D7)

**Access/Parking:** There are a few different access points that can be used to begin this route. The main access is the Kawawaymog Lake interior access point. The access point can be found on Kawawaymog Lake, at the end of Chemical Road from South River.

The Nipissing River travels through Algonquin Park from Big Bob Lake on the park's western side all the way to Cedar Lake on the park's north side. The river was once used as a transportation vein for the early log drives inside the park. Remnants of this era can still be found along the shoreline to this day. The Nipissing is now a remote river that meanders through the park, with several whitewater sections that can be portaged around. This route is a moderate to difficult eight day trip due to the distance traveled and the many portages.

Day one includes a long paddle east on North Tea Lake to Mangotasi Lake. two portages travel to and from the small Hornbeam Lake into Biggar Lake, where 21 wilderness campsites can be found. From Biggar Lake, you must travel up the Loughrin Creek to Lawren Harris Lake. En route to the lake there are two portages. The first being somewhat steep and 2,010m (6,590ft). The other is 640m (2,100ft). Lawren Harris Lake is named after Lawren Harris, who was one of the original members of the 'Group of Seven' Canadian artists.

There is a short portage south into Loughrin Lake and then a 495m (1,620ft) portage to Barred Owl Lake. A short carry over takes you to Nod Lake, the Nipissing River can be found south of there at the end of a challenging 1,950m (6,400ft) portage. If you plan ahead, you can take a different route from Nod Lake through Gibson Lake and then down to the Nipissing. The advantage of this route is that you can spend the next night at the Highview Cabin, which is found off the portage to the Nipissing. Otherwise, your second night can be spent on Loughrin, Barred Owl or Nod Lake. Each of the small lakes offers a rustic campsite in a remote setting.

The next day involves travel solely on the Nipissing River. From your river put-in, you will travel all the way to High Falls. There are a few campsites along the route, however, the High Falls makes an ideal overnight setting. The river along this stretch meanders through a sleepy forested setting until it meets the Allen Rapids. The rapids can be avoided via a 2,715m (8,910ft) portage. From the Allen Rapids to the High Falls, it is over 9km down the Nipissing interrupted by three portages (495m, 365m and 1,300m). The last portage travels around the picturesque High Falls. Be alert for the last portage, as it

can be easily missed. The High Falls is a series of cascading ledges and are a natural treasure of the park's interior.

The following day will take you through a marshy, meandering stretch of the Nipissing River. En route to Cedar Lake, the river travels over 25km and six portages, which skirt four different dams and one whitewater section. Keep your eyes open for moose.

Once at Cedar Lake you can make camp at one of the many sites available on the lake. If you like, you can also visit the Brent Store on the north shore of the lake. From the eastside of Cedar Lake, Little Cedar and Aura Lee Lakes can be reached. Two short portages (275m and 130m) are found between Cedar and Little Cauchon Lake. Another 440m portage links Cauchon and Mink Lake.

Mink Lake has 11 campsites lining its north shore near an old railway bed. Can you imagine the Algonquin experience rattled by a steel clad train rolling down the tracks every few hours? This was reality until November 15, 1995, when the last train finally passed through the park.

The second last day is a journey from Mink to Manitou Lake via Kioshkokwi Lake. There are two portages (450m and 730m) between Mink and Kioshkokwi Lakes then another three (275m, 485 and 200m) between Kioskokwi and Manitou Lakes. The last night of your trip can be spent on Manitou Lake. A number of beach areas along the shore make an ideal spot for an evening dip. There are also several campsites located on islands.

The last day involves a short portage to North Tea Lake and the long paddle to the access point. Wind can be a major hindrance to travel on these last three lakes. Be sure to take advantage of low wind conditions whenever possible.

## Oxtongue River Route (Map 2, 3, 12)

**Access/Parking:** Off of Hwy 60 in Algonquin Provincial Park a short road takes you to the north end of Smoke Lake and the access point and parking area. For the river only route to Lake Of Bays, access is provided at Oxtongue Provincial Park.

From Smoke Lake, travel west to Tea Lake to access the mouth of the Oxtongue River. The river meanders slowly at times, although there are a few areas where some rapids speed up the flow and heighten the excitement of the trip. The river parallels Hwy 60 until the portage to Park Lake, which crosses the highway at the west entrance to the park. From the portage point you can travel in a loop back to Smoke Lake or continue down the Oxtongue River past Oxtongue Lake and on to Lake Of Bays.

There are a few short portage points along the river before the Hwy 60 crossing that are well marked and maintained. There are a number of portages along the loop back to Smoke Lake which are more rustic, although still easy to find. The longest portage is a grueling 2400m trip from Norman Lake to the south end of Smoke Lake. The loop is moderate in difficulty and takes at least two days to complete with campsites scattered along the river and on a few of the lakes along the loop.

If you choose to continue along the Oxtongue River to Lake Of Bays, be alert at all times for fast water and potential hazards. A portion of the river is classified as grade III-IV whitewater, which is difficult and can be treacherous if unprepared, especially in spring.

## North Depot Lake Route (Map 31/F6)

**Access/Parking:** The North Depot Lake Route is an Algonquin Park interior canoe trip. The access point and parking area can be found at Wendigo Lake on the northern side of the park. Interior camping permits can be acquired from the Access Point Office at the turn off towards Wendigo Lake.

This lake route is a short, easy 2-3 day trip that can be done in one day. The route is popular in spring after trout season opens. During summer, when lake and brook trout are more difficult to catch, canoe traffic on the route slows considerably. For anglers looking for seclusion, the best time to travel this route is in late September when the trout begin to bite again.

From the access point on Wendigo Lake, paddle to Wendigo's southern most tip to the first portage. The portage is an easy 180m (590ft) traverse to Allan Lake. If you plan to spend some time on Allen Lake there are nine interior campsites including a very nice island site. At the southern tip of Allen Lake lies the portage into North Depot Lake. The 255m (840ft) portage travels around a set of rapids found on a small stretch of the North River. North Depot Lake is a long lake that is part of the North River system. There are nine well spaced campsites on the lake, with three of the sites lying on an island. Travel via the same access route to get back to Wendigo Lake.

## Pinetree Lake Route (Map 13/F6)

**Access/Parking:** Both the Sunday Creek and the Pinetree Lake access points provide access to this canoe route. By beginning at the Pinetree access, you can shorten the route by a day. Our description begins at Sunday Creek. This access is found off Hwy 60 about 0.5km west of the Algonquin Visitor Centre Road. Park your first vehicle at the Spruce Bog Boardwalk Trail entrance. A second vehicle can be left at the Galeairy Lake public boat launch in the town of Whitney. Purchase your interior camping permits at the East Gate.

This route is an ideal weekend trip since it is not frequently used due to its short length and the need for a second vehicle. A second vehicle is not needed if you retrace your route back to the put-in. The put-in for this moderate route is Sunday Creek, just before it crosses under the highway. The creek meanders through a wetland habitat and into Norway Lake. A short paddle south of Norway Lake lies Fork Lake. Each lake has two interior camping sites. In spring, the marshy habitat of the lakes provide an ideal viewing area for moose.

The first portage of the next day is a large one at 1,550m (5,080ft), which can be muddy. The portage takes you to the small Rose Lake where a 915m (3,000ft) portage to Pinetree Lake waits on the other side of the lake. Your second night can be spent on one of three rustic campsites on Pinetree Lake. The last leg of the trip begins with a gruelling 1,825m (6.000ft) portage into Fraser Lake, where a single campsite is available.

From Fraser Lake, there are two portages (860m and 220m) and a short paddle to access David Thompson Lake. The lake is named after David Thompson who was a renowned Canadian mapmaker who once explored this part of the park for a possible canal route from Ottawa to Georgian Bay. A 1,580m (5,180ft) portage from the lake takes you to Galeairy Lake. The take-out is about a 5km paddle from the portage.

## Red Pine Lake Loop (Maps 3/C7)

**Access/Parking:** Access and parking is available for a small fee at the marina on Big Hawk Lake off Big Hawk Lake Road.

This easy loop is set amid the Leslie M. Frost Centre property and covers over 19km and four different lakes, including Big Hawk, Nunikani, Red Pine and Clear Lakes. There are four portages along the route with the longest being 440m from Nunikani Lake to Red Pine Lake. During high water this portage can sometimes be reduced to about 30m.

Many of the lakes do have cottages on them, although secluded Nunikani Lake is quit scenic. There are campsites on both Nunikani and Red Pine Lakes can be used as a base for exploration into some of the other ponds and lakes close by. For fishing enthusiasts, there is fair to good fishing on all the lakes in the loop. If you enjoy island camping, Red Pine Lake has a few nice spots to choose from.

## Rosebary/Longbow Lake Route (Map 11/C1, 20/F7)

**Access/Parking:** The put-in for this Algonquin interior trip is the Tim River access point. To find the access point, take the Forestry Tower Road from the village of Kearney and follow the signs to the access area. Park permits can be acquired at the Park Office in the Kearney Community Centre.

The Rosebary/Longbow Lake Canoe Route is an easy 2-3 day trip. From the put-in on the Tim River, the route meanders into Tim Lake. There are six rustic campsites on the lake, with three of the sites located on the lake's only island.

If you arrive early enough at the put-in, you can travel all the way to Rosebary Lake in a day. The Tim River flows out of Tim Lake's northeastern side and offers a slow but relaxing paddle. There is only one portage on the river, which

is an easy 120m (390ft) trail around a set of falls. Rosebary Lake is a scenic Algonquin interior lake that is surrounded by a park nature reserve zone. These zones are restricted from logging and have a natural significance to the region.

Longbow Lake can be found through a narrows on Rosebary's southeast shore. The lakes are located close together and you can plan your itinerary to camp at either lake. If you plan to stay a few nights, you can take a day trip into Floating Heart Lake to the north or explore the Tim River further to the south.

The route is a popular trip throughout the year, especially with anglers in spring. To return to the access point follow your route back to Tim Lake.

## Sec Lake Trip (Map 25/C6)

**Access/Parking:** The access is located south of the Sand Lake Gate at the Sec Lake interior access point. Algonquin Park permits can be picked up at the Sand Lake Gate.

Sec Lake can be busy on long weekends during the summer, although during most of the year it is generally quiet. The access road leads right to Sec Lake, where 16 campsites are available. Sec Lake can be used as your base camp for further exploration of the area or you can do a short one day loop through Wet and Norm's Lakes. There is an 805m (2,640ft) portage into Wet Lake from Sec Lake that can be muddy in spring. There is also a wilderness campsite available on Wet Lake, near the portage to Norm's Lake.

The portage to Norm's Lake is 750m (2,460ft) and a 1,005m (3,300ft) portage takes you back to Sec Lake to complete the loop. Little Sec Lake and Log Canoe Lake can also be accessed from Sec Lake. The portage to Little Sec is 1,370m (4,490ft) and to Log Canoe it's 770m (2,530ft). Log Canoe Lake has a campsite. Overall, Sec Lake provides a great 2-3 day Algonquin experience.

## South River Paddling Trail (Map 19/G5, 20/A5)

**Access/Parking:** There are a few access points along this route with the main access point located near Algonquin's boundary. The bush road passes over the river near the confluence with Craig Creek. Your canoe can be put-in on the west side of the bridge. A second vehicle can be left down river at one of four other access areas off River Road.

The South River Paddling Trail is a historic canoe route. For centuries before the first settlers arrived, the river and the surrounding hillsides were the hunting grounds of Algonquin, Ojibway and Huron natives. The river was also one of Tom Thompson's favourite access points to the Algonquin Park. The river travels through the scenic Almaguin Highlands offering travelers beautiful scenery and the chance to experience the solitude of nature.

In spring, the higher water level of the river allows you to travel from the Algonquin put-in all the way to Forest Lake. In summer, low water levels pose problems for travel in a number of areas. Extra portaging or lining your canoe is often required. The route is currently under development; therefore, portages may not be marked along the route. Stay alert for any dangers such as sweepers, rocks or spring debris. The main portage areas along the river are the bridge crossing points, which are readily noticeable. Otherwise, in spring much of the river involves moderately challenging travel with little portaging.

## Tim River Route (Map 11/G1, 12/A1, 20/E1, 21/B7)

**Access/Parking:** The access point for this Algonquin Park interior trip is the Tim River near Tim Lake. Interior camping permits can be picked up a the park office in the Kearney Community Centre.

The Tim River Route is moderately difficult and can be traveled a few different ways. You can start at Magnetawan Lake and make your through Little Trout Lake to the river. Our route begins on the river outside the park near Tim Lake.

If you arrive late the first day you can stay on Tim Lake. Otherwise, continue down the Tim River to Rosebary Lake, which offers six campsites. There is only one short portage along this stretch. In spring, the water level is usually high enough for unimpeded travel, although in summer the river can be quite low. Be sure to call ahead before your trip.

The Tim River flows out of Rosebary's south side over a small dam. A short portage takes you around the dam. For anglers, the river is a prime brook trout spot. The meandering river has numerous log jams and deep pools that hold brookies. The river is also ideal for spotting moose. The odd canoeist has even been stopped by a big bull moose standing in the middle of the river.

From Rosebary Lake the river slowly winds rolls through the Algonquin wilds. Your second night can be spent at one of the river's three rustic campsites. It is recommended to stay at the last available site on the river in order to increase the distance you cover on the second day. There are four short portages (90m, 410m, 275m and 460m) before the last campsite.

About 6.5km from the last campsite you will find the portage to Stag Lake. The portage is a grueling 2,860m (9,380ft) to the small lake. After the short paddle across Stag Lake, there is another difficult 2,000m (6,560ft) portage to the beautiful Devine Lake. Devine Lake used to be referred to as 'Camp Lake' by poachers. Poachers would camp in the hollow on the lake's island, which would provide a natural cover, hiding them from park rangers. The current site on the lake's island makes a great place to spend your third night. You can also camp at Ranger or Stingman Lake, found west of Devine Lake.

On the fourth day of the trip you can travel all the way back to the access point, although you should start early. Alternatively you can spend another night on Rosebary Lake. To reach Rosebary from Devine Lake you will pass through Ranger, Stingman and Longbow Lakes, with five generally easy portages en route (415m, 510m, 120m, 700m and 300m). From Rosebary Lake it is an easy paddle back to the Tim River access point.

## Welcome Lake Loop (Map 4/D1, 13/D7)
**Access/Parking:** The access area is the Rock Lake interior access point, which is found on a road off the south side of Hwy 60, west of the visitor centre road. The put-in is located on the Madawaska River between Rock and Whitefish Lakes. Permits can be picked up at Rock Lake Campground.

This moderate 2-3 day Algonquin Park route is great for a weekend or long weekend trip, although it can also be busy during these times. For solitude searchers, the best time is during the week or in the fall. If you arrive late on the first day you can camp at Coon Lake or Rock Lake Campgrounds.

Beginning at the put-in on the Madawaska River, paddle onto Rock Lake. Rock Lake is a pretty lake with several cottages along its shoreline. The cottages and campground keep the lake active throughout the summer months. Be sure to check out the native pictographs on the lake's western shore. The paintings are faint, although you can make out the various shapes of animals.

Once at the southern tip of Rock Lake, there is a short 375m (1,230ft) portage around the Pen Lake Dam. If you wish to stay on Pen Lake there are 18 interior campsites available. For this route, the first day of paddling ends at Welcome Lake, which can be found via the Galipo River from Pen Lake's southwestern shore. Most of the river is not canoe worthy and requires a bit of portaging. The first portage travels around a pretty waterfall and is quite easy at 295m (970ft). The second portage is much more challenging at 2,170m (7,120ft).

Welcome Lake is a picturesque interior lake with a sandy beach and rocky outcropping. The long portage helps keep the lake from being overcrowded with summer trippers, however, in spring it is a popular fishing destination. There are six wilderness campsites on the lake. If you prefer, you can continue north along the Galipo River to Harry and Rence Lakes. A few campsites on Harry and Rence lie on beautiful granite points.

To complete the loop, you you follow a small stream from Rence Lake north to Frank Lake. There is one 320m (1,050ft) portage before the lake. Continue onto Florence Lake, where you have a choice of two different portages to Lake Louisa. A 1,725m portage or a 3,455m portage. The longer route will shorten your paddle considerably on Lake Louisa. If winds are heavy this could be an advantage. Otherwise, nobody enjoys carrying their gear an extra 1.7km!

Lake Louisa is one of the larger park lakes south of Hwy 60. The popular lake offers 23 interior campsites. The last portage of the trip is a grueling 2,895m (9,500ft) back to Rock Lake and the access area.

## Wilkins Lake Route (Map 14/G2, 15/B2)
**Access/Parking:** The access to this Algonquin Park interior canoe route can be found outside of the park on Aylen Lake. Interior camping permits can be purchased from the Aylen Lake Marina, off Aylen Lake Road.

The Wilkins Lake Route is a moderate route with a number of challenging portages. The portages on the route are not regularly maintained and deadfall may hinder your progress. The trip takes 4-5 days and is seldom used. Seclusion is usually easy to find, especially after the spring trout fishing season.

Aylen Lake is a very large lake and it is a long paddle from the access point to the first portage. It is recommended to take a water taxi up the lake to the O'Neill Lake portage. The portage is 1,425m (4,670ft) to O'Neill Lake and then there is another 1,235m (4,050ft) portage into the park to Robitaille Lake. If you plan to camp on Robitaille Lake there are six wilderness campsites to choose from. The lake's northern shore is quite weedy and is a great area for moose spotting. From Robitaille Lake, it is a 695m (2,280ft) portage into the smaller Breezy Lake, where another campsite is available. A challenging 1,475m (4,840ft) portage takes you west to Wilkins Lake, a large lake with six well spaced and secluded campsites. Wilkins Lake can be reached in the first day of travel if you arrive at the O'Neill Lake portage early.

A 970m (3,180ft) portage leads to the Aylen River, a slow, meandering river. About 3km up river there are two portages (780m and 670m) before you reach Alsever Lake. There are seven rustic campsites at this lake with two sitting on a large point that juts out from the lake. If you plan to spend some time at Alsever Lake, Roundbush Lake to the north makes a good day trip.

To return to Aylen Lake access point, follow your route back out. To shorten your trip, a second vehicle can be left at the end of the cart trail from Wilkins Lake. The trail is about 3km from the lake to the park boundary.

## York River Route (Map 5/A7)
**Access/ Parking:** From Hwy 648 take Elephant Lake Road to Kingscote Lake Road. Follow the north branch just after Benoir Lake, to the Pine Grove Point Lodge, where park permits can be purchased and a second vehicle can be left. Go back to Kinscote Lake Road and follow it west to the Kinscote Lake Access point. If you are not going to use a two vehicle system, for a marginal fee an attendant at the lodge will give you a ride to the access point.

This moderate route is seldom used since the panhandle portion of Algonquin Park has never been very popular. The panhandle still offers good fishing and camping opportunities. From Kingscote Lake two portages will take you to Byers Lake and to the mouth of the York River. Camping is available at Byers Lake and there are a few sites along the York River, if you wish to divide the river trip over a few days. Brook trout fishing along the river is quite good in some areas. There are five short portages along the river, which has grade II-III whitewater sections. two of the portages avoid dams and one skirts around the magnificent High Falls.

# River Routes

Whitewater abounds in the Algonquin Region. For whitewater enthusiasts of Southern Ontario, the Algonquin Region offers some of the best whitewater rivers in the province and even the country! The Algonquin and Madawaska Highlands are responsible for this great collection of Ontario rivers. The rivers flow from the top of the watersheds down to the lowland valley areas producing amazing whitewater runs. The Madawaska and Opeongo Rivers are a good example of this phenomena. The rivers are renowned for their rolling runs and attract adventure seekers from as far as the Unites States. The Petawawa River is another good example and is perhaps one of the country's greatest whitewater rivers. The Petawawa River offers scenery, solitude and adventure all in one package. For those who are a little timid of rapids, several good novice rivers can be found in the region. Once you experience the thrill of whitewater, you'll be counting the days before you can run it again!

*We have used the International River Classification system to grade whitewater areas on rivers:*

**Grade I:** Novices in open canoes or kayaks. Riffles and small waves with virtually no obstructions.

**Grade II:** Intermediate paddlers. Manoeuvering is required. Medium rapids, channels can be clearly spotted without scouting.

**Grade III:** Advanced Paddlers. Rapids can swamp open canoes. Waves are unpredictable. Scouting should be done before approach. Skilled manoeuvering is required.

**Grade IV:** Expert paddlers, closed canoes & kayaks only. Long, challenging rapids with obstructions requiring manoeuvering. Eskimo roll ability is recommended. Good swimming skills. Scouting required.

**Grade V:** Professional Paddlers, closed canoes or kayaks only. Scouting always required. Long, violent rapids through narrow routes with obstructions. Eskimo roll ability essential. Errors can be fatal.

For detailed whitewater information on the Madawaska River and the Opeongo River, pick up a copy of the "Madawaska River and Opeongo River Whitewater Guide," published by the Friends of Algonquin Park.

*Please remember that river conditions are always subject to change and advanced scouting is essential. The information in this book is only intended to give you general information on the particular river you are interested in. You should always obtain more details from your local merchant or expert before heading out on your adventure.*

## Amable Du Fond River Route (Map 29/F4)

Access/Parking: The route begins at Kiosk within Algonquin Provincial Park. Parking is available at the access point and park permits must be obtained to leave your vehicle behind. A second vehicle can be left at Samuel De Champlain Provincial Park or the Eau Claire Gorge Conservation Area.

The Amable Du Fond River Route is currently undergoing further development. Although there are no portage markers along the river bank, there are 11 established portages along most of the needed sections. Therefore, you must be alert when approaching whitewater in order to spot the portages.

The route is moderate in difficulty, due to the grade II-III whitewater sections and rustic nature of the portages. It is about a 40km trip from Kiosk to Samuel De Champlain Provincial Park.

The river begins in the highlands of the park and slowly travels downward to the lowlands of the Mattawa River. It is recommended to allow at least 2 full days to complete this entire stretch. This route travels through mainly crown land, although does pass through private land sections. There are no organized campsites on the route, although no-trace camping is permitted. Fishing is good along the river for small trout.

## Big East River Route (Map 1, 2/A2)

Access/Parking: From Hwy 60 follow County Road 8 past Brooks Mill and travel north to Distress Dam. Access and parking is located at the dam area. A second vehicle can be parked at Arrowhead Provincial Park.

This moderate to difficult (grade II-III) whitewater route is not well used and portages are very difficult to locate. You may have to line or bushwhack a portage around some areas of the route depending on your experience. The route travels about 17km from the dam to Arrowhead Provincial Park and can be done in a full day. Wilderness camping is available along the route, although an actual site may be difficult to find. The route travels through some rapid areas including the McArthur Chute, a waterfall that must be portaged around. It is recommended to scout any areas that may be a problem before attempting to run any rapids. Overall, the route is a rustic and exciting experience.

## Hollow River Route (Map 3/C5)

Access/Parking: Follow Kawagama Road to the first fork and turn left to Russell Landing. Parking and access is available off the road. A second vehicle can be parked at Rabbit Bay, off Hwy 35 near Dorset or at any one of the public boat launch areas on Lake Of Bays.

The Hollow River Route is a moderate (grade II-III) whitewater route that is about 20km in length and can be done in a day. From Russell Landing travel north to the mouth of the Hollow River. You then follow the river past Dorset before heading north to Rabbit Bay and to the take-out point. There are 4 distinct sets of rapids along the river with the last 2 sets, The Hollow River Rapids, being the most difficult.

When traveling the river, it is recommended to scout any rapids or tricky areas to avoid potential problems. The route is user maintained only and portage points are not marked and may be difficult to locate. Based on your skill level, you may not need to portage around certain areas. For a longer trip, you can travel to one of the alternative access points on Lake Of Bays.

## Lower Madawaska River Route (Map 7/G6, 8/A7)

Access/Parking: There are three put-in and parking areas for the Lower Madawaska River Route. The first put-in can be found just west of the village of Jewelville. Follow Palmer Rapids Dam Road, off Hwy 515 to the Ministry of Natural Resources access point and parking area. The other put-ins can be found down river, south of Erneas Creek at Aumond's Rapids and south of the village of Quadeville, off the Green Lake Forest Access Road.

There are two take-outs on the river. One is located at the end of Buck Bay Road between Quadeville and Griffith. The other take-out can be found 0.5km west of the town of Griffith, off Hwy 41. A two vehicle system must be used on this route.

The Madawaska River is one of Ontario's premier whitewater rivers. This great river offers over 40km of thrilling whitewater fun along with wonderful scenery as it flows through farmland, wetland and scenic forests. It is difficult to rate the entire river as one particular grade but overall the Lower Madawaska is rated a grade II, with grade III and IV rapids, in low water. During spring run-off the river is a grade III route, with grade IV and V rapids. Be sure to scout all rapids before attempting to run the river.

The stretch of the river from the Quadeville put-in to Griffith is a part of the Lower Madawaska River Provincial Park. Campsites are found scattered along the shoreline of this portion of the river, allowing you to divide your whitewater trip into multi-day adventures. All campsites are user maintained, so please ensure you leave your site clean for future visitors. This great whitewater river also offers fishing opportunities. After a day of whitewater fun you can take a few hours and try to catch dinner.

Portages are marked along the river, making take-outs a little easier. Along with the camping, the river also has a number of different areas you can explore. Just past the first take-out area, an old ranger cabin lies near the river's northern bank. The cabin was a base for rangers looking for poachers. About 5km past the ranger cabin there is a portage around Crooked Rapids. From the portage, the Jameson Mountain Hiking Trail can be found. The trail makes a fine addition to a whitewater river trip.

## Mattawa River Route (Map 28/G1, 29/D1)

Access/Parking: There are a number of different ways to access the Mattawa River. Since this route requires a two vehicle system, it is recommended to leave one vehicle at the public campground up river and the other vehicle at Samuel de Champlain Provincial Park.

'Mattawa' is native Ojibway for 'meeting of the waters'. The Mattawa River flows from Trout Lake, near North Bay, to the Ottawa River, near the town of Mattawa. You can relive a bit of history on a 2-3 day paddle down the historic Mattawa River route. The river is easy to moderate in difficulty depending on the distance you choose to travel. For whitewater grading, the river is regarded as a grade I-II river.

If you are travelling from Trout Lake all the way to Mattawa, it is recommended to take 3-4 days. The stretch from Trout Lake to Samuel de Champlain Provincial Park can be done in 2 days. From Trout Lake to Samuel de Champlain Provincial Park, the river is protected by the Mattawa River Provincial Park. This is a waterway park, therefore there are no facilities other than user maintained campsites at various points along the river bank. Portages are usually marked, however, in spring some may be difficult to see due to fallen branches.

There are also a few grade I and II whitewater sections along the river that can be run, adding some excitement to your trip. Between Trout Lake and Pimsi Bay, the river meanders by numerous cottages and homes, although the stretch from Pimsi Bay to Samuel de Champlain Provincial Park is more secluded.

The cave found on the north side of the river near the Elm Point camping area is known as "La Porte de L' Enfer" or "Hell's Gate". It was rumoured by the Voyageurs that the cave housed a flesh-eating demon that the natives worshiped.

The annual Mattawa River Canoe Race is a popular recreation event on the river. The race begins at the west end of Trout Lake and ends some 64km down river at Mattawa Island. The race is usually held during mid-summer. Check locally for exact dates and times.

### Middle Madawaska River Route (Map 6/D1)
**Access/Parking:** There are two put-ins onto the Middle Madawaska River. The first put-in is found at the bridge where Siberia Road crosses over the river. The second put-in is found further up river at the Bark Lake Dam. A small parking area is located at the dam. The main take-out for this part of the river is located near River Road before the river enters Kamaniskeg Lake. If you prefer, you can continue on to Kamaniskeg Lake. A public access point is located on the lake's western shore off River Road.

This stretch of the mighty Madawaska River is about 5km in length. The route begins at the Bark Lake Dam and flows all the way to Kamaniskeg Lake. The river travels through rolling forested hills and is a popular whitewater paddling area. During summer, the water level on the river varies greatly. The Bark Lake Dam usually only releases water into the valley between Monday and Thursday from 9:30am to 3:30pm. At other times, the river is practically non-existent. It is recommended to check river conditions before heading out for a day of paddling.

Overall, the river is rated a grade II-III difficulty, although during high water there is a stretch of grade IV whitewater at the Staircase Rapids. All of the larger rapids can be portaged around. Be sure of your skill level and scout all whitewater before attempting to run it. For middle river conditions, call the Madawaska Kanu Centre at (613) 756-3620.

### Opeongo River Route (Map 14/G3, 15/A5)
**Access/Parking:** The Opeongo River Route travels from within Algonquin Provincial Park south to Bark Lake. The access to the route is the Shall Lake Algonquin interior access point, found at the end of Major Lake Road. There are two take-outs along this route. The first take-out is located at the Aylen River/Opeongo River confluence. You can park just off Aylen Lake Road, near the confluence. The other take-out is found where the river flows under Hwy 60. Algonquin Park permits are required and can be purchased at the Access Point Office at the river.

The Opeongo River is an exciting river to travel. In spring, the whitewater runs are sensational. The river flows over 30km from the put-in point in Algonquin Park to the Hwy 60 take-out. The 30km stretch can be paddled in one day, however, you must have good endurance and get an early start on the route. A scenic riverside campsite found before the first take-out can be used to split the trip into two days. The river travels through mainly wooded hills, with the odd cottage or camp found on the last few kilometres.

The section of the river from Victoria Lake to the Aylen River confluence is an almost never ending whitewater ride! The river drops over 80m (260ft) in this stretch creating grade II to grade IV rapids. Portages can be spotted from the river. Be sure to scout all whitewater before attempting to run it. If you are uncertain of your skill or of a particular run, portage around. Kayakers and whitewater canoeists alike will definitely enjoy the great Opeongo River. For river conditions call Algonquin Park at (705) 633-5572

### Ottawa River Whitewater (Map 18/G1)
**Access/Parking:** The main put-in for this whitewater section is located south of Rocher Fendu, off County Road 43. The put-in is privately run by the Madawaska Kanu Centre and Owl Rafting, although there is no fee for use of the area. Bathrooms are available as well as parking.

The main take-outs are located about 7km down river on the western shore. The first take-out is privately owned and operates on the honour system for maintenance. Donations are accepted and needed to keep the site in good shape. There are no facilities other than a parking area. The second take-out is operated by River Run and there is a fee for use of the area. Facilities at the take-out include parking, camping, toilets, showers and a store.

The Ottawa River from the south end of Sullivan Island to the south end of Isle Lafontaine contains some the greatest whitewater runs in the world! Year after year, the area is home to countless competitions for both kayaking and open canoeing events. You must have good whitewater skills in order to attempt

most of the runs on this stretch of river. In fact, some of the runs are rated grade V whitewater. This section of the river travels through a natural setting of forested and rocky shoreline and osprey can often be spotted hovering overhead. A number of companies operate whitewater schools on the river as well as guided rafting trips.

### Petawawa River Whitewater Route (Lower)
### (Maps 22, 23, 24, 25, 32, 33)
**Access/Parking:** The Petawawa River is an Algonquin Provincial Park whitewater river. There are several access points, which depend on the distance and difficulty you wish to travel. Cedar Lake is the uppermost access to this route, while Radiant Lake and Lake Travers double as access points/take-outs. Radiant Lake can only be accessed by canoe from the Wendigo Lake interior access point. A road travels to Lake Travers from the east side of the park. The last main take-out on the river is McManus Lake in the park's southeastern side. The road north of the Sand Lake Gate leads to the lake.

The Petawawa River is perhaps the best known river of Algonquin Provincial Park. The river travels from one side of the park to the other, taking on a different character with every kilometre. From the marshy meandering flow in the west to the rushing rapids of the east, the Petawawa is a dynamic and exciting river to travel. It is difficult to rate the river's overall difficulty since it is made up of many different forms of whitewater that change throughout the year. From Cedar Lake to Rapid Lake the river offers grade II-IV whitewater as it flows through a steep valley. This section can be run in one day. From Radiant Lake to Lake Travers, the river is very rigorous as the majority of rapids are rated as grade III-V. In one location just before Lake Travers, falls called "the Fury," are unrunable during most of the year. Allow two days for this scenic section of the river. Several campsites can be found on the rocky shorelines surrounded by pine forests.

The Petawawa River between Lake Travers and Lake McManus is the most popular stretch of the river for whitewater trippers. The main reason is due to the proximity of the put-in and take-out from each other. The road north to the Lake Travers put-in passes right by the short road to the McManus Lake take-out. From Lake Travers to The Natch (a large rapid), the scenery along the Petawawa is set amid a forested valley. It is recommended to allow at least three days to complete this section. Down river from the Natch, the scenery begins to change to a more southern feeling with maples and other deciduous trees lining the shoreline. You can camp along the shore in several locations.

The rapids en route vary from grade I whitewater to grade IV. The grade also depends on the water level encountered. Regardless, there are portages around each whitewater area. Be sure to always scout whitewater before attempting to run it. Portions of the Petawawa River can be traveled by novice canoeists but know your limits before attempting any part of the river. Many areas can be treacherous.

*Note: Travel beyond Lake McManus is strictly prohibited. From the southern end of Lake McManus the Petawawa River travels through a live artillery training range at Canadian Forces Base Petawawa.*

### Upper Madawaska River Route (Map 14/D7)
**Access/Parking:** There are two access points to the Upper Madawaska River. The first put-in is located in the village of Whitney, off Hwy 60. The parking area and put-in is found at the west side of the river. The second access point is located east of Whitney, off a short road from Hwy 60, just after the power lines cross the highway. The take-out is located down river off Victoria-McCauley Lake Road, north of the town of Madawaska.

The Upper Madawaska River is an exhilarating whitewater river. The river has a number of grade IV and V rated whitewater, although all rapids can be portaged around via the old railbed that follows the river. The railbed also doubles as a trail to scout the difficult chutes and rapids. The river can really only be traveled in spring until about the end of May. After May, the river level drops to a point where many areas are impassable.

The Upper Madawaska River travels through forested highlands with a few camps along its shoreline. Unfortunately, there are no campsites along the river, however, the entire run can be done in a day, especially if you begin at the power line access. The first portion of the river has several difficult rapids and you must have whitewater experience to challenge them. In the last 5km, the river begins to slow considerably leading to the take-out. Be alert at all times in order to ensure a successful take-out and scout all whitewater before attempting to run it.

# Multi-use Trails
## (Summer and Winter Routes)

The Algonquin region is blessed with several great recreation trails. From the Western Uplands Hiking Trail of Algonquin Park to the Pakkotinna Trail of Renfrew County, the opportunities abound. Hiking trails make up a large portion of the trail systems in the region, however, cross-country skiing trails are also quite popular. The best thing about the Algonquin Region is that there are a variety of recreation trails available. The snowmobile trail system in the region is world class and there are even alternative type trails for activities such as snowshoeing.

Algonquin Provincial Park is well known for its interpretive trails that can be found throughout the park's main usage areas. The trail system is designed to inform you about Algonquin Park's many characteristics, while you enjoy the intrinsic benefits of the hike. In the summer, extensive backpacking trails and a few great mountain biking routes are available. In winter, the park offers a number of different trail systems, which include cross-country skiing, snowshoeing and dogsledding. All trails are well maintained and are set amid the magnificent park setting.

Areas outside of the park are quickly becoming recognized for their recreational trail systems. Communities are becoming more aware of the benefits of eco-tourism and are continually upgrading and developing trails in their area. Hiking and biking are the main uses of trail systems during summer months, while snowmobiling and cross-country skiing are the more popular uses of trails during the winter. Many of the trails have not been widely publicized and are underutilized, especially during the summer period. This makes them all the more attractive to adventure seekers.

Included on the maps contained in this book are symbols that identify which mode of travel is available on a trail system. An individual trail may be able to be used by a number of different users including: cross-country skiers, hikers, horseback riders, mountain bikers, snowmobilers and ATV's. In the reference section each of the trails have been rated according to difficulty as follows:

*Easy:* The route is well marked and involves very little uphill or downhill travel. The terrain is generally easy to traverse and has few natural obstacles. These trails are ideal for inexperienced users.

*Moderate:* The trail could require some strenuous climbs and may not be marked. The terrain could be challenging due to obstacles such as fallen trees or sharp corners. Be prepared, as these trails can challenge even experienced users.

*Difficult:* These routes are rarely marked and involve challenging climbs or descents. Orienteering skills may be required to track the trail. The routes are usually rustic with fallen trees or grown-in sections.

Please note that all distances are for round trips unless otherwise noted.

*Note: Day-use or overnight-use passes must be purchased and displayed on your dashboard for use of all facilities and trails within Algonquin Park.*

## Algonquin Provincial Park Dogsledding Trails

Algonquin Provincial Park is quite a different place in winter. The first difference you will notice is the lack of people compared to summer months. This is expected because it is cold! However, just because there is snow and it is chilly, it does not mean you can not still enjoy the great outdoors. Many of us try to enjoy the outdoors year round and Algonquin is a great place for winter recreation. Along with the park's popular system of cross-country ski trails, there are endless snowshoeing opportunities and even dogsledding trails. The park, in conjunction with independent operators, maintains a fabulous series of dogsledding trails just waiting for you to experience. One thing is for sure, you will always remember an Algonquin Park dogsledding expedition.

**Biggar Lake Dogsledding Trail (Map 20/E3, 29/E7)** system has two access areas: Kawawaymog Lake access and the Kioshkokwi Lake-Kiosk access. This system traverses over 65km of rustic trails through the frozen Algonquin Park. The system is made up of old trails and logging roads that are only passable during icy winter months. The trip varies by preference and/or accessibility and all routes pass by water bodies of various sizes. The trip is a little more rustic, although quite exhilarating.

**Brule Lake Dogsledding Trail (Map 12/B4)** trip begins at Hwy 60 across from Smoke Lake and can be traveled up to 22km (one-way) through the majestic Algonquin Park. The trail passes a number of lakes including Teepee Lake, Potter Lake and, of course, Brule Lake. Much of the trail follows the old Ottawa, Arnprior and Parry Sound railbed, which was built in the late 1800's by the lumber baron J.R. Booth.

**Sunday Lake Dogsledding Trail (Map 13/C4)** begins from the north side of Hwy 60 at about the 40km point from the park's West Gate. The trail is made up of a number of different loops and can be traveled for 10km-49km. The route crosses near a number of small water bodies including Blackfox and Redfox Lakes. Much of the trail travels on old forest access (logging) roads once used to haul lumber out of the park.

If you are looking for a different winter adventure, a dogsled trip is highly recommended. To take a guided dogsledding trip on an Algonquin sled trail, contact Algonquin Park Information at (705) 633-5572 for a list of companies that organize dogsledding outings.

*Please note that these trails are not year round recreation trails and are off limits during non-winter months. Most of these trails can be overgrown and almost impossible to orienteer during non-winter periods. Parts of the trails also travel over frozen marsh areas and/or lakes, which are impassable at other times.*

## Arrowhead Provincial Park Trails (Map 1/G2)

Arrowhead Provincial Park is located off Hwy 11, north of Huntsville. The park offers four easy trails for hiking and interpretive brochures are provided to enhance your visit. In winter, the trails are groomed for cross-country skiing. There is also one section that can be skied at night.

**Beaver Meadow Trail** is approximately 3km in length, although it may take a little longer than normal due to the wet conditions, especially in spring. The trail is an easy route that travels over a few streams and through some boggy areas.

**Homesteader Trail** passes by the remains of an authentic pioneer settlement and is a short, generally easy route.

**Mayflower Lake Trail** is an easy 30-40min nature walk through a forested area and past Mayflower Lake.

**Stubbs Falls Trail** is an easy short hike along the Little East River. The trail also passes a beautiful set of waterfalls.

## Barron Canyon Trail (Map25/A4)

The Barron Canyon is one of Algonquin Provincial Park's natural treasures. This easy 1.5km trail takes you to the edge of the canyon where a breathtaking panoramic view is offered. From the canyon edge, you can view the sheer canyon walls and the river that flows through it. Various bird species can be spotted on the trail, including Red Tailed Hawks, swallows and Eastern Phoebes. An interpretative brochure, which explains the history, ecology and geology of the canyon is available at the trailhead. The trail is located in Algonquin's eastern side just past the Sand Lake Gate. Be sure to take caution when walking along the cliff edge.

## Bat Lake Trail (Map 13/A5)

This Algonquin Park trail is an easy 5km loop that travels through a bog area and past Bat Lake. The trail is located off Hwy 60 across from Mew Lake or about 30km from the West Gate. A parking area is available off the highway and trail brochures can be found at the trailhead. The interpretative guide is co-ordinated with various checkpoints along the route and informs users about the basic ecology of the area. The trail passes through a mixed forest and a towering stand of Eastern Hemlock. There is also a lookout along the trail, which provides a good view of Sasajewan Lake and the surrounding area.

## Bear Mountain Hiking Trail (Map15/A6)

This trail was established by a local association and was once maintained, although the group that established and maintained the trail no longer exists. Regardless, this hidden gem is definitely worthwhile and has plenty to offer hikers. The route consists of two connecting loops for a total of 8km and traverses through some rustic terrain. You can travel a short loop past the first lake or there is a longer loop that extends all the way to Spectacle Lake and back. Shortly after the start of the trail there is a small side loop that takes you to Kluke's Lookout. The lookout gives you a fantastic view of a chain of lakes and the distant rolling hills. The first loop is used more often than the longer loop and is moderate in difficulty. The longer loop is difficult due to the rarely used trail that could be tricky to follow the further you venture into the forest. The unmarked trailhead is found about 19.2km west of Barry's Bay, off the south side of Hwy 60 and is only an opening in the trees. You can park your vehicle on the shoulder of the Highway.

## Beaver Pond Trail (Map 13/E4)
This easy 2km Algonquin Provincial Park trail passes through a mixed forest and past a couple of beaver dams. The beaver and their dams are the focus of the trail and the trail's interpretative guide. In the guide, you will learn more about the nature of the beaver, its dam building instincts and the ecology of the area. If you're lucky you may even see a beaver but be sure to be quiet or they will quickly head for shelter. The trail also passes Amikeus Lake, which is the result of the work of the beaver. Before returning to the parking area, you will pass a natural lookout that provides an exceptional view of the pond and the meadow below the dam. The trail can be found at about kilometer 45 on the south side of Hwy 60. A parking area and trail guides are available at the trailhead.

## Berm Lake Trail (Map24/E4)
At the Achray Campground in the eastern portion of Algonquin Park you will find a number of trails including the Berm Lake Trail. This easy 2km loop travels around Berm Lake and through some brilliant stands of red and white pine trees. At one point along the trail, you will pass through a stand of white pine that is over 150 years old. The trees in this area measure over 30m (100ft) tall and 80cm (31in) in diameter. Amazingly when the first loggers arrived in this area in the early 1800's, stands of white pines would have been over 300 years old and more than 53m (175ft) high. Unlike the maple dominated forests of the western portion of the park, this part of the park has its own unique ecology. Along with the trail guide, the trail will help you learn more about the ecology of the pine forests and the drier climate that is common to this side of the park. This part of the park is also a prime area for blueberries.

## Bonnechere Provincial Park Trails (Map16/B2)
There are three separate trail loops available at Bonnechere Provincial Park. The park, which offers camping and other facilities, can be found off Hwy 62, west of Pembroke. At the main park gate, attendants can direct you to the trailheads.

Beaver Marsh Loop is an easy 1km loop that travels through a mixed forest and past an old beaver pond.

Meandering River Loop passes through dense forest at times and is an easy 2km loop.

Oxbow Loop circles around an old river oxbow and through a lush forest area for an easy 2km loop.

## Bondi Village Resort Trails (Map 2/D5)
Bondi Village Resort, located off Hwy 35 on Muskoka District Road 21, offers 16km of cross-country ski trails and over 8km of hiking trails. The trails vary in difficulty from easy to moderate as they traverse through a mixed forests with great viewpoints of the beautiful Lake of Bays. Although there is no fee for use of the trails, donations are always welcome. Detailed maps are available at the resort office.

## Booth's Rock Trail (Map 13/D6)
Booth's Rock Trail is an Algonquin Provincial Park trail that was named after the famous lumber baron J.R. Booth. J.R. Booth was responsible for most of the early logging in the park and was instrumental in building the Ottawa, Arnprior and Parry Sound Railway (O.A. & P.S.). The railway stretched from Ottawa to the Georgian Bay and traveled right through present day Algonquin Park. In fact, the last leg of Booth's Rock Trail is part of the old railbed. The railway was used as a transportation line but more importantly, it was a main artery for shipping lumber out of the park. The trail passes other remnants of the railroad era including the old site of the Barklay Estate. This estate was built by Judge George Barklay, a relative of J.R. Booth, in the late 1800's and was used until 1953. All that remains today is subtle remnants of the estate, including the old asphalt base of the tennis court! The trail traverses through a mixed forest and past Rosepond and Gordon Lakes, which both offer fishing. Shortly after Gordon Lake you will climb up to a large rockface, accordingly named Booth's Rock. The cliff offers a beautiful view of Rock and Whitefish Lakes as well as the sprawling highlands of the park. The trailhead and parking area is located just past the Rock Lake Campground off Hwy 60. The trail is a moderately difficult 5km loop. The trail brochure will help you learn a little history of human activity in the park. Brochures are available at the trailhead in the parking area.

## Brent Crater Trail (Map 31/B7)
Located within Algonquin Provincial Park's northern boundary is the Brent Crater Trail. The trail is an easy 2km loop that travels from the ridge of the crater to its present day floor. The trailhead and parking area can be found en route to the Cedar Lake-Brent access point. At the parking area, trail brochures are available for your hike. There is also a lookout tower to help provide a better view of the crater. From the lookout, you can see the far rim of the crater and Tecumseh Lake, which is in the crater. The crater was discovered in 1951 from aerial photographs of the area. A strange circular pattern imbedded in the earth was noticed in the photos and further investigation revealed that this indeed was a phenomenon. After extensive study, the surviving theory of the crater is that a large meteorite hit the area creating the huge depression. It is estimated that this occurrence happened over 450 million years ago. Amazingly, the huge hole is still evident today.

## Burk's Falls Heritage River Walk (Map 10/B4)
This trail is found in the village of Burk's Falls and is an easy 1.5km walk along the graceful Magnetawan River. The route begins at the Burk's Falls Welcome Centre off Hwy 520 and travels to the racetrack in the village. Much of the route is made up of an old railway spur that once played an integral role in shaping the growth and settlement of the village. Today, the railbed is maintained as a walkway for visitors and locals to enjoy. Look for wild strawberries, raspberries and rhubarb along the way.

## Centennial Ridges Trail (Map 13/C5)
The Centennial Ridges Trail of Algonquin Provincial Park was established in 1993 to coincide with the 100th birthday of the park. The trail can be found 2km off Hwy 60 at about 37km from the West Gate of the park. A parking area and trail guides are available at the trailhead. The guide depicts short biographies of a number of individuals who were instrumental in developing the park. From the original park founders to Tom Thompson, you will be a little more enlightened on the park's evolution after this hike. The trail is a moderately difficult 10km loop that traverses through a mixed forest and along a number of cliff tops. From the cliffs, magnificent views of the park's rolling highlands and a number of lakes can be seen.

## Driftwood Provincial Park Trails (Map 33/C3)
Driftwood Provincial Park is located on Hwy 17, north of the Town of Rolphton on the historic Ottawa River. The trails are used mainly for hiking and cross-country skiing. The access points can be found at the parking areas just past the park office. Both trails are also a good area for blueberry and raspberry picking when they are in season.

Chevrier Creek Trails are a 9.5km series of moderate trails that venture through a mixed forest and along a number of rocky areas. Four different loops make up these trails that offer a few scenic viewpoints of the Ottawa River along the route.

Oak Uplands Hiking Trail is comprised of two interconnecting loops that follow moderately difficult terrain for a total distance of 3km. There are a few areas where you can catch a nice view of the Ottawa River. There is an interpretive trail guide available at the main gate for this route.

## Eastern Pines Backpacking Trail (Map 24/F5)
The Eastern Pines Backpacking Trail is an Algonquin Provincial Park Trail that is located in the eastern side of Algonquin Park. The trailhead can be found at the Achray Campground and permits can be obtained at the Sand Lake Gate as you enter the park. The trail is made up of two connecting loops for a total of 15.9km. From the parking area, the trail travels along Johnstone Lake for about 2km. Once at the east tip of the lake you can choose to travel onto the larger loop or you can continue in a circle around Johnstone Lake. On the north shore of the lake overnight campsites are available for hikers. There is a short trail off the Johnson Lake loop that leads down to the lake where five interior campsites are offered. The larger loop travels over a lookout with a great view of Johnstone Lake. Not far from the lookout, the trail heads towards Stratton Lake, where five more hike-in campsites are available. From here, the trail crosses over some fairly hilly terrain before coming down to the northern tip of Stratton Lake. Three more hike-in campsites are available at the tip of the lake as well as a 2km side trail. The side trail makes a great afternoon trip and follows the Barron River to High Falls. Once back on the main loop, the trail travels past a few marshy areas and past an old logging camp location on Buckholtz Lake. The trail circles the lake and passes through some glacial boulder gardens. The gardens consist of large rocks scattered on the ground by retreating glaciers thousands of years ago. There is one hike-in campsite on Buckholtz Lake, where you can have the lake all to yourself. Just over 2km from the lake, the trail meets up with the first loop and heads back towards the parking area. You can choose how far and which loops you like.

wish to travel. Overall, the trail is moderate in difficulty due to the distance involved and a few challenging climbs. The trail is monitored under Algonquin Park's quota system and the route can be busy at certain times of the year. It is recommended that you make reservations well in advance of your trip to avoid disappointment. Call (888) 668-7275 for reservations and availability.

### Fairy Vista Trail (Map 1/G4) 🚶 🎿 🚴 🎿
The Fairy Vista Trail is an easy 6.8km paved route that can be accessed from the north side of Hwy 60 at Fairyview Drive, near Huntsville. The trail is for non-motorized use only and is great for hiking, biking, cross-country skiing or snowshoeing. The route passes through a variety of farmland and forest tracts and ends at Canal Road. Near the east end of the trail you can see some ruins of an old farmhouse, a reminder of past attempts to settle the area.

### Fen Lake Cross-Country Ski Trails (Map 3/B1) 🎿 🚶
The Fen Lake Ski Trails in Algonquin Park are comprised of a number of interconnected loops varying from easy to difficult. There is a total of 18km of groomed trails available. There is also a warm up shelter with a toilet available off the trail at Fen Lake. Watch for moose tracks in the snow, as the large animal is known to frequent the area during winter. All routes traverse through a mainly hardwood forest of maple, beech, birch and hemlock.

From the parking area at the West Gate south of Hwy 60, there are two possible routes you can choose from. The loop to the north is an easy 1.25km trail that travels past Heron Lake. It is often used as a warm up trail for those intending to venture out onto the larger circuits. The trail to the south of the parking area is the first main loop. It is an easy 4.5km trip back to the parking area. At about the 3km mark on the loop you can continue on to the next series of longer and more difficult trails. The first additional loop adds another 8km to your trip and is moderate in difficulty. The longest additional route will add another 8.9km to your trip and traverses over challenging terrain. This route is rated difficult and is recommended for more advanced skiers. An Algonquin Provincial Park day pass is required. A detailed map of the trail and day passes are available at the West Gate.

### Forest Lea Trails (Map 26/A6) 🚶 🎿 🚴 🎿
The Forest Lea Trails are located about 13km west of the town of Pembroke off Forest Lea Road. The system is suitable for cross-country skiing, biking and hiking and is maintained by the Pembroke Ministry of Natural Resources and the Pembroke & Area Cross Country Ski Club. There is parking available and a picnic area, along with a small chalet in winter. All trail distances are from the parking area.

Southwestern BC   Vancouver Island   Kamloops/ Okanagan

The Kootenays   The Cariboo   Southwestern Alberta

*Let us show you the way out West!*

**Beaver Ridge Trail** is found in the north end of the forest and can be accessed from the Tall Pine Trail or the Poplar Grove Trail. This trail can be difficult on a bike/ski or moderate on foot as it travels for 7km across many hilly sections.

**Lookout Ridge Trail** can be found off the Beaver Ridge Trail and traverses over a number of short downhill sections and a few long uphill climbs. The route is a moderate hike or difficult biking/skiing route and travels a total of 8km before joining with the Tall Pine Trail.

**Poplar Grove Trail** is a moderate biking/skiing route or an easy hiking trail that is located off the north portion of the Tall Pine Trail. The 5.1km trail travels over a number of small hilly sections and past a swamp before ending at the junction with the Beaver Ridge Trail.

**Ruffed Grouse Trail** is a 3.3km route that begins at the parking area off Forest Lea Road and is a moderate biking/skiing route or an easy hike. The trail traverses over generally flat terrain, although there is one fun downhill section shortly after the trail begins.

**Tall Pine Trail** provides access to the Beaver Ridge Trail and travels over hilly terrain for 4.9km. The trail begins off the west side of the Ruffed Grouse Trail, travels in a "C" formation and rejoins the Ruffed Grouse Trail. The trail is generally moderate in difficulty for biking/skiing or easy for hikers. If you are looking for more of a challenge, the route is a good addition to the Ruffed Grouse Trail.

### Granview Inn Nature Trails (Map 1/G4) 🚶 🚴 $
Located off Hwy 60, 5km from Huntsville, Grandview Inn resort offers 15km of trails that can be used for hiking or biking. Nature tours along the trails are also available for a modest fee. The trails vary in difficulty from easy to moderate. A detailed map is available at the resort.

### Haliburton Forest Reserve Trails (Map 3/F5) 🚶 🚴 🎿 ⛺ $
The Haliburton Forest Reserve has long been an established recreation area for a variety of outdoor activities. This wonderful nature reserve is privately owned and encompasses over 50 lakes, 300km of trails and access roads, in over 50,000 acres of beautiful natural habitat. The reserve is open year round and charges a nominal fee for daily and overnight use. In summer, the Forest offers mountain biking, hiking, canoeing, camping and the spectacular forest canopy tour. The canopy tour takes you along an exciting suspension bridge that is mounted over 20 metres high amid a beautiful old growth white pine canopy. In winter months, many of the trails are groomed and provide endless cross-country skiing and snowmobiling opportunities. The Forest rents snowmobiles and mountain bikes and there is a small supply store open daily. The main gate to the Haliburton Forest and Wildlife Reserve can be accessed from Kennisis Lake Road off Hwy 118. Call (705) 754-2198 for trail conditions or more information.

### Hardwood Lookout Trail (Map 12/D6) 🚶 🥾 📋
This easy 0.8km Algonquin Park trail loops through a hardwood forest typical of the western side of the park. Along the trail you will pass a number of different hardwood tree species including Red Maple, Black Cherry and Yellow Birch. Along with the interpretative brochure, the trail will help educate you on the ecology and significance of the hardwood forest. You will also pass a natural lookout area that offers a great view of Smoke Lake and a backdrop of rolling hills that are typical of much of Algonquin. At the parking area there is also a short side trail called the **Red Spruce Side Trail**. The Red Spruce is quite rare in Algonquin and is only occasionally found in solitary pockets on the park's west side. Along the side trail you will learn a little more about this tree and why it is found in Algonquin. The parking area for these trails can be found off Hwy 60, across from Canoe Lake. Trail brochures can be picked up at the trailhead.

### Hastings Heritage Trail (Map 5/E2, 6/A7) 🚶 🎿 🚴 🎣 🎿 🐎 🏍
The Hastings Heritage Trail is made up of an old railway bed, which stretches from Trenton past the town of Wallace. The Hastings Heritage Trail Association currently maintains the 156km stretch of trail from Wallace to the town of Glen Ross, although almost all of the old railway bed can be used for a variety of outdoor recreation activities. This includes hiking, biking, horseback riding, cross-country-skiing, snowshoeing, ATV and snowmobiling. The trail passes through a wide variety of terrain, including towns and rustic forest tracts. Access points to the trail can be found at numerous areas along the route. Since the route is set upon an old railbed, the grade is quite gentle, making the trail accessible for everyone. Snowmobile users must have a valid permit to travel the trail (see the Ontario Snowmobile Trails).

## Hemlock Bluff Trail (Map 12/G5) [icons]

This Algonquin Park trail can be found about 27km from the West Gate on Hwy 60. There is a parking area across the highway from the trail and trail brochures are available at the trailhead. The trail is an easy 3.5km route that leads through a predominantly hardwood forest including an enchanting stand of Yellow Birch trees. Shortly after you begin the trail, you will ascend a cliff to a lookout providing a gorgeous view of Jack Lake. Along the trail, the guide gives you valuable information on research in Algonquin Park. Many park research programs have played a significant role in shaping our views today. One prime example is the extensive studies done on wolves in Algonquin Park.

## Highland Backpacking Trail (Map 12/A6) [icons]

The Highland Backpacking Trail is one of three Algonquin Provincial Park interior hiking trails. This route is generally moderate in difficulty, although some sections can be more challenging due to steep terrain. The trailhead and parking area can be found near the Mew Lake Campground off Hwy 60. The trail is made up of two connecting loops totaling 40km of trail. The two loops give hikers some flexibility in the distance they wish to cover. Rustic camping is offered at a number of areas along the trail, although site reservations must be made in advance.

From the highway, there is a 3.8km stretch to the first (blue) loop of the trail. This section traverses over a few challenging hills and past a scenic lookout over the Algonquin Highlands. The Blue Loop is 10.9km in length and travels around Provoking Lake. The lake is about 1.5 square km in size and hosts thirteen hike-in campsites. Smallmouth bass fishing is available at the lake. The Blue Loop can be completed in two days, although a two night trip would be a more leisurely and comfortable pace.

The larger second (yellow) loop can be found 1.6km after traveling on the Blue Loop. The Yellow Trail is more difficult than the blue due to more challenging terrain and the distance involved. It is recommended that you have someone with backcountry experience in your group and know your limits before committing to this route. The loop is 21.6km in length and requires at least two days of hiking to complete. This does not include the first 5.4km section of the Blue Trail. Shortly after beginning the Yellow Loop you will pass a small lake named Faya Lake. A secluded campsite is available at the lake. After Faya Lake the trail travels to the top of a natural lookout where a splendid view is offered. After 7.1km on the Yellow Loop you will arrive at Head Lake. There are a number of rustic campsites available at the lake, including four hike-in sites. For fishing enthusiasts, there is a population of lake trout in the lake. Not far from Head Lake lies Harness Lake, with five more hike-in sites. Lake trout also inhabit this interior Algonquin lake. From Harnes Lake it is at least 8km back to the Blue Trail. En route, you will pass a small, secluded hike-in campsite just off the trail. The site lies along a small brook and is perfect for secluded camping.

*Please note that the trail is monitored under Algonquin Park's quota system and the route can be busy at certain times of the year. It is recommended that you make reservations well in advance of your trip to avoid disappointment. For reservations and availability call (888) 668-7275.*

## Lake St. Peter Provincial Park Trails (Map 5/E3) [icons]

Lake St. Peter Provincial Park can be found off of Hwy 127, just south of Whitney. There are two connected hiking trails totaling about 5.5km. Permits can be picked up at the gate and parking is available at the trailhead. In winter, the trails can be used for cross-country skiing or snowshoeing, although they are not groomed.

**Lookout Trail** leads to the Shanty Trail and is an easy loop of about 1.5km in length. The trail traverses through less rugged terrain than the Shanty Trail. The route passes by a lookout that provides a wonderful view of Lake St. Peter and the surrounding hillsides. Before rejoining the Shanty Trail, you will pass by a small kettle pond, which was formed after the glaciers retreated thousands of years ago.

**Shanty Trail** is the second trail loop and is about 4km in length. The trail passes an old cabin that was constructed many years ago. The trail is generally easy.

## Leaf Lake Cross Country Ski Trails (Map 13/F6) [icons]

The Leaf Lake Trails are a large series of Algonquin Provincial Park Trails that are maintained in the winter. The entrance to the trails can be found off Hwy 60 about 1.5km from the East Gate, where permits can be purchased. The trail system is a collection of loops and there are many different combinations you can choose from to vary the distance and difficulty of your trip. Toilets and small shelters are available along a few of the trails.

**Clarke Lake Loop** is a nice addition to the Leaf Lake Loop or the Jack Rabbit Loop. The trail is easy and adds an additional 3.4km to the Jack Rabbit Loop as it passes by Clarke Lake.

**David Thompson Loop** is a difficult 12.4km loop that can be found at the 3.3km mark of the Thistle Lake Loop. The trail travels past David Thompson Lake and to the shore of Galeairy Lake. From Galeairy Lake the trail follows an old railway bed and leads to the Galeairy Lake Loop before returning to the Thistle Lake Loop.

**Farm Loop** can be accessed from the Galeairy Lake Loop and leads to the Moose Trail. The loop is a moderate 1km addition to the David Thompson Loop and provides access to the shore of Galeairy Lake.

**Fraser Lake Loop** is a difficult section that can be added on to the Thistle Lake Loop. The trail is 4.4km and traverses over some steep terrain with a number of challenging turns.

**Galeairy Lake Loop** is a moderately difficult loop that leads to the Farm Loop. The loop is 4.5km back to the David Thompson Loop, although the loop can be shortened to 2.9km.

**Jack Rabbit Loop** is the first loop of the series of trails and is the only access to the rest of the trail network. The trail is an easy 5km loop and leads to the Leaf Lake and Clarke Lake loops. A toilet is available at about the halfway mark.

**Leaf Lake Loop** is a good addition to the Jack Rabbit Loop and leads to the Pine Tree Loop, where a toilet is available. The loop is an easy 3.9km.

**Moose Trail** is a moderate 2.2km (one-way) from the Farm Loop to the shore of Galeairy Lake.

**Pine Tree Loop** is a challenging addition to the Leaf Lake Loop and travels past Pinetree and Thistle Lakes. The loop is an additional 11.5km and is rated difficult due to the terrain it traverses. A number of the turns are quite sharp and the trail ascends two challenging hills to natural lookout areas. There are two toilets along the route and a small shelter available at the last lookout. Although the trail is challenging, it is one of the most scenic routes available in the park. Wildlife tracks are usually abundant in the area.

**Thistle Lake Loop** is an addition to the Clarke Loop and leads to the larger Fraser Lake and David Thompson Loops. The loop is an easy 5.2km.

## Leslie M. Frost Centre Trails (Map 2/G7, 3/B7) [icons]

The Leslie M. Frost Centre has long been a training area for Ministry of Natural Resources employees and recreation trails have been developed over time for education purposes and public use. It offers over 14km of trails through a beautiful portion of the Haliburton Highlands. All trails to the east of the centre are for hiking and snowshoeing use only, due to the difficult terrain. The series of trails across the highway from the centre offer access to 21km of cross-country ski trails. These trails can also be used for hiking or biking in the summer. A more detailed map (available at the centre) will help you easily locate all of the trails. The Leslie M. Frost Centre can be found on Hwy 35, south of Dorset.

Although a portion of the centre is covered in this book, the actual trail systems lie to the south of the Algonquin Region. Please refer to the Cottage Country, Ontario Backroad Mapbook for more information.

## Linda Lake Snowshoe Trail (Map 12/G4) [icon]

Although you can snowshoe virtually anywhere in Algonquin Provincial Park, this is the only designated snowshoe trail. The Linda Lake trail can be accessed off Hwy 60 at the parking area to the Minnesing Trail. Since much of the trail crosses frozen water bodies, our maps have not indicated the routes other than the name. This description will give you a good idea of where it travels so you can locate the route on our map. The trail is about 8km and it is not recommended for inexperienced users. Due to the many frozen water bodies on this route, previous winter waterway experience is highly recommended before heading out on this trail.

The trail starts at the parking area and travels to the south of Canisbay Lake. You travel across the frozen lake to its northern tip where you'll find a beaver dam. From the dam the trail travels along the frozen waterway to a treed bog at the southern tip of Linda Lake. The waterway from Cannisbay Lake is made up of a collection of bogs and ponds and a number of winter portages (land travel) are required to follow the route. The ice on the route is normally safe between the first week in January to the third week in March. Day pass permits are required to travel the trail and can be picked up at the West or East Gates. For trail conditions and more information call (705) 633-5572.

*Note: the ice from the beaver dam at Cannisbay Lake to the first winter portage is often unsafe. Traveling on the west side of the bog is recommended.*

## Lookout Tower Trail (Map 2/D5) 🚶 ⛵ 🚴

The Dorset lookout tower and trails can be found off of Hwy 35 just north of Dorset. The tower is over 30 metres high and offers a stunning panoramic view of Dorset and the surrounding hills. The connecting trails are easy and generally short in distance. Signs are posted along the trails, which describe various points of interest and natural information. There is also a picnic area available at the base of the tower.

## Lookout Trail (Map 13/C5) 🚶 🚴 📷

The Lookout Trail is an Algonquin Park trail that can be found off Hwy 60 approximately 40km from the park's West Gate. The trail is an easy 1.9km loop that has an informative interpretative guide. There are numbered posts along the trail that co-ordinate with the guide. The main feature of the trail, however, is the natural lookout. The lookout sits approximately 525m (1,700ft) above sea level offering a spectacular view of the park. From the lookout, you can see the rolling hills of Algonquin along with Kearney Lake, Little Rock Lake and Lake of Two Rivers. Parking is available at the trailhead.

## Loxton Beaver Trail (Map 19/F3) 🚶 ⛷ 🚴

The Loxton Beaver Trail is found off Chemical Road north-east of the town of South River. This easy 8.5km loop travels through a mixed forest past the Loxton Lake Dam. The trail is maintained as a cross-country ski trail in the winter and doubles as a hiking/biking trail during summer months. The route passes both Loxton and Beaver Lakes before returning to the trailhead.

## Mattawa Golf and Ski Resort (Map 30/G1) ⛷ 🏃

The Mattawa Golf and Ski Resort is located about 13km east of Mattawa off Hwy 17. The resort offers over 20km of cross-country ski trails that vary in difficulty from easy to difficult. A chalet is available at the resort offering a restaurant, bar, change rooms, washrooms and ski rentals. For trail information call (800) 762-2339.

## Minnesing Mountain Bike Trail (Map 12/F5) 🚴 🏃

The Minnesing Mountain Biking Trail is solely dedicated for mountain biking. The trail can be found about 23km from the West Gate to Algonquin Park off of Hwy 60. There is a parking area off the highway or alternatively the trail can be accessed from the Canisbay Campground. For your convenience, toilets and a small cabin are available at the parking area. The trail is named after the Minnesing Road, which ran from Cache Lake to the Minnesing Lodge on Burnt Island Lake. The lodge was demolished in the early 1950's and the old road now makes up much of the western portion of the Minnesing Trail. The trail is comprised of four interconnecting loops for a combined total distance of 55.3km. A park vehicle permit or overnight permit is required for use of the trail. In spring and late fall, the route is extremely muddy; therefore, the trail is only open from late June to the Canadian Thanksgiving. This is to ensure the condition of the route is both safe and manageable for future seasons. However, depending on weather, the trail could be open earlier in the year. Check with the Park Information Office for conditions. (705) 633-5572.

1ˢᵗ **Loop** is an easy 4.7km loop that travels to the bottom of Canisbay Lake and back to the parking area on Hwy 60.

2ⁿᵈ **Loop** travels just west of Canisbay Lake for a moderately difficult 10.1km. About halfway along the trail, a toilet and small cabin are available.

3ʳᵈ **Loop** is a moderate 17.1km route that passes Polly Lake. There are three toilets available on this route along with a cabin at about kilometer 12. Be aware of portaging canoeists on this route.

4ᵗʰ **Loop** is the largest loop in the Minnesing Trail system and is a moderate 23.4km. The trail passes Canisbay, Linda and Polly Lakes before returning to the parking area. A picnic area is available at about the half way mark on Linda Lake. Be aware of portaging canoeists on this route.

## Mizzy Lake Trail (Map 12/D5) 🚶

The Mizzy lake Trail is located across from Smoke Lake off Hwy 60 in Algonquin Park. Parking is available along with trail guides at the trailhead. The trail is 11km in length and is rated moderate in difficulty due to the distance of the trail and the sometimes soggy terrain. The trail travels past nine different water bodies of various sizes and is one of the better routes for spotting wildlife, especially in the early morning or towards evening. A few of the notable species that can sometimes be spotted on this trail are otters, beavers, deer, moose and more rarely, wolves and bears. Do not be alarmed if you see any of these animals, they are afraid of humans and will quickly scurry away. There is also plenty of smaller wildlife that can be seen on the trail including the Great Blue Heron, Painted Turtles and many different species of birds. For a little added adventure you can travel down the **Bear's Nests Side Trail** found just after West Rose Lake. The trail is an additional 2km loop where you will find Beech Trees

that have been ravished by black bears in their attempts to fatten up on the trees tasty nuts.

## Moose Mountain Trail (Map 19/E3) 🚶 📷

This 3km loop is moderate in difficulty due to the climb that is required to ascend Moose Mountain. Moose Mountain is not a mountain per say, although it can be challenging. Once on top, you will be rewarded with a picturesque view of Loxton Lake and the surrounding countryside.

## Ontario Snowmobiling Trails (TOP Trails) 🛷

There are over 175,000 snowmobilers and 49,000km of trails in the Province of Ontario. In winter, you can literally travel continuously from one corner of the province to the other on snowmobile trails. Local groups and clubs that are part of the Ontario Federation of Snowmobile Clubs (OFSC) maintain the majority of the trail systems throughout the province and are stewards of safety on the routes. The OFSC is a non-profit organization with the primary goal of providing the best possible snowmobile trails for Ontario riders. The federation has made dreams such as the TOP (Trans Ontario Provincial) Trail system a reality.

A user fee system helps pay for the maintenance of trails by local clubs and for other services such as safety patrols. Trail permits, which give you unlimited access to all OFSC trails in Ontario, must be purchased to travel on OFSC trails. Trail wardens can issue substantial fines if you are caught traveling without a pass. Passes can be bought at most snowmobile dealers and local sports retailers across the province.

The snowmobiling season in the Algonquin Region is generally from mid-January to late March. Inquire locally about ice conditions if you plan to travel on lakes. For additional information call the OFSC at (705) 739-7669

On our maps, we have tried to differentiate the snowmobile trail systems from the other trail systems. We have done this because most of these snowmobile trails are for winter use only. These trails often cross private property and marshy areas or water bodies. Further, due to the very nature of the sport and the ambiguous trail information, a lot of these trail locations are only approximated on our maps.

If you are exploring these trails in the off season, please respect all private property. Closing all gates and leaving no-trace will help ensure the trail systems can be enjoyed by future visitors.

## Pakkotinna Recreation Trail (Map 16/F2) 🚶 🚵 🛷 🎣

The Pakkotinna Trail can be found about 8.5km west of the town of Golden Lake on the south side of Hwy 60. There is a small parking area available at the trailhead. The trail is a rustic, multi use recreation trail that is compiled of old logging roads and trails. The route is moderate in difficulty and travels through dense forest at times. Hiking and biking are the main uses of the trail in summer, while in winter, the trail is a popular snowmobile route. During summer months, the west loop should be avoided due to very wet conditions along many parts of the trail.

"Pakkotinna" means high, hilly ground and not surprisingly, the trail does ascend a large hill where there is a panoramic lookout of the Golden Lake area. The route also leads to Dan Lake, a small, secluded semi-wilderness lake. In winter, it is possible to travel the entire 40km of the trail. During summer, marshy conditions limit the trail to mainly the 10km section that stretches from Hwy 60 to Dan's Lake.

## Peck Lake Trail (Map 12/E6) 🚶 📖

The Peck Lake Trail in Algonquin Park is an easy 1.9km loop that travels around Peck Lake. Along with the trail brochure, you will learn a little more about the ecology of an Algonquin Provincial Park Lake. The hike will help give you some insight on the complexities of freshwater lakes and how they support life. The parking area and trail brochures can be found about 4km past Smoke Lake, off the north side of Hwy 60.

## Petawawa Crown Game Preserve (Map 26/B4) 🚶 ⛷ 🚵

The Petawawa Crown Game Preserve is located off Laurentian Drive, which can be found off Hwy 17, north of Pembroke. The Preserve is great for cross-country skiing, in fact a number of local athletes have used the area for training in the past. There is a small parking area and a detailed route map at the trailheads. The trails are also suitable for hiking and biking during summer months.

    **Green Loop** is an easy 2.3km loop that begins at the parking area near the entrance to the Preserve. The route passess through a mixed forest. Look for fox tracks that can often be seen in the snow along the trails.

    **Orange Loop** begins at the parking area north of the Green Trail trailhead and is an easy 4.4km loop. The Orange Trail travels around the old fish hatchery and past a few ponds including an old hatchery pond.

## Petawawa National Forestry Institute Trails (Map 34/G2)
🚶 ⛷ 🚵 🏂 📖

North of the town of Petawawa, just off Hwy 17, lies the Petawawa National Forestry Institute. The Institute is comprised of 98 square kilometres of land and was established in 1918 as a base for forestry research. At the Forest Visitor Centre there is a series of trails that guide you through a towering pine forest and a boardwalk along the winding Chalk River. The Institute trails are a perfect way for travelers to loosen up their legs. There are also picnic areas available to the public. The Forestry Visitor Centre is open from June to September and offers hiking and a newly developed mountain biking trail system. The easy bike route travels 10km along old bush roads through the research forest. During winter months, a number of trails are groomed for cross-country skiing. There are also snowshoeing opportunities.

## Port Sydney Cross-Country Ski Trails (Map 1/E7) ⛷

The Village of Port Sydney offers over 11km of easy groomed cross-country ski trails for recreational pleasure. The trailhead can be found off of Muskoka Road 10 on Clark Crescent just past the tennis courts. There is a detailed map available at the trailhead to help you pick a preferred route.

## Powassan Trails (Map 28/C7) 🚶 ⛷ 🚵 🏂

The Powassan Trails are part of the Discovery Routes Partners, which is a collection of multi recreation trails and canoe routes. The idea of the Discovery Routes is to establish and update recreation opportunities in the North Bay area. The Powassan Trails can be found just southeast of Powassan shortly off Hwy 11. The trails were developed for hiking, biking, snowshoeing and cross-country skiing. Trail maintenance is in its early stages, although cross-country routes are in fairly good shape throughout the season.

    **Porcupine Trail** is a moderate 3.5km loop that travels past the water tower and over Powassan Mountain before heading back to the trailhead.

    **Squirrel Trail** is an easy 2.5km loop that passes a water tower and eventually follows Big Bend Avenue back to the beginning of the trail.

## Oxtongue River/Ragged Falls Provincial Park Trail (Map 2/G2) 🚶 ⛺ 🎣

This non-operating provincial park was established to protect a stretch of the Oxtongue River. The park joins Algonquin Provincial Park at its western boundary and follows the river up to Hwy 60. There is a short turnoff off Hwy 60, where parking is available with public toilets. From the parking area there is an easy 2km trail that leads to a lookout over the magnificent Ragged Falls.

## Old Railway Bike Trail (Map 13/C6) 🚵

The Railway Bike Trail is an easy Algonquin Park trail that travels along the old O.A. & P.S. (Ottawa, Arnprior and Parry Sound) railway. This section of the railbed is about 10km in length and can be ridden from the Mew Lake Campground off Hwy 60 to the southern tip of Whitefish Lake. The trail travels through the Algonquin forest and along Whitefish Lake. It also follows the Madawaska River and Lake of Two Rivers. The old railbed makes travel quite easy and is ideal for all skill levels.

## Renfrew County Forest Walking Trails (Map 18/E2) 🚶 ⛷

The Renfrew County Forest Trails are two connected loop trails that can be found near the intersection of Township Road 39 and the Westmeath/Ross Townline Road. The trails were established in 1984 and along with interpretive signs describe the local history and forestry practices. The trails are generally easy and are suitable for hiking and cross-country skiing. There is a small parking area at the trailhead.

## Ridge Trail (Map 19/G4) 🚵

The Ridge Trail is an easy 19km tour along old logging roads throughout the Almaguin Highlands. The exhilarating bike ride begins at the Algonquin Provincial Park access point on Kawawaymog Lake. From the access point, the route takes you past a number of small semi-wilderness lakes and through some quiet forests. The route also passes the trailhead to the Tower Trail, which can be a fun side trip.

## Samuel de Champlain Provincial Park Trails (Map 29/G1)
🚶 ⛷ 🎣 📖

There are a number of different trails within Samuel de Champalin Provincial Park that are mainly used for hiking during summer months. These trail systems include the Etienne Trails and the Kag Trail. For winter recreation enthusiasts, the roads throughout the park are transformed into a great cross-country ski trail system. The groomed cross-country trail lengths vary from year to year and difficulties range from easy to moderate. Donations are requested for the use of the trails in winter. The park is located off Hwy 11 just west of the town of Mattawa. Parking is available at the main gate to the park.

    **Etienne Trail System** can be found at Samuel de Champlain Provincial Park off Hwy 17 west of Mattawa. Four separate trails totaling over 25km make up the Etienne Trails, with each set of trails offering a different educational theme for users. Be wary of poison ivy along the trails. Before heading out be sure to pick up a copy of the comprehensive Etienne Trail System booklet from the main gate.

    **Ecology Trail** is an easy 2.5km loop that takes the user through a display of the ecology of the area dating back over two billion years. You will travel through impressive stands of red and white pine, which was the prized logging fare of the 18th Century. The trail will explain and help you understand the delicate balance of nature and the need for proper resource management. Along the trail, you will also pass a lookout offering a picturesque view of the Mattawa River.

    **Geology Trail** takes you around Long and Coco Lakes while explaining the geological development of the area. The trail is a moderate trek and travels about 5km along sometimes rugged terrain. The trail explains the development of the Mattawa River area and the role the area played in shaping the geography we are familiar with today. Shortly after beginning the route, there is a short trail to a lookout area where a nice view of the Mattawa River can be found. The lookout stands over 250m (825ft) above sea level offering an excellent view of the surrounding area. There are many interesting sites along the route including a bedrock ridge, mineral deposits and a glacial 'kettle'.

    **Nature Trail** is an addition to the Geology Trail, creating a total loop of 8.5km. The trail is moderate in difficulty, although it does traverse over challenging terrain at times. On this trail you will learn about the natural features of the park and the surrounding area. You will travel through a mixed forest indigenous of the transitional north/south nature of the Mattawa area. There are many signs of the beaver, as they are very active in this part of the province. Other wildlife may also be spotted but birds and smaller mammals, such as squirrels, are more prevelant. There are also many wildflowers to be viewed along this route at various times of year.

**History Trail** is the longest trail of this system at 9km. The route can be classified as moderately difficult due to the distance involved and the sometimes challenging terrain. The loop is made up of portions of both the Geology and Nature Trails and along with the trail brochure, provides insightful information on the history of the area. The river has played an integral role in shaping native history and folklore for thousands of years. It is even believed that natives traveled the Mattawa River over 12,000 years ago. The trail also explains the significance of the Mattawa River as a part of one of the main trade routes between Montreal and Western Ontario and other parts of Canada. Many explorers have traveled this river including the infamous Samuel de Champlain.

**Kag Trail** takes you along a 2.5km loop through a majestic forest setting and a trail guide will teach you a little about the history and nature of the area. The trail is moderate in difficulty due to a few steep climbs before passing Gem Lake. Along the last leg of the trail there are numerous chances to catch splendid views of Moore Lake to the south. The trail also passes the former home of Amable Du Fond, the head of a group of natives who once had hunting and fishing rights for the area. The building was built by Du Fond for his family in 1864. The word "Kag" is native for porcupine.

## Seguin Trail (Map 10/B7) 🚶 ⛷ 🏂 🛶 🎿 🏇 🚵 ⛺
The Seguin Trail is part of an old railway line that has been abandoned since 1955. The railway spanned from Ottawa to the Georgian Bay. The trail stretches 61km (one-way) from the Hwy 69/400 access point at the Parry Sound Visitor Centre to the Fern Glen access point on Fern Glen Road, west of Hwy 11. The route can also be accessed from the many access points along Hwy 518, where the trail intersects with the highway. This rustic trail is a popular snowmobile and ATV route and is becoming increasingly used for hiking, biking and horseback riding, especially in the stretch closer to Hwy 69/400. The trail is currently maintained by the Parry Sound MNR and is well groomed for winter activities including cross-country skiing and snowshoeing. The route passes through both private and public lands and if you plan to do some camping, it is essential to organize your trip to avoid trespassing on private property. The geography of this great trail is based in the beautiful Canadian Shield, where you'll travel over rocky areas, through dense forest and past many lakes and wetland areas. Please practice low impact camping at all times so future users can enjoy the beauty of the route.

## Shaw Woods Trail (Map 17/G3) 🚶
This moderate 5km hiking trail travels through an older forest. The forest floor is not that dense, although the canopy above is remarkably thick. The trailhead lies off of County Road 9, east of Lake Dore. About 1km from Hwy 41 you will see the Shaw Woods protected area. Your vehicle can be parked on the side of the road.

## Silver Spoon & Cranberry Lake Trails (Map 34) 🚶 ⛷ 🏕 🚻
There are three different trail systems in this area each that can be used for hiking or cross-country skiing. The MBL and King's Road Trails can be accessed from the Information Centre found on Hwy 17 just north of Deep River. The RXC Trail is found a little more north of the Information Centre on McGelligott Drive off Town Line Road. There is a small parking area available.

**MBL Trail** is a moderately difficult trail on skis or an easy trail for hikers. The loop travels past the Cranberry Lakes and over a few streams for 4.5km. There is a scenic lookout along the route and a beach at Cranberry Lakes.

**The King's Road Trail** travels over easy terrain from the Information Centre to the Ottawa River. The trail is mainly an old logging road, although it also follows a portion of the RXC Trail to reach the river. There is a picnic area at the river.

**The RXC Trail** can be a muddy route in spring or after heavy rainfall. This easy route is made up of three separate loops that total 7km. The northern portion of the trail passes by some scenic lookout areas with a great view of the Ottawa River and Laurentian Mountains, in Quebec. The north portion of the system also has a picnic area and beach.

## South Himsworth Trails (Map 28/C7) ⛷
This 10km cross-country ski loop is set amid a charming forest setting. Most of the trail is over easy terrain, although the last few kilometers of the route is a little more challenging. This loop is perfect for a family outing or just to get some exercise. The trailhead and parking area are on the south side of Linquist Line, north of Powassan. Donations to aid in the maintenance of the trail system are always welcome.

## Spruce Bog Boardwalk Trail (Map 13\D4) 🚶 🚻 📖
A spruce bog is indeed a rare place in nature. This Algonquin Park trail helps to explain some of the mysteries of the bog and why it is truly unique. The 1.5km loop trail begins by traveling through a spruce forest and then proceeds along a boardwalk across the Sunday Creek Bog and a smaller kettle bog. With the trail booklet and trail markers, you will be learn about the different stages of a bog and the ecology of the area. The forests of the bog are also a great place for bird lovers. A number of species inhabit the spruce forest including the Golden-Crowned Kinglet, the Grey Jay and, of course, the Spruce Grouse. Near the end of the trail there is a lookout area with a view of the bog in its entirety. The parking area for the trail can be found off Hwy 60, across from the road to the Algonquin Park Visitor Centre. Interpretative booklets are available at the trailhead.

## Tawingo Nordic Trails (Map 1/D3) ⛷ 🎿
The Tawingo Nordic Trails are located off of Hwy11 on Ravenscliff Road and are maintained by the private school. There are over 15km of groomed cross-country trails that vary in difficulty and length and are available to the public from Friday to Monday throughout the winter season. A detailed map at the trailhead and a warm up hut will help you enjoy your visit. There are no fees for use of the trails, although donations are always welcome.

## Tower Trail (Map 19/F4) 🚶 🚻
The Tower Trail can be found off the Forest Access Road northeast of South River. The trail was originally used to travel to a tower which helped monitor forest fire activity in the area. The tower is now gone but the cement blocks where it used to stand still remain. The 5km trek is somewhat difficult due to the steep ascent.

## Track and Tower Trail (Map 12/G5) 🚶 🚻
This Algonquin Park trail offers a number of different hiking options. The main trailhead can be found at about kilometre 25 along Hwy 60. A parking area and interpretative guides are found at the trailhead. It is an easy 7.5km hike from the parking area and back, unless you choose to venture down one of the side trails. A short side trail is available at the 3km mark of the main trail. The 1.6km side trail leads to the site of the former Skymount Tower, a fire tower that was torn down in the early 1950's. Shortly after the tower site, you will pass atop a cliff where a fine view of Cache Lake is offered. Once back on the main trail you will travel along an old railbed that was once the base for a railway. The railway was built by the famous lumber baron J.R. Booth. It stretched from Ottawa to the Georgian Bay and, during World War I, was the busiest railway in all of Canada. A larger side trail off the main loop can be taken at about the 3.9km point of the main loop. The side trail travels for 4.4km to the Mew Lake Campground area. It follows the old railbed and along the Madawaska River before reaching the campground. It is recommended to park a second vehicle at the Highland Trail parking area off Hwy 60 in order to return to the Track and Tower trailhead. The main trail also passes Grant Lake, a small picturesque lake, before returning to the parking area. Overall, this trail system is a great way to experience the Algonquin wilderness and, along with the interpretative guide, learn a little history about Algonquin Provincial Park.

## Tramore Cliffs Trail (Map 16/G4) 🚶 🚻
The Tramore Cliffs Trail is situated 1.2km north on Tramore Road off of Hwy 60. The trailhead is on the east side of the road and can be difficult to locate at times. From the road the trail is a moderate 2km one-way hike that climbs through a mixed forest and over rocky sections to the top of the Tramore Cliffs. At the top, a wonderful view of the Bonnechere Valley is offered. Both Round and Golden Lakes can be seen from the cliffs as well as the Madawaska Hills in the distance.

## Two Rivers Trail (Map 13/A5) 🚶 🚻
The Two Rivers Trail is an Algonquin Park trail that is located across from the Mew Lake Campground entrance off Hwy 60. There is a parking area and interpretative guides available at the trailhead. The trail is an easy 2km loop that traverses through a mixed forest and to a lookout area on top of a cliff. Along with the interpretative guide, you can learn more about forest ecology in and outside of Algonquin Provincial Park. The hike informs users about the effects humans have on the forest and natural events such as fire and predatory insects. From the lookout, you will find a great view of a pine forest set amid the rolling highlands of Algonquin.

## Wasi Cross Country Ski Club Trails (Map 28/C4) ⛷ 🎿
To find the Wasi Ski Club Trails take Lake Nosbonsing Road from Hwy 11 and you'll see the parking lot on the left just before Groulx Road. There are 6 different loops available totaling over 47km of groomed ski trails. The trails vary in difficulty from beginner to advanced, providing an option for everyone.

A warm up hut is located at the parking area to take the bite off those extra chilly winter days. For trail conditions and information call (705) 476-5717.

## Western Uplands Backpacking Trail (Map 3/A1, 12/A7, 11/G4)

There are numerous trails within Algonquin Provincial Park, although the most famous trail in the park is the Western Uplands Backpacking Trail. It is comprised of three large interconnected loops and spans over 100km through the interior of the park. There are rustic campsites at numerous areas along the trail that are usually set on the shore of lakes. Be sure to practice low impact camping and leave your site as clean or cleaner than when you arrived. The trail can be accessed from either the Oxtongue River picnic area off Hwy 60 or from the Rain Lake Access Point at the east side of the park. The trail is regarded as a moderate to difficult route depending on the distances traveled and the terrain. The trail is well marked and can be busy during the months of August and September. Trail use is regulated under the Algonquin Park quota system, which limits trail users. Included in this quota is a maximum of nine people in your camping party. Larger groups may travel together, although only nine people per campsite is permitted. This helps to reduce overcrowding on the trail and at the sites, which helps maintain a positive experience for visitors. You can choose how far and which loops you wish to travel. It is recommended to make reservations well before your trip date to reserve your space on the trail. Call (888) 668-7275 for reservations or (705) 633-5572 for more information.

**Highway 60 Access Point** is found off the north side of Hwy 60 about 3km past the West Gate, where park permits are available. The parking area includes a picnic area. You begin travel on the 32.4km Blue Loop. After crossing the Oxtongue River, which may have to be waded through in spring due to flooding, the trail travels to Maple Leaf Lake. Nine interior campsites are available on the lake and fishing for stocked splake can be rewarding in spring. Not far from Maple Leaf Lake the trail passes South Leach Lake. The lake is small but offers a great interior campsite where you can have the lake all to yourself. The trail continues past a few more small lakes before you'll find a short trail to Little Hardy Lake, where a single campsite is available. Hardy Lake is also a common first night camping area. Maggie Lake, a little further up the trail, offers eight hike-in campsites for trail users. Also, just before Maggie Lake, there is a short side trail to Steeprise Lake, which hosts a secluded campsite. Maggie Lake's water is an uncanny crystal blue and is great for swimming. The lake has no fish, however, due to its inability to neutralize acid rain. From Maggie Lake, it is only about 2km to the junction with the Yellow Trail. If you choose to continue to follow the Blue Trail, after about 2.2km you will traverse past a short side trail to Norah Lake. An exquisite, secluded campsite is available at the lake. From Norah Lake to the next Yellow Trail junction is about 6km. Through this stretch there are two short side trails with one leading to Oak Lake and the other to Panther Lake. Both Lakes offer two hike-in campsites. From the junction, it is 8.2km back to the parking area on Hwy 60. The last stretch passes Guskewau Lake, which should not be overlooked. There are three campsites available at the lake, which would make a perfect last stop before your trip home the next day.

**Rain Lake Access Point** is found at the end of Rain Lake Road at the southern tip of Rain Lake. Parking is available at the access area and permits can be picked up at the park office in the Kearney Community Centre. The Red Trail loop begins by following the old O.A. & P.S. (Ottawa, Arnprior and Parry Sound) railway bed. After about 2.5km on the trail you will come to a small clearing where an old logging camp once was. A rustic campsite is found at the old site and another across the bay of Rain Lake. A population of lake trout and smallmouth bass are present in the lake and fishing can be rewarding. The trail travels on the old bridge over the small bay and continues for about 4km before reaching Islet Lake. This part of the trail was once the site of one of the parks largest trestles. The trestle here stood over 7.5m (25ft) high. The trail follows the lake's shoreline and provides a number of camping locations (five in all) along the shoreline. Smallmouth bass are found in Islet Lake and can be quite active in the mornings and evenings. Just past Islet Lake lies Weed Lake, where another rustic campsite is offered. The trail then traverses past Stammer Lake and over a natural lookout. The lookout gives you a good view of the lake and the surrounding hillside. From here the trail passes one more small lake, named Stuter Lake, before coming to Pincher Lake. Pincher Lake is at the first Yellow Trail junction. The lake provides six hike-in campsites for trail users. Only about 1km from Pincher Lake lies Tern Lake and two more hike-in campsites. From Pincher Lake to the next Yellow Trail junction, which is found between Gervais and West Otterpaw Lakes, is 5.7km. Both lakes offer hike-in campsites. The junction is the site of a short cut. This trail follows a portage most of the

way for a 2.9km route to the other side of the loop. You will shorten your trip by 9.4km if you choose to take this route. If you choose to follow the main route, from West Otterpaw Lake it is 4.7km to the next junction. En route, you will pass the East River. From the Yellow Trail junction, it is about 2km to Loft Lake where another hike-in campsite is available. Brook trout inhabit this beautiful lake and you may have success catching a few, especially in spring. From Loft Lake, the trail travels another 5.6km to the junction of the Red Trail shortcut. En route, you will pass East End Lake, with a secluded hike-in campsite. From the short cut junction it is a little over 7km back to Islet Lake and the old rail trail. At about the halfway mark you will pass Brown Lake where you'll find two more hike-in campsites. Just before Islet Lake, you will pass Ishkuday Lake and the last hike-in campsite of the trail. The rail trail heading back to Rain Lake is only about 0.5km away from the lake.

**Yellow Trail** connects the Red and Blue Trails together. They provide hikers with the opportunity to add another loop to their trip, extending it over several days. We have broken up the trail into two separate routes to simplify our descriptions.

**The East Yellow Trail** travels 10.9km from the easterly red junction to the corresponding blue junction. From the Red Trail, the Yellow Trail passes Rainbow Lake only about 1km from the junction. Two rustic hike-in campsites are available at the lake and are well spaced apart. Brook trout inhabit Rainbow Lake and fishing could be successful in spring. From Rainbow Lake, the trail passes Susan Lake where two more hike-in sites are located. The trail then passes by a magnificent lookout just after the lake. From the lookout it is just over 7km to the Blue Trail junction. En route, you will pass Redwing, Lupus and Thunder Lakes. All three lakes offer two hike-in campsites along their shoreline.

**Yellow Trail West** is 10.4km from the Red Trail junction to the Blue Trail. Beginning at the Red Trail, the route passes by Cashel and McCormack Lakes. There is no campsite at Cashel Lake but there is one site at the small McCormack Lake. From McCormack Lake it is about 1km to Clara Lake, where two more hike-in campsites are offered. These sites are the last campsites on the west Yellow Trail before the Blue Trail junction. It is over 6km from Clara Lake to the Blue Trail.

## Westmeath Provincial Park Trails (Map 27/C7)

Westmeath Provincial Park is a non-operating provincial park, although it offers a number of different recreation opportunities. To find the park, take County Road 21 to County Road 12. About 6km south of Westmeath, you can park near the park gate. Although there are no actual marked trails within the park, there a number of trails that zigzag throughout. The most used route is the old road that leads from the park gate through the park to the beach area. The trip is about 4km and generally easy. The route can be biked, hiked, snowshoed or even cross-country skied, although there is no trail maintenance throughout the year. Be sure to stay to the left at any trail junction in order to make it to the beach. There are a number of areas where you could stray off the main trail. The trail passes a causeway before the beach area, where there is a fine view of the Ottawa River. If you plan to explore other trails within the park, use caution to avoid getting lost.

## Westmeath Scenic Lookout Trail (Map 27/D7)

The parking area for this route can be found off of County Road 12 at the Township of Weastmeath's Administration Building. From the building it is an easy 3km hike along County Road 11 then on County Road 31 to the lookout. On the south side of County Road 31 there is a short hike up a hill to a gazebo and the spectacular lookout. There are panoramic views of the historic Ottawa Valley. There is also a bench at the gazebo for a relaxing view.

## Whiskey Rapids Trail (Map 12/B7)

This Algonquin Provincial Park trail is located just inside the park's West Gate off Hwy 60. The parking area is off the highway and interpretative brochures are available at the trailhead. The trail is an easy 2.1km loop that traverses through a mixed forest along the Oxtongue River to the Whiskey Rapids. The theme of the trail and its corresponding trail guide is the ecology of rivers of Algonquin. You will learn how algae, insects, fish and birds and how they co-exist in the river environment. The last leg of the trail follows a tote road built in the late 1800's. Horse drawn wagons once carried supplies to Canoe Lake down this old road. From Canoe Lake, the supplies were disbursed to the logging camps.

## Yonge St. Trail (Map 1/F5)

This easy 3km multi-use trail travels from Chubb Lake Road to Young Street South through a beautiful part of Huntsville. The trail passes through some dense forested areas and is popular with bird watchers. The main access point is approximately 1.2km north on Young Street South from Main Street West.

# INDEX

This comprehensive index is intended to help guide you to the map or reference page you are interested in. If the specific item is not labelled try picking the most prominent land feature in the area. This will guide you to the right map and reference page.

# IMPORTANT NUMBERS

## Ministry of Natural Resources

General Inquiry ................................................. (416) 314-2000

(416) 314-1665 (French)

www.mnr.gov.on.ca

Outdoors Card Customer Service ................... (800) 387-7011

Aurora, Greater Toronto Area ........................ (905) 713-7400

Minden ............................................................. (705) 286-1521

North Bay .......................................................... (705) 475-5550

Pembroke ......................................................... (613) 732-3661

Invading Species Hotline ............................... (800) 563-7711

Sportfish Contaminant- Monitoring Program . (800) 820-2716

Crimestoppers (Poaching) ............................... (800) 222-TIPS

## Parks

Ontario Parks (Reservations) ........................ (888) 668-7275

www.OntarioParks.com

Algonquin Park (Information) ........................ (613) 633-5572

Samuel de Champlain (Information) .............. (705) 744-2276

## Tourism Ontario

Resorts Ontario................................................. (705) 325-9115

Travel Ontario .............................................. (800) ONTARIO

## Help Us Improve Your Mapbook

In order for us to ensure the accuracy of this mapbook, we invite you to continue to provide feedback on the maps and reference section. If you see any trails, road systems, lakes, etc. that are missing or wrongly noted, please let us know.

All comments from you, the reader, will be used to update this valuable guidebook from time to time. Please contact us at:

**Mussio Ventures Ltd.**
232 Anthony Court
New Westminster, BC
Canada, V3L 5T5

Tel: (604) 520-5670  Fax: (604) 520-5630
Email: updates@backroadmapbooks.com

Go to our website to learn about the latest updates to the mapbooks.

**www.backroadmapbooks.com**